THIS CONTESTED LAND

THIS CONTESTED LAND

THE STORIED PAST AND UNCERTAIN FUTURE OF AMERICA'S NATIONAL MONUMENTS

McKenzie Long

UNIVERSITY OF MINNESOTA PRESS
Minneapolis
London

The publication of this book was assisted by a bequest from Josiah H. Chase to honor his parents, Ellen Rankin Chase and Josiah Hook Chase.

An earlier version of chapter 1 was published as "Voices of Bears Ears," in *Alpinist Magazine* 60 (Winter 2017). A different version of chapter 3 was published as "The Alphabet Effect," *Nowhere Magazine* (2018).

Maps were created by Ann Piersall Logan and the author.

Photographs on pages ii–iii and 310 (Valley of the Gods, Bears Ears National Monument, Utah) by Veronica Palmer; pages x, 1, and 278 (Grand Staircase–Escalante National Monument, Utah) by the author; pages 67 and 171 (Grand Staircase–Escalante National Monument, Utah) by Veronica Palmer.

Published by the University of Minnesota Press
111 Third Avenue South, Suite 290
Minneapolis, MN 55401-2520
http://www.upress.umn.edu

ISBN 978-1-5179-0982-6 (hc)
ISBN 978-1-5179-1536-0 (pb)

A Cataloging-in-Publication record for this book is available from the Library of Congress.

Printed in the United States of America on acid-free paper

The University of Minnesota is an equal-opportunity educator and employer.

30 29 28 27 26 25 24   10 9 8 7 6 5 4 3 2 1

Contents

Introduction *A Closer Look* | *xi*

National Monuments Visited in This Book | *xxxi*

PART I. ROCK

1. The Heart of Bears Ears | *3*
   Bears Ears National Monument, Utah

2. The Conflict of Dreams | *27*
   Katahdin Woods and Waters National Monument, Maine

3. The Meaning of Monuments | *45*
   Berryessa Snow Mountain National Monument, California

PART II. RIFT

4. Seeing | *69*
   Cascade-Siskiyou National Monument, Oregon and California

5. Digging | *87*
   Castle Mountains National Monument, California

6. Shifting | *97*
   Sand to Snow National Monument, California

7. Expanding | *119*
   Papahānaumokuākea Marine National Monument, Hawaii

8. Layering | *145*
   Grand Staircase–Escalante National Monument, Utah

PART III. RIPPLE

9. On Sharing | *173*
   Rio Grande del Norte National Monument, New Mexico

10. On Reactions | *193*
    Hanford Reach National Monument, Washington

11. On Walls | *215*
    Organ Mountains–Desert Peaks National Monument,
    New Mexico

12. On Patterns | *239*
    Basin and Range National Monument, Nevada

13. On Possession | *257*
    Gold Butte National Monument, Nevada

   Epilogue *Looking Forward* | *279*

   Acknowledgments | *287*

   American Antiquities Act of 1906 | *291*

   Presidential Monument Proclamations | *293*

   Selected Resources | *311*

   Index | *337*

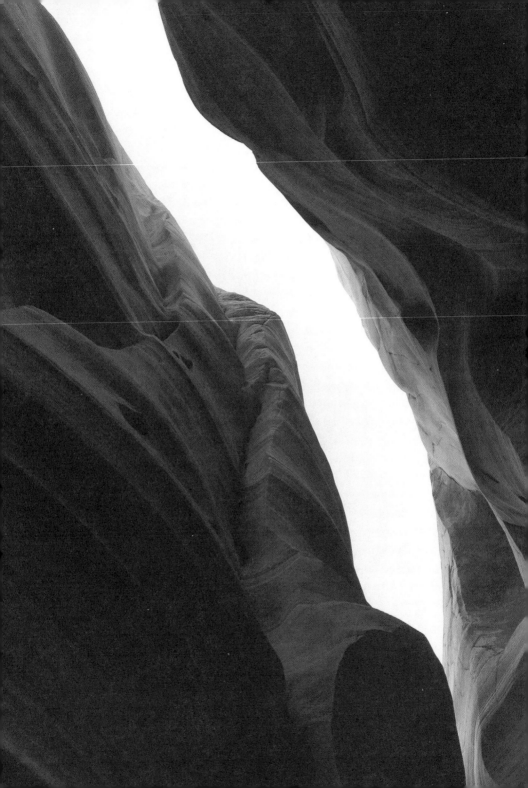

A Closer Look

L ook behind you," my younger sister Veronica called from below. I stood up on the sandstone ledge where I had been crouching to examine ancient bricks balanced on a cliff's edge. Behind me, a gold wall was spattered with faint ochre handprints, from the base to well above my head. Large, masculine hands imprinted next to tiny, childlike hands. "I need to see that up close," Veronica said, and climbed up the angular boulders that guarded the ledge to join me.

In silence, we stood shoulder to shoulder and contemplated the people who had left these marks. I imagined families dipping their hands into homemade paint, feeling cool wetness squish between their fingers, then pressing palms to grainy stone. "I feel so connected to them right now," Veronica whispered. I hovered my hand above one of the prints. The fingers ended where my fingers ended, the base of the palm curved where mine curved. Palm to palm, the unique ridges of our hands reached across centuries.

It was April 2017, and Veronica and I were in Bullet Canyon in the newly designated Bears Ears National Monument in southeastern

Utah. For the past six years, I had spent almost every spring and fall rock climbing in Indian Creek, north of Bullet Canyon, and had fallen in love with Utah's desert. But when President Barack Obama designated the 1.3-million-acre national monument the December before, I recognized that I had seen only a tiny part of this enormous new protected area. I hoped to rectify that. We had taken this trip together in Veronica's last weeks of free time before she started a full-time job. A photographer about to transition to office work, Veronica woke for every sunrise and paused for every sunset to capture the landscapes while I wrote in my journal. In between we would hike and explore, our trip schedule dictated by light.

We hiked out of Bullet Canyon and drove north to find a place to camp. Bears Ears Buttes, the namesake for the monument, rose in front of us, tilting toward each other like the ears of a mischievous cub peeking over the horizon. The sun slipped down the sky. Veronica wanted to photograph the buttes, so we parked and hauled camp chairs into the sagebrush. She assembled her tripod. I cinched a hood over my ears as the dry air cooled. Minty, evergreen sage surrounded us as the sun daubed the buttes persimmon and magenta. We watched in the meadow until the tips of our noses and ends of our fingers were numb with cold.

The next morning I rolled out of the fluffy warmth of my sleeping bag and lit the stove to brew coffee. As I waited for water to boil, I turned on my phone and received a flicker of signal. "Trump orders review of national monuments, vows to 'end abuses and return control to the people'" read the *Washington Post*. On April 26, 2017, President Trump signed an executive order to review twenty-seven national monuments, calling them "surreptitious land grabs" and "an abusive use of the Antiquities Act." He wanted to reevaluate all monuments designated between 1996 and 2017 that were more than

100,000 acres in size, suggesting that he might reduce or abolish them completely. This included Bears Ears.

I felt a prickle along my neck. I looked around at the rabbitbrush and juniper, the crumbly, ivory Navajo Sandstone, the rust-colored Wingate Sandstone. Red sand hid between my toes, tinged my hair with a hint of strawberry, and darkened my skin to a false tan. I sat underneath the shadow of Bears Ears Buttes, breathing in sage-scented air, caressing the land with the soles of my feet, while miles away a politician made an abstract decision that would change this desert. Suddenly my interest in this place felt urgent and relevant. The intricacy of this landscape, of its history, the stories of the people who live here and love it seemed much deeper and more layered than the politics controlling it. I had to know more.

IN THE 1890S, entrepreneur Charles Cary Graham led an expedition into Grand Gulch, Utah, in search of antiquities to sell. His route took him through Bullet Canyon, where he most likely encountered the same two-story ruins where Veronica and I had seen handprints. Graham's expedition inspired two more, led by Richard Wetherill, the Colorado rancher who excavated and sold pottery and ancient skulls from Cliff Palace in Mesa Verde. These explorations occurred at a time when the science of archaeology was relatively new, demand for Native American relics was high, and many Indigenous people had been killed or forcibly removed from their homelands. Ancient structures seemed abandoned or empty, leaving them vulnerable to looting. Many didn't think twice about raiding an eight-hundred-year-old cliff dwelling. It was like striking a gold vein or unburying a treasure.

These explorers smashed the walls of hand-bricked buildings to let in light and expedite the search for pots. They ripped off timbers that had held roofs for more than seven centuries to build campfires on cool desert nights. They dispersed arrowheads and clothing without any record of where items had been found, and offered no respect for the dead or their burial customs. Archaeologists at the time began to express alarm at the rapid ruin of irreplaceable cultural sites. Groups petitioned the government to act. The final straw came when Gustaf Nordenskiöld, Wetherill's Swedish excavation partner, shipped pottery, ancient tools, and skeletal remains found at Mesa Verde to a museum in Finland. Anger that American archaeological treasures were sent abroad, the fact that no law prevented that from occurring, and growing dismay at destruction caused by pothunters like Graham and Wetherill contributed to the passage of the Antiquities Act, signed into law by President Theodore Roosevelt in 1906.

This law was written with two primary objectives: to protect antiquities by making it illegal to excavate, deface, or remove artifacts from public land without a proper permit, and to give the president power to further protect areas controlled by the government that contain "objects of historic or scientific interest" by declaring them national monuments.

The second clause of the act was intended to allow presidents to claim land that was open for settlement and save cultural sites from looting. More than one hundred years after its passage, the Antiquities Act has become a contested piece of legislation that has been applied to much more than the law's title might imply. In addition to cultural sites, the Antiquities Act has been used to preserve natural areas and to enhance protection of regions vulnerable to mining, logging, and development. Scholars have observed that this law has had more influence on the preservation of America's land and culture than any other law. "The law is the tool by means of which the broadest category of park areas ever created has been established," wrote public land historian Hal Rothman in *America's National*

Monuments: The Politics of Preservation. He notes that the Antiquities Act "has given federal administrators a flexibility that no other piece of legislation has allowed." This flexibility is exactly why some lawmakers dislike the Antiquities Act today.

After signing the act into law, Roosevelt designated Devils Tower in eastern Wyoming as the United States' first national monument. The proclamation emphasized the "scientific interest" of the tower as "such an extraordinary example of the effect of erosion . . . as to be a natural wonder." It wasn't until his second proclamation several months later, establishing El Morro National Monument in New Mexico, that he used the act to protect an archaeological site. From the very beginning, Roosevelt interpreted the law broadly and used it to preserve unique land formations and fragile environments in addition to antiquities.

NATIONAL MONUMENTS are like the scrappy younger siblings of national parks. With a well-established management philosophy and emphasis on tourism, national parks are sleek, alluring, and beloved. Many parks have glamorous marketing campaigns and host huge numbers of people. Popular parks like Yosemite in California and Zion in Utah see an average of four million visitors each year. By contrast, Grand Staircase–Escalante, one of the most popular national monuments and a neighbor to Zion, sees only around nine hundred thousand visitors per year. Many people just don't know about monuments, and if they do, they often confuse them with parks.

This might be because the language we use to describe parks and monuments is muddy. The term *monument* often refers to a built structure that honors something or someone specific, like the Statue of Liberty. The word also carries a connotation of remembrance; monuments are aids to public memory. Many national monuments created under the Antiquities Act are parklike natural land designations, and these are what I discuss in this book. The matter is further confused because the distinctions between a monument and a park are subtle and invisible.

National monuments differ from parks primarily in the way they are created. Congress approves national parks by vote, which requires broad public support. Under the authority of the Antiquities Act, the president declares national monuments by proclamation. This does not require consensus, can be done quickly, and often leads to controversy. According to Rothman, "there are no intrinsic features that separate national monuments from the national parks. The difference is in the mode of establishment. Congress must pass bills authorizing new national parks, whereas the president can proclaim national monuments by the stroke of a pen."

While Congress establishes national parks to protect remarkable landscapes, emphasis is placed on scenic beauty. When a new park is considered, lands and waters are evaluated for their inspirational, educational, and recreational value. The National Park Service also strongly encourages visitation, allowing people to see and experience these inspirational places.

National monuments are established to protect something specific, and unlike for a park, this protection is prioritized over tourism. The "objects" a monument protects are listed in its proclamation and range from geologic features such as columnar basalt in Devils Postpile National Monument, to ancient ruins like the cliff dwellings of Montezuma Castle National Monument. Congress has created some monuments with a specific protection aim through legislation, but most are established without a vote through presidential proclamation.

Monuments can be created only on land that is already controlled by the federal government, such as U.S. Forest Service or Bureau of Land Management (BLM) land. They cannot be designated on private land unless a land exchange takes place or the land is gifted to the government, as was the case with Katahdin Woods and Waters in Maine. Opponents frequently call national monuments "federal land grabs," which, strictly speaking, is inaccurate. A monument designation does not change ownership but does change the land's management status, which often reduces extractive uses and enhances its level of protection.

One reason many Americans are unaware of national monuments is that people often think of all public land as a park. This comes with an assumption that all protection of public land attempts to preserve it in a wild and natural state. Instead, the level of protection is determined by the managing agency. The National Park Service (NPS) restricts land use the most, places a heavy emphasis on preservation and visitation, and provides scripted recreation with paved trails lined with wayside exhibits and scenic viewpoints from parking pullouts. The U.S. Forest Service focuses much of its work on timber and watershed management and allows for unscripted recreation; people can drive down winding dirt roads and camp just about anywhere for free for two weeks. The BLM has a more-or-less all-bets-are-off strategy. Unless something is specifically prohibited, anything goes: mining, grazing, off-road vehicle use, shooting ranges, camping, hunting, biking, and hiking.

Monuments are managed by each of these agencies and reflect these different priorities. Usually, monument proclamations prohibit mining and drilling but allow for an array of other uses from recreation to grazing to strict environmental regulation in certain areas. In this way monuments prioritize the goals of both conservation and preservation. Conservation is a management strategy that aims for sustainable human interactions with land, allowing for multiple uses, such as recreation and road building, while not destroying the land in the process. Preservation is focused on leaving land natural and without human influence. This perspective discourages roads and any resource extraction. Though they seem contradictory, both approaches exist simultaneously in all public lands, especially in monuments.

Yellowstone, America's first official national park, was established by Congress in 1872, but the National Park Service was not created as a central managing agency for parks until 1916, ten years after the Antiquities Act became law. In the 1930s, existing monuments were transferred to NPS jurisdiction; this was the first time any significant management plans were applied to monuments. For many years after, when a monument was established, it was transferred to the NPS to administer. Since the late 1990s, it has become common to leave a new monument under the jurisdiction of its previous managing agency. As of 2022, there are 129 national monuments managed by eight federal agencies, including the BLM, U.S. Forest Service, U.S. Fish and Wildlife Service, and the National Oceanic and Atmospheric Administration—as well as the NPS. The NPS oversees 423 units; 84 are monuments, 63 are parks, and the rest are national battlefields, national recreation areas, and other parklike designations.

In the early 1900s, monuments were thought to be parks-in-waiting. While Congress moved slowly to finalize a vote on park status, monuments were declared quickly by presidents when the issue of protection was time sensitive. Congress did convert many early monuments into national parks: Grand Canyon, Grand Teton, and Joshua Tree all started as monuments. Occasionally monuments are still converted into parks. Death Valley in California and White Sands in New Mexico, for example, were designated as monuments by President Herbert Hoover in 1933. Congress converted Death Valley to a national park in 1994, White Sands in 2019. However, most recent monuments are seen as entirely different entities than parks and are not thought to be waiting for a change in status.

THE ANTIQUITIES ACT CAN BE INTERPRETED in different ways, which has enabled its wide-ranging use but has also caused conflict. The two clauses that are most often debated are "objects of historic and scientific interest," which sets the standard for the creation of a monument, and the stipulation that a monument "shall be confined to the smallest area compatible with proper care and management of the objects to be protected." Though some argue that the law's intention was to protect only archaeological sites, President Theodore Roosevelt set an immediate precedent with his broad interpretation of the first phrase. He used the Antiquities Act to designate eighteen monuments during his presidency, and less than half offered specific protection of archaeological sites such as cliff dwellings and petroglyphs. The rest preserved interesting examples of geology such as sandstone arches in Natural Bridges, rare forests such as old-growth redwoods in Muir Woods, and impressive landscapes like the Grand Canyon.

Even with Roosevelt's generous vision of what could be protected, the first monuments were small, their boundaries drawn precisely around the features to be protected without concern for or understanding of ecological implications. The original boundary of Devils Tower was drawn with the tower in mind and included only a couple bends of the Belle Fourche River. Now more of the river is included. Both El Morro and Gila Cliff Dwellings in New Mexico started as a mere 160 acres each, with boundaries drawn tightly around cliff dwellings and ancient pueblos. Though still relatively small, both monuments have been expanded to include land around the sites themselves. As scientific understanding grew about biodiversity, ecological connectivity, and wildlife corridors, monument designations became larger and larger. By the time Presidents Bill Clinton, George W. Bush, and Barack Obama began designating monuments, a size of over a million acres per monument was common. As Rothman wrote, "the evolution of the monument category reveals the gradual awakening of government officials and the public to the importance of a broadly based approach to federal preservation, while the areas preserved mirror the changing values of American society."

Since the Antiquities Act allows presidents to act without public input, some designations have resulted in such vehement controversy that the law itself has been challenged. As a result, two restrictions have been placed on the law.

In 1943, President Franklin D. Roosevelt established Jackson Hole National Monument in Wyoming, which included land from Grand Teton National Forest and private land donated by John D. Rockefeller Jr. The proclamation outraged Wyoming politicians, Jackson residents, and even Forest Service employees, all of whom viewed the monument as a restriction of their use of the land. The State of Wyoming sued the federal government. Local ranchers, along with Hollywood actor Wallace Beery, protested with a cattle drive across the new monument and into the mountains, without proper permits and with an arsenal of guns. A bill was even brought to the U.S. Senate calling for the abolition of the Antiquities Act.

The federal government successfully proved the "historic and scientific interest" of the area and won the lawsuit. Jackson Hole National Monument stayed in place and was rolled into the boundary and management of the now adored Grand Teton National Park in 1950. But to relieve tensions, the government agreed to a compromise. The bill that designated Grand Teton National Park included an amendment to the Antiquities Act that exempts Wyoming from any further monuments by proclamation within that state.

Rothman called the battle over Jackson Hole National Monument "the last of the first generation of conflicts between the interests of conservation/preservation and unregulated use of land." Now a new generation of conflicts over land use and protection is repeating on a strikingly similar loop. In the past twenty-five years, almost every time a president has unilaterally proclaimed a national monument, it has been met with resistance.

IN 1978 President Jimmy Carter created fifteen massive monuments in Alaska, totaling 56 million acres. Legislation concerning the protection of this same area had reached a standstill, and stalling tactics were being used in hope of enabling extractive uses in some regions. Carter's quick political maneuver forced legislators back to the table to develop a compromise. Only a few of his original proclamations remain as national monuments; most were turned into parks or preserves. Carter's enormous designations also resulted in a requirement that Congress ratify the use of the Antiquities Act for any future reservations larger than 5,000 acres in Alaska.

After Carter, Republican presidents Ronald Reagan and George H. W. Bush did not establish any monuments by proclamation. A few monuments, such as Mount St. Helens Volcanic in Washington and Poverty Point in Louisiana, were established by Congress in the 1980s, but because these were the result of a legislative vote, they were not as controversial as monuments created by executive order.

Before Grand Staircase–Escalante was established in 1996, a monument had not been created by proclamation in almost twenty years. When President Clinton announced Grand Staircase–Escalante National Monument, Utah politicians were caught by surprise. Clinton's new monument included land that was slated for a coal mine, and this designation ended those plans. The monument was perceived by some as a muzzle on Utah's economy, which made many Utahans furious. The uproar in response to Grand Staircase–Escalante renewed the long-standing controversy over the Antiquities Act. Twenty years after Clinton's Utah monument, President Barack Obama's designation of Bears Ears was equally inflammatory. State politicians were still sore over Grand Staircase–Escalante, and Bears Ears was yet another large reservation that limited resource extraction and economic development in Utah.

These two divisive Utah monuments bookended Trump's 2017 review. Both were over 1 million acres in size and both housed coal and uranium deposits that were inaccessible as long as the land retained monument status. The Trump administration argued that large designations like these were not "the smallest area compatible with proper care and management of the objects to be protected." The review suggested the president's desire to open this land up for mining and his intention to either eliminate the monuments or alter them in some way. This came to fruition in December that year, when Trump issued proclamations that reduced Bears Ears by 85 percent, and Grand Staircase–Escalante by 45 percent.

These reductions were just as controversial as the monuments' inceptions. The Antiquities Act includes only directives for the creation of monuments, not their dissolution. Environmental groups claimed the president did not have the authority to significantly alter a monument made by a previous president. No president has issued a proclamation that completely abolished a monument made by another, and many argue that only Congress has that authority. Yet, the media portrayal of Trump's reduction of these monuments as "unprecedented" was not entirely accurate. In 1911, William Howard Taft, the first president to follow Theodore Roosevelt and the

Antiquities Act, reduced Petrified Forest National Monument by 40 percent, declaring the acres he removed not "worth preserving." At the beginning of World War I, Woodrow Wilson reduced the size of Mount Olympus National Monument by over 300,000 acres, citing the country's need for timber during wartime. Franklin D. Roosevelt and Dwight Eisenhower also modified the boundaries of several monuments created by previous presidents.

So, while President Obama's use of the Antiquities Act to designate large swaths of land for ecological protection was preceded by Theodore Roosevelt (Grand Canyon, 808,120 acres), Calvin Coolidge (Glacier Bay, 1,379,316 acres), Jimmy Carter (Wrangell–St. Elias, 10,950,000 acres), and Bill Clinton (Grand Staircase–Escalante, 1,885,800 acres), among others, Trump's disputed move to reduce large monuments also had historical precedent.

The problem with these reduction precedents is that legislation passed in the 1970s seems to void them. A huge lands bill called the Federal Lands Policy and Management Act of 1976, known commonly as FLPMA (pronounced "flip-ma"), set new rules for how public land should be managed. It included a clause in its final amended form that states, "The Secretary [of the Interior] shall not . . . modify or revoke any withdrawal creating national monuments under the Act of June 8, 1906." So, while FLPMA does forbid the secretary of the interior from modifying monuments, it does not mention what the president can or cannot do. The vagueness of this language concerning presidential power leaves considerable room for interpretation. Many hoped that lawsuits filed on behalf of the reduced monuments would answer this question with finality.

Complicating matters further, when President Joe Biden took office in 2021, his administration signaled a reversal of Trump's anti-monument policies. On Biden's first day he signed an executive order initiating another review, this time of the national monuments that

President Trump altered. His administration also requested a stay of court proceedings in the lawsuits contesting the reduced monument boundaries. On October 8, 2021, Biden reinstated the boundaries of both Grand Staircase–Escalante and Bears Ears. But the story is unlikely to end here. Monuments seem doomed to wild back-and-forth swings depending on the preferences and priorities of the administration in power.

THIS BOOK EXAMINES twelve large monuments and one small one designated by presidential proclamation. Each falls within Trump's review time frame beginning in 1996. This includes monuments made by three presidents: Clinton, who established nineteen during his presidency; George W. Bush, who created six; and Obama, who expanded or established thirty-four, more than any other previous president. These places encompass deserts, forests, mountains, rivers, and oceans. They consist of private land gifted to the government and Department of Energy land reserved to build nuclear bombs. They include timberland, fishing territory, pasture, a gold mine, and a life-size sculpture. Many of the questions these recent monuments raise regarding size, the interests of the public, and the well-being of the land itself are still unresolved.

I come to this topic as a recreationist: a rock climber, mountain biker, and backcountry skier. Recreating on public land brings abstract concepts about conservation and policy into focus for me. It is through climbing and backpacking that I have formed deep bonds with these places. Only after spending time in a place and with people who love a place does a more complex picture of how humans and the natural world interact begin to surface. Scholarship about public land policy and in-depth histories of our national landscape—though both important—too often do not convey the feeling of a place and the urgency, the desperate need some people feel to be in a place or to protect it.

National parks and monuments preserve more than natural environments: they preserve stories. We learn about the bloody Civil War through Gettysburg National Military Park in Pennsylvania. We learn about the fight for equality at Women's Rights National Historical Park in New York. We learn about the often-hidden history of Black soldiers in the west at Golden Gate National Recreation Area in California. Since the 1930s, the National Park Service has emphasized education, interpretation, and public history as, in the words of historian Denise D. Meringolo, a way to "raise important questions about the meaning of the past and impose order on a diverse and otherwise incoherent landscape."

Intermingled with stories is the fact that people become attached to places. Stories and experiences anchor people. "The physical environment and the emotions generated at sites of public memory have serious implications for not only how we remember the past, but how we understand the present," writes Jennifer K. Ladino in *Memorials Matter*. America's protected spaces evoke many emotions: wonder at the improbably tall and smooth side of El Capitan in Yosemite, grief and fear at the National September 11 Memorial, shame and anger at Manzanar National Historic Site.

Making sense of an "incoherent landscape" is perhaps an impossible task, but there is room to explore these landscapes more deeply. The past is complicated, and the stories told have too often been one-sided, the narrative controlled by a privileged few. The Antiquities Act was written with an intent to preserve history, but society's ideas of what that history is and who should tell it are changing. The original language of the act erased Indigenous peoples. In 1906, lawmakers' attitudes were that the Indigenous peoples of America had been removed and that ancient human history was a curiosity to be studied. While the law protected physical historical evidence, it deliberately ignored the lives, customs, and rights of the people to whom these artifacts and the land belonged. Modern uses of the act have begun to counter this attitude by recognizing Indigenous connection to land, the importance of Indigenous stories, and the need for Indigenous-led decision-making concerning land use.

The following chapters are an exploration in storytelling—the stories people tell about themselves, about places, the way stories shape our understanding. The conservation of ecosystems, endangered species, and natural beauty twists around the preservation of human history, narrative, and emotion like tangled vines growing from the same seed. On the surface, the science of natural conservation seems separate from subjective human attachment to place, but the two are inseparable. The natural world and its stories are branches of the same bush.

I share the stories of these monuments in different ways to provide the opportunity to read differently and, I hope, to understand differently. This book is not the definitive history of national monuments and not even close to the whole story about any one place. Rather, I offer sketches of people and places. There is room, and need, for more stories from people with different perspectives, histories, and backgrounds. My hope is that the sharing of these stories, from the viewpoint of someone who sought intimacy with each place, will inspire a reframing of how people see themselves in relation to land and each other.

Discussion of public land is often dominated by an us-versus-them rhetoric. People are either for national monuments or against them; they are environmentalists or oil drillers, conservationists or preservationists, Republican or Democrat, local or outsider. This black-and-white portrayal does us all a disservice. Throughout my travels I found that strongly worded political messages often obscured what was really happening in each monument. I wanted to understand the gray area, the complexities and nuance about what is really at stake if monuments lose protection and who is harmed by certain land policies and decisions. I began to wonder if I could find common ground among dissenting groups, or if opinions really were as polarized as the news made them seem.

Monuments are quintessentially American. After all, what is more American than disagreement over the scope of governmental power? Composed of the physical soil and sand and water within this country's border, they also represent more than the literal. They are shadowed by American tragedy, reminding us of acts of slavery, the slaughter and displacement of Indigenous peoples, and the cruel detainment and treatment of immigrants of many ethnicities. But they also serve as monuments to American possibility by preserving natural beauty and encouraging human connection to land, reclaiming areas that have been mined or polluted, and working to halt the effects of climate change and development through conservation. These contested lands contain important stories of our past and, I believe, a hopeful promise for our future.

ANOTHER MORNING ON OUR TRIP, Veronica and I sat inches away from petroglyphs on penny-colored boulders in Basin and Range National Monument in Nevada. I sipped coffee as dawn light pinked distant mountain ranges. Above amber and lavender clouds rose a tiny sliver of the moon, the slim glowing edge of a larger secret. Veronica balanced her tripod on a boulder next to me and frowned as she looked from the colorful sunrise to the screen on the back of her camera. "A camera can detect only about eight stops of light," she said. "Your eye can see a much larger range. We'd have to check, but I think it's twenty-two stops of light. That is why a photograph is never as beautiful as what you actually see. It is impossible to capture."

Over the course of several photography classes I took in art school, I learned that to achieve balance in a black-and-white film image, a photographer needs to set the correct aperture and shutter speed. If done correctly, the image will contain the entire gradient from true black to bright white. To do this, the lens is aimed at something neutral, and a reading is taken, which informs the settings. If the camera's settings are adjusted while aiming at something black, the camera tries to adjust that dark tone to a more even one, and the resulting image is overexposed, washed out and wimpy. If the camera is adjusted while aiming at something white, the image becomes underexposed and too dark to interpret. Photographers determine the correct settings by aiming the camera at an even tone called middle gray. Starting with gray allows the camera to expose a complete, rich image.

Middle is an indescribable state. It is not large or small, tall or short, wide or slim, or any definite edge of any spectrum. *Medium* is what people say when they lack a more precise word for description, as in medium build or medium height. *Middle* describes something that is neither here nor there, hot nor cold, just something lost in ambiguity. Even the word *middle* lacks distinctive, declarative notes; the sound gets lost between the tongue and the roof of the mouth.

Gray is the most boring color. It is the absence of more saturated hues. The lack of something vibrant, memorable, and intriguing. But there can be a beauty to it. It is the color found between velvet night and day's illumination. It is solid stone between spongy earth and cobalt sky. Middle gray is a painterly mix of many pigments: slate blue and dusky plum and rosy granite flecked with gold.

The cellist Yo-Yo Ma has said that music happens in the space between notes. Thich Nhat Hanh teaches that meditation happens in the quiet moments between thoughts. Perhaps a map of place can be drawn between footsteps. In these monuments I search for the truth between place and politics, for meaning hidden in crevices, for what is contained in the space between landscape and people. By focusing on gray, on what is in the middle, I hope to achieve a more complete vision of both dark and light.

NATIONAL MONUMENTS
VISITED IN THIS BOOK

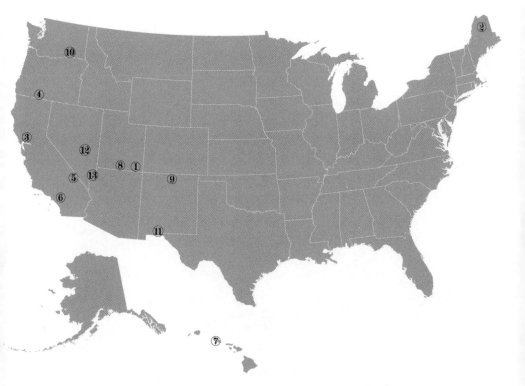

1. Bears Ears National Monument
2. Katahdin Woods and Waters National Monument
3. Berryessa Snow Mountain National Monument
4. Cascade-Siskiyou National Monument
5. Castle Mountains National Monument
6. Sand to Snow National Monument
7. Papahānaumokuākea Marine National Monument
8. Grand Staircase–Escalante National Monument
9. Rio Grande del Norte National Monument
10. Hanford Reach National Monument
11. Organ Mountains–Desert Peaks National Monument
12. Basin and Range National Monument
13. Gold Butte National Monument

Part I. Rock

ROCK (noun)
: a large mass of stone forming a cliff, promontory, or peak

ROCK (verb)
: to daze with or as if with a vigorous blow
: to astonish or disturb greatly

It seems the right words can come only out of the perfect space of a place you love.

ELLEN MELOY
The Anthropology of Turquoise: Meditations on Landscape, Art, and Spirit

1. The Heart of Bears Ears

BEARS EARS NATIONAL MONUMENT, UTAH

I sit in soft red sand and squint at orange rock silhouetted against blue sky. Golden light drapes the cliff behind me. The contents of deflated backpacks litter the ground: climbing shoes with their sour smell, a tangle of metal gear, and half-eaten pieces of fruit now resting on rock ledges. Climbers dip between sun and shadow as they try to maintain balance on the wall. I prepare for my own attempt on the crack that rises and thins above me. I trace the shape with my eyes, memorizing each curve, each notch in the edge, each subtle change in width. I've done this before: fixate on a single route until eventually my body and mind unite and I push through some invisible barrier to enter a realm as unexpected and enchanting as a delicate bloom on a cactus. I hope to do this again on this climb, embrace the process of learning and power that mimics the power of this wide-open-sky place.

BY MY SECOND CLIMBING TRIP TO INDIAN CREEK, I had fallen deeply in love. Indian Creek is a basin in San Juan County, Utah, in the southeastern corner of the state. The land is managed by the

BEARS EARS
NATIONAL MONUMENT

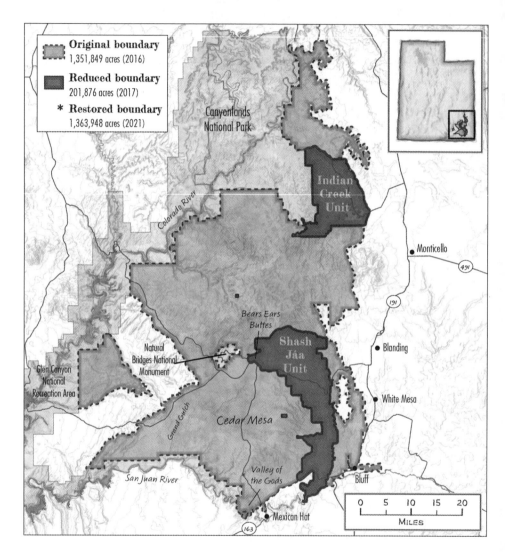

Original boundary
1,351,849 acres (2016)

Reduced boundary
201,876 acres (2017)

* **Restored boundary**
1,363,948 acres (2021)

Canyonlands
National Park

Indian
Creek
Unit

Colorado River

Monticello

491

191

Bears Ears
Buttes

Shash
Jáa
Unit

Natural
Bridges National
Monument

Blanding

Glen Canyon
National
Recreation Area

White Mesa

Grand Gulch

Cedar Mesa

San Juan River

Valley of
the Gods

Bluff

Mexican Hat

163

0   5   10   15   20

MILES

Bureau of Land Management (BLM) and encompasses a cattle ranch, world-class climbing, ancestral pueblo ruins, and an intricate desert ecosystem.

My first glimpse of this heartbreak-red desert was from a truck, driving an open road with flat, sagebrush plateau on either side. The road wound into a narrow, sandy canyon and turned a corner. Suddenly, the canyon opened to expansive basin rimmed with round, ruddy cliffs following round, ruddy cliffs, each lined with shadow-filled cracks; cliffs and cracks, cliffs and cracks multiplied to the horizon. It felt endless. I parked and leaned against the tailgate as the day cooled into evening. A car rattled over a cattle guard on its way northwest to Canyonlands National Park. I watched the sunset paint the stone blush pink then brick red then blood orange. My heart stuttered.

That first trip left me frustrated. Though the desert was mesmerizing, the smooth, featureless cracks felt impossible to climb, and it hit my ego hard. I left after four days, sunburnt and subdued, and didn't return until more than a year later. Enticed by a new partner, I gave desert cracks a second chance and fell headlong into passion in more ways than one.

To climb here required different techniques than I was used to. Instead of toeing small crystals, curling fingers around edges, and scaling a rock face, here the climber ascends cracks. Cracks with nothing to grab onto. The Wingate Sandstone in Indian Creek is smooth and hard and fractures evenly to form parallel-sided cracks that soar up stone for hundreds of feet and remain nearly the same width the entire distance. The challenge is to determine how to fit your body into that crack and gain purchase so you can inch yourself upward. Each size crack requires a different approach. A hand crack is easiest; it is the size that most hands and feet can flex into and feel secure. "Cupped hands" is wider, less secure for hands but easier for feet. "Tight hands" is harder still; both hands and feet barely fit, and a climber must keep the body close to the wall using careful tension. Cracks get smaller, down to fingers and tips, and they get larger, to fists then offwidth then chimneys that can envelop an entire body. Some climbers seem to have an easy time with crack climbing, but for me it was hard-won. I spent months learning how to climb different sizes.

While I was falling on climbs, I fell for my climbing partner too: a man equally passionate about climbing but with a different vision for a future than mine. We didn't agree on topics such as marriage, kids, and family, but at the time those matters took second place to climbing.

I fell for the flushed Utah desert too: colorful stone, strong sunlight and dry air, extremes of heat and cold, the way it storms on one side of the sky while sun pierces the other. I hardly noticed, because this love grew alongside romance, but the connection that developed was perhaps deeper than love between humans. Certainly deeper than my relationship with my climbing partner.

This desert is cherished by many, and for different reasons. Indigenous communities have ancestral and contemporary connections to southeastern Utah and consider it sacred. In the region known as Bears Ears there are over one hundred thousand cultural sites, including petroglyphs, cliff dwellings, granaries, and kivas, evidence of a long human history there. As European settlers moved westward in the 1800s, they forced the Southern Paiute people, Diné, Hopi, Zuni, Ute Mountain Ute, and Uintah and Ouray Ute off the land inhabited by their ancestors. Today the Indigenous people of the area collect herbs, plants, and firewood and perform spiritual ceremonies on the same land. "We are a spiritual people. However, our holy practices happen right here on earth, not in a church, but in special places like Bears Ears," reads *Bears Ears: A Native Perspective*, a publication of the Bears Ears Inter-Tribal Coalition.

BEARS EARS

Many members of the Church of Jesus Christ of Latter-Day Saints also have a spiritual connection to this land. Mormon settlers first came to Utah in the 1840s to escape religious persecution elsewhere and held the belief that Utah was a land promised to them by God. The Book of Mormon, 2 Nephi 1:5 reads, "we have obtained [the] land of promise, a land which is choice above all other lands; a land which the Lord God hath covenanted with me should be a land for the inheritance of my seed. Yea, the Lord hath covenanted this land unto me, and to my children forever." So just as many Indigenous communities are caretakers of this sacred land that is their home, many descendants of early Mormon settlers also call this place home and view its development as a god-given right and a way to honor their descendants.

Indigenous communities were betrayed by the U.S. government with unhonored treaties, which has created a lasting distrust of the government and its intentions. Similarly, many followers of the Mormon faith distrust the U.S. government because of past persecution. It is an attitude that overlaps with that of many other rural westerners. In the 1970s the BLM and U.S. Forest Service began to evaluate areas to designate as wilderness throughout the western United States. These actions received pushback from those who supported land uses like logging, mining, drilling, and ranching, none of which are permitted in wilderness areas. People who felt their livelihoods were threatened by an overreaching federal government advocated for state and local control of the land. They argued that land management decisions should be made by those who lived near the land and not be mandated by distant officials. This vocal movement became known as the Sagebrush Rebellion.

As the Sagebrush Rebellion gained traction in the West, so did the American conservation movement. The Wilderness Act was signed into law in 1964, the Environmental Protection Agency began operation in 1970, and the Endangered Species Act was passed in 1973. A growing number of people and groups across the country focused on protecting land, plants, and animals before development, pollution, and shrinking habitat caused them to disappear. In contrast to the Sagebrush Rebel perspective, conservationists typically pushed for more federal regulation to achieve their goals.

This soup of views about how to live with land converges in southeastern Utah, where gorgeous landscapes could be either protected or mined and where histories overlap. Disagreements about management, control, and economic futures stretch back decades here. Some point to the passage of the Antiquities Act, with its uncommon grant of presidential power over land, as the origin of these disputes. In 1936, Secretary of the Interior Harold Ickes proposed a 4.5-million-acre national monument in southeastern Utah that included much of what later became Bears Ears National Monument. World War II sidelined his proposal. Then, after years of political discussion, Congress created the much smaller 257,400-acre Canyonlands National Park in 1964. Yet, many still believed that the remaining area from Ickes's proposal should be protected in some form.

I knew nothing of this, but my passion for the same place was growing. In 2010, I moved from Wyoming to California to be with my desert-loving man. Twice a year, we made the long drive across Nevada, what we dubbed the "in-the-way state," on our way to Utah, the state of color, love, and wild. My life ticked to the rhythms of month-long climbing trips: sleep until the thumps of cooler lids and clatter of cookstoves wake me, drink coffee in a thick, puffy jacket as the sun warms night-chilled stone, wait in line at the bathroom, stuff my jacket into the backpack still loaded with gear from the previous day, cram as many friends into one truck as possible, and bounce down dirt roads to the cliff. Then, spend the day trying hard until my skin is scraped raw and my muscles are weak with exhaustion.

In 2012, Utah Congressman Rob Bishop decided to try to forge a "grand bargain" of land use to settle ongoing disputes. Modeling his tactics after a successful compromise made by Senator Bob Bennett in the St. George region, Bishop aimed to bring together ranchers, environmentalists, recreationists of all types, extractive industry representatives, and Indigenous tribes in a compromise called the Public Lands Initiative (PLI). His efforts to find common ground were undermined somewhat by his own outspoken rebuke of Interior Department decisions, especially national monuments. At a public event in the midst of the PLI effort Bishop announced, "If anyone here likes the Antiquities Act the way it was written, die."

The same year informal conversations for the PLI began, the Diné (Navajo) formed a nonprofit called Utah Diné Bikéyah (UDB), which means "people's sacred lands" in the Diné language. UDB wanted to protect off-reservation lands important to Indigenous communities. In explaining the impetus for its inception, UDB's website reads, "Utah Senator Bob Bennett asked Native people in San Juan County, UT, if they had any interest in how public lands were managed. White Mesa Ute and Utah Navajo grassroots people responded that the depth of their connections are so deep that they had been afraid to speak out for fear of what might still be taken away."

Bishop initially invited UDB to partake in the PLI planning process. After many years of work, research, and cultural mapping, UDB created a four-pronged land protection proposal that drew a boundary for a 1.9-million-acre national conservation area, nominated sections of wilderness within that boundary, established tribal and federal comanagement, and ensured continued access for

9

Indigenous people to their sacred land. This proposed area bordered Canyonlands National Park and encompassed the climbing area of Indian Creek. It was named after the distinctive twin buttes central to the region they hoped to protect: Bears Ears.

This proposal was presented to the Utah congressional delegation and San Juan County but was ignored. At the final planning meetings for the PLI, Utah Diné Bikéyah and the Navajo Nation were not invited. In response to this exclusion, five tribes formed an official Bears Ears Inter-Tribal Coalition composed of elected members from the Hopi, Ute Mountain Ute, Navajo Nation, Pueblo of Zuni, and Ute Indian Tribes. With the promise of the PLI bargain broken, this coalition decided to move forward with a plea for a national monument.

*

I've been attempting this climb for several seasons with no success. As the crack jogs horizontally, my feet slip on the featureless stone and I fall. One morning I wake up and the sand is two shades darker from rain. Sweet sage fragrance hangs in the air. The stone is wet; I can't climb. Instead, I let my mind rest as I hike through freshly scrubbed air along a pink slab, long views of saffron earth patched with dark green juniper on either side. Water fills potholes in the rock slab, reflecting pale blue from the clearing sky. Isolated from the rest of the world, these ephemeral pools contain creatures like fairy shrimp who can withstand drought and loss of body water, but come alive when it rains. Thunder rumbles in the distance while I crouch with my nose near the water's surface, watching the swimming shadows of desert life.

THE YEAR 2016 WAS THE ONE THAT SCRAMBLED. After six years, my relationship unwound. Tentatively, gently, almost reluctantly, we untangled the threads of our lives. They were deliberately tied together in complicated knots—the lifesaving kind used in climbing. But the underlying threads were weak. Instead of the climbing ropes that were our lifelines on rock, we had tied ourselves together with mere string. We had stayed together because we made great climbing partners, but we could not find a way to be good life partners. So we worked our knots loose. They came apart frighteningly easily. The day we ended our relationship, he climbed into his truck with tears in his eyes and drove to Indian Creek. I stood alone on the steps of our California apartment, consumed with loss. Not only had I lost my partner, I had lost my place. That was the first spring I didn't spend in Indian Creek in years.

In July of that scrambled year, Congressman Bishop introduced the Public Lands Initiative to Congress. The bill would set aside 1.28 million acres of southeastern Utah as a national conservation area and facilitate several land exchanges between the federal government and the state with the intention of opening areas to mining and development. Comanagement with Indigenous nations was not included. Later that month, amid an increasingly divisive presidential campaign, Secretary of the Interior Sally Jewell hosted a meeting in Utah to gauge public interest for protecting part of San Juan County as a national monument. Over fifty people testified, including ranchers, rock climbers, environmentalists, members of the Mormon Church, and Indigenous leaders. The overwhelming mood was support for Bears Ears National Monument.

In November, Donald Trump was elected president of the United States, and in December, Congress adjourned without voting on the Public Lands Initiative. After the election but before Trump's inauguration, President Obama invoked the authority of the Antiquities Act to designate Bears Ears National Monument. The proclamation struck a compromise between the Inter-Tribal Coalition's proposal and the PLI. It protected 1.35 million acres of federal land, directing that it be comanaged by the U.S. Forest Service, the BLM, and, in an unprecedented move, a commission composed of one elected officer from each of the five tribes unified in the Bears Ears Inter-Tribal Coalition.

Obama's lengthy proclamation opens with a description of "abundant rock art, ancient cliff dwellings, ceremonial sites, and countless other artifacts." It also makes specific mention of the ways in which Indigenous communities currently use the land. By including this in the proclamation, these cultural sites and land uses become objects protected by the monument along with fossils, a dark night sky, claret cup cactus, mountain mahogany, balsamroot, bluegrass, mule deer, pinyon mouse, red-spotted toad, eastern fence lizard, and the Mexican spotted owl.

The designation of Bears Ears was a joyous occasion for many. It was the result of years of work by UDB and the Inter-Tribal Coalition, and it was seen as a sign of healing, "healing of the land, healing of the wounds between tribes, between tribes and the federal government, and between tribes and local Anglos," wrote Rebecca Robinson in *Voices from Bears Ears*. It was a way of giving agency and voice to sovereign Indigenous nations that had been severely mistreated by the U.S. government in the past.

But while many felt joy, others were outraged. Some San Juan locals felt their land was being locked up by a greedy federal government. A campaign emerged to revoke what had just been created. Utah's conservative governor and lawmakers argued that management of land in their own state should be decided by legislative process and not imposed by presidential proclamation. The monument had been in existence for only a couple months when in February 2017 Governor Gary Herbert urged President Trump to rescind Bears Ears and shrink Utah's other controversial monument, Grand Staircase–Escalante.

Perfect Kiva, Bullet Canyon, Bears Ears National Monument, Utah.
Photograph by Veronica Palmer.

The dispute over Bears Ears bled across the country. Everyone seemingly had their own take on this monument, and the important fact that it was conceived by and for Indigenous people was often lost in the scuffle. Even outdoor industry retailers got involved, recognizing that reducing public land access across the nation will reduce the need for products like tents, hiking shoes, and backpacks. The clothing company Patagonia led a boycott of the Outdoor Retailer Show (the outdoor industry's largest conference held biannually in Salt Lake City) unless Utah legislators backed off their petition to remove the monument designation. Utah's politicians did not change their position, so the conference with its $50 million in local revenue was relocated to Colorado in protest.

Not all Indigenous people supported the new monument either. Ryan Benally, a member of the Navajo Nation and son of anti-monument San Juan County Commissioner Rebecca Benally, published an editorial in *Indian Country Today* arguing that the language of the proclamation relegated the Bears Ears Commission to providing "guidance and recommendations" but prevented their suggestions from being legally binding. Benally viewed it as yet another governmental betrayal of Indigenous people. In another op-ed, which appeared in the *San Juan Record,* Shoshone writer Darren Parry worried that the monument designation would increase tourism to the region and visitors would trample sacred sites even more.

I paid attention to these developments because they affected a place that I loved. I wasn't yet sure what the monument would mean for Indian Creek. I ached to reconnect with the place that made me feel alive and most myself, so I began asking people how they felt about the monument. By understanding others' closeness to the desert, perhaps I could find my way back to it.

The town of Monticello, surrounded by open, sage-covered hills, is less than twenty miles from the Bears Ears border. In late 2016, Monticello city council passed a resolution stating the town's official opposition to the monument. I contacted George Rice, the former chair of the Recreation Committee, to ask why. "If you look at the rules and regulations of other monuments in the country, they are very restrictive as to the type of activities that you can do. . . . I think that's how a lot of us feel, that it is more of an overreach and a restriction than a protection," he said. George and his neighbors were concerned about access to land to hunt game, graze cattle, and drive off-road vehicles. He thought that new rules could make it difficult for them to earn a living from the land and could dampen ATV-driven tourism. "If the land is restricted to the point where no one can use it, then it hurts us worse than it hurts someone else. . . . We live here. We would like a little bit of a say in how the land is managed," George said.

Nothing in the proclamation actually diminished these land uses. Existing roads and existing rights, such as for grazing, were left untouched by the monument designation. Yet, I understood what George was getting at. He chafed against the idea of Washington telling small towns what to do, but he was also fearful of change, afraid that this new thing would disrupt the way he interacts with land that is his home.

"No one here locally wants to see access restricted," said Josh Ewing, executive director of Friends of Cedar Mesa, a conservation-focused nonprofit that supports the monument. "We just want to see people using the area responsibly."

Josh is a resident of Bluff, a tiny town built beneath tall, red towers. Unlike in Monticello, Bluff residents overwhelmingly support the monument. "There are a lot of threats to the Bears Ears area," Josh explained. "There's use that's a threat, there's growing visitation that's unmanaged that's a threat, you have irresponsible motorized recreation that's a real challenge, you have continued looting and vandalism of sites which has been an issue for more than a century. So there are many reasons why a place that's this special, this beautiful, this full of archaeology ought to receive some special attention and be set aside for future generations to enjoy the way we do today."

Josh, though contradicting George's stance on the monument designation, seemed to be saying much the same thing: we don't want things to change. George's fear that his interactions with the land around his home would change is the same fear that motivated the push for the monument: fear that the place would be altered if it wasn't preserved.

*

The rocks themselves are alive. Colonies of microbes live on the surface of the stone where they secrete manganese and iron, forming a tawny varnish. Early desert inhabitants scratched pale, intricate shapes into this medium. Malcolm Lehi, a Ute Mountain Ute, says, "Native People relate to rock art with our hearts. . . . We do not view these panels as just art, but almost like a coded message that exists to help us understand . . . our life and reality as humans." The living varnish also creates the clean surfaces of the best climbs, which allow me to understand my reality. I look up at my chosen climb, place my hand on the smooth stone, and feel the pulse of the desert.

IN SPRING 2017, President Trump issued an executive order requiring a review of all national monuments over 100,000 acres that were designated after 1996, implying that he planned to remove protection from some of them. This included Bears Ears and twenty-six other monuments. As a response to this order, Secretary of the Interior Ryan Zinke embarked on what he called a "listening tour" through the monuments under review. In May, as I read about his visit to Utah's monuments, I saw a link to a personal video that had gone viral. In the clip, Secretary Zinke is shaking hands with onlookers at the Butler Wash Trailhead when a dark-haired woman wearing red lipstick and a "Protect Bears Ears" T-shirt approaches. "When are you going to meet with the tribal leaders?" she demands. "It's kind of unfair that you have only met with them for one hour. Sir, is there a reason that you are not listening to them more?" After first ignoring her, Zinke turns, shoves a finger in her face, and scolds, "Be nice. Don't be rude." He walks off.

I decided to talk to her. I reached Cassandra Begay on the phone, and as we spoke, her GPS navigation squawked in the background. "I'm so sorry . . . I'm driving for Lyft at the same time I'm talking to you," Cassandra said. "You don't make a lot of money in activism." She told me that she used to work in the corporate world, but "since I went to Standing Rock, for me as a Native American woman, that was the first time I actually felt like I belonged somewhere. I've had to live in two different worlds: the way I was raised traditionally and then in the more modern world."

Cassandra is a member of the Navajo Nation and grew up on a reservation near Bears Ears. "As a Native American people, we have always been one with the land." She described memories of growing up in a traditional hogan, eating deer meat that her stepfather hunted, and walking with her grandmother along a red-banked creek, where they collected willow branches to weave into baskets. "We see that land as a living organism with a heartbeat and a pulse."

Cassandra explained that the monument designation was the result of large-scale tribal cooperation: protecting this land was an important-enough cause to unite sovereign nations that hadn't typically worked together in the past. To her, the designation of Bears Ears with tribal comanagement was a symbolic gesture by the U.S. government to return stolen land to Indigenous peoples. "We were the first caretakers of these lands, and it's an absolute must that we have a seat at the table in every decision regarding these lands," she said.

In other places, Indigenous and federal government cooperation has resulted in better care for land and the communities connected to it. In 1958, Congress established Grand Portage National Monument in northeastern Minnesota. Grand Portage, or Gichi Onigaming, "the great carrying place," is a footpath that bypasses rapids and waterfalls on the Pigeon River as it feeds into Lake Superior.

This path has been used by Indigenous people for thousands of years. Later it became an important route for fur traders. This 710-acre monument differs from Bears Ears in that it lies entirely within the boundary of the Grand Portage Band of Minnesota Chippewa reservation and was created partly with land donated from the band and the larger Minnesota Chippewa Tribe. In 1999, the Grand Portage Band and the National Park Service agreed that all maintenance of the monument would be done by enrolled band members. Since then, band members have also been hired for interpretation and resource management roles. This cooperation allows the band to control and participate in decisions regarding land that is vital to their heritage, their daily life, and their future. Comanagement of Bears Ears could have been similar.

On June 10, while Zinke was still reviewing Bears Ears, an intertribal gathering took place beneath Comb Ridge to celebrate the monument and Indigenous relationships to lands that lie outside reservations. "The Bears Ears region is not a series of isolated objects, but a connected, living landscape that must be protected," the president of the Navajo Nation, Russell Begaye, told *Native News Online*. "You cannot reduce the size without harming the whole."

Secretary Zinke's monument review was largely perceived to be a sham. He traveled the country and met with people who stood to benefit from shrunken monuments and increased resource extraction, then claimed the Trump agenda had local support. He ignored tribes and the many people and groups who shared the opinion that the land should retain monument status. Documents accidentally released by the Department of the Interior confirmed that Zinke's review prioritized logging, ranching, and mining potential over any other interests.

On December 4, 2017, President Trump traveled to Salt Lake

City and signed an executive order shrinking Bears Ears and Grand Staircase–Escalante National Monuments. The Antiquities Act, which allowed President Obama to establish Bears Ears, was invoked in its resizing.

"The previous administration designated more than a half a billion acres of land and water, including Bears Ears. It did so over the loud objections of the people of this state and their elected representatives. Governor—right?" President Trump said in his speech before signing the proclamation. "The results have been very sad and very predictable. Here, and in other affected states, we have seen harmful and unnecessary restrictions on hunting, ranching, and responsible economic development. . . . These abuses of the Antiquities Act have not just threatened your local economies; they've threatened your very way of life. . . . With the action I'm taking today, we will not only give back your voice over the use of this land, we will also restore your access and your enjoyment. . . . We will put our nation's treasures to great and wonderful use."

In contrast to Obama's descriptive proclamation, which celebrates a vibrant human history and the ruggedly beautiful landscape, President Trump's proclamation modifying the monument is short and defensive. It states that some of the "objects" outlined in the original proclamation are not unique to that area or under direct threat of damage and concludes that Bears Ears was not the smallest area required for protection.

The 1.35-million-acre monument was divided into two smaller parcels, removing 1,150,860 acres: an 85 percent reduction. The Shash Jáa unit ("Bears Ears" in the Diné language) includes Bears Ears Buttes, Comb Ridge, and several other popular cultural sites, while the Indian Creek Unit encompasses the climbing area, rock art sites such as Newspaper Rock, dinosaur tracks, and other fossils.

Places left out are Bullet Canyon and Valley of the Gods, as well as miles upon miles of canyons, juniper and pinyon pine forest, and cultural sites.

The reduction order renamed the Bears Ears Commission the Shash Jáa Commission and relegated the group to providing guidance on the management of the Shash Jáa unit only, a significant reduction to tribal input and a removal of the comanagement that was so important to the original designation. This commission would now include the elected San Juan County commissioner, a person who had historically not cooperated with tribal representatives.

Utah lawmakers and residents opposed to the Antiquities Act and who staunchly claim that land-use decisions should be made through a legislative process rather than presidential order welcomed and celebrated this presidential order.

Immediately after the reduction, lawsuits were filed that challenged the president's authority to modify a previous president's monument. But these cases move slowly through the courts. In just a little over two years, a management plan was hastily approved for the smaller units, officially opening up removed land to new mining leases before the courts ruled on the legality of the reduction. All the national attention caused an influx of visitors to the Bears Ears region, even to parts of the original monument that were now excluded. The impact of numerous hikers, climbers, Jeepers, and others weighs heavily on a fragile, sacred desert.

I struggled to separate my love for a person from my love for the desert. I wanted to let go of one love but keep the other. I returned to Indian Creek and climbed routes I had never tried before, went to walls I had never been to, sifted grains of sand through my heart muscle, and examined what varnish remained.

Love develops and reaches new depths when there is shared vulnerability. Relationships grow when both parties reveal weakness and accept each other despite those weaknesses. Bears Ears and I, we were both vulnerable. Somehow this deepened our solidarity.

*

I stare up at my climb and take a breath, inhaling clean desert air. A bead of sweat rolls down my forehead. I think about purple flowers that bloom in spring and cottonwood trees that glow yellow in autumn. I think about living, lumpy cryptobiotic soil, a community of fungi, algae, bacteria, and lichens that takes decades to grow and guards the desert floor from erosion and invasive species. I think about wind and sudden rain, sand dunes from long ago and the heated pressure that formed these rocks and cracks. In comparison, rock climbing seems so trivial.

I AM AN OUTSIDER, an interloper. My ancestors did not live here for thousands of years, or even live here at all. I am not a resident of Utah. I have no claim to this land whatsoever. And yet, inside my heart are canyons that mirror Canyonlands. My blood is rust and salmon and copper and terra-cotta, the colors of sandstone. The story of this monument soaked into my own story until eventually my own narrative took on a deeper, more complex shade, and I could no longer separate it from this place. My connection to this desert is flimsy compared to people who have hundred-year history with the area. But I still feel the desert's pull.

In the center of Indian Creek is a startling patch of green surrounded by dry, rosy sand: the Redd family ranch. I have driven past it countless times, sometimes waiting in my car as glossy black cattle meandered across the road. It is the only ranch in the Indian Creek basin and has been operating here for generations. When I called Matt Redd, I caught him by surprise. It was evening, and a chorus of crickets chirped in the background. Hesitant at first to speak with me, he eventually opened up, using reverent language to describe the landscape. "This place is very, very special to me. . . . It is my church, my temple."

Matt referred to himself and other ranchers as "mature land users" because they come from a line of people who have worked this land for over a century. He told me about Al Scorup, one of the first cowboys in the area. In the 1890s Scorup ranged livestock throughout southeastern Utah, over land that is now Canyonlands National Park, Bears Ears National Monument, and the Redd family's ranch. After Scorup had spent years living in the intense heat and numbing cold of the desert, navigating canyons on horseback, and sleeping in caves, he was asked by a journalist what he thought of the land. "It has been my worst enemy," he said. Then after pausing a moment, he added, "And my best friend too."

"Talking to other ranchers who operate on Bears Ears, I would say we've all felt that way," Matt said, indicating the intense, complex bond between land and people.

Ranchers are often portrayed in the media as anti-monument and anti-land protection. Matt was careful not to express an opinion for or against Bears Ears, but it was apparent that he loves this place as much, if not more, than I do. "In my lifetime I have seen parts of the landscape that I hold sacred degraded by recreation," he said. "It is subjective, but what I consider to be the experience that people should have in the landscape isn't available anymore. What I consider an intact landscape, unpolluted by noise or excessive vehicles or traffic or people, is not available. Part of the reason for that is the [Canyonlands] National Park infrastructure put in to make things accessible for the public. As you do that you remove a fundamental aspect of the landscape that you are trying to preserve and protect."

Matt's lament, which ignored the impact of ranching, made me confront some truths I had been ignoring. Climbing was hurting this place that I loved. By being there I was destroying it. Climbing introduced me to the intricacies of this place, birthed my intimacy, made me care about protecting it. And yet, climbing can be destructive in its own ways, just like ranching. Matt complains about climbers; climbers complain about ranchers.

It is easy to demonize people with different opinions, to say that everyone who does not agree on the same approach to land use is wrong. But after these conversations I became convinced that people who are intimately tied to this place all want the same thing: to maintain that intimacy.

In 2018 the Access Fund, a nonprofit dedicated to protecting climbing areas, released a list of the ten most threatened climbing areas in the United States. Each of these areas was being loved to death, trampled by unprecedented numbers of visitors as the sport of climbing exploded in popularity. Indian Creek was on this list.

When I first visited, the Creek felt freer, more open, less crowded. And so was my heart. I fell in love with a man despite early signs that we would end in disaster. I took a wild and glorious leap to be with him, accepting beauty in the moment, disregarding the weightiness of the future. I also enjoyed the desert without concern for what the future would look like. Bathrooms hadn't yet been built at the camping areas. The main parking lot was yet to be paved. There were no numbered campsites or fees. No lines for routes at the cliffs.

But there are now.

The debate about the monument embodies a longing to preserve this place exactly as it is now, like a fading diorama in a museum. But the desert is different every day. Erosion slowly shapes the mesas, buttes, and towers, while humans inscribe their own lives into the landscape: paintings on stone and dwellings hidden in rock alcoves, roads, signed trailheads, and pit toilets. Cattle chewing grass, ATVs spitting dust, climbers on unusually parallel cracks, and visitor centers built on the roadside all leave a mark. The Diné believe that the landscape is not a collection of separate objects but a connected living whole. People and their accompanying infrastructure, good or bad, are part of this living whole too.

"I come from the Navajo Nation. My family are traditional healers and farmers and ranchers. A lot of my early outdoor experience was through herding sheep. We would climb around and look for medicinal plants," writes Len Necefer, founder of the nonprofit Natives Outdoors. Len is a climber and a backcountry skier who promotes inclusion and respect within the outdoor industry. "When I went to college, in Kansas, I started mountain biking and running. I found that so much of the outdoor recreation community's relationship with nature was about conquering it. To me this particular relationship felt empty. I grew up with practices that are based on an ethic of reciprocity with the land—with everything you take, you give something back. We were also taught the history of this place; we weren't just out there to have fun. These stories and relationships are what have allowed us to live in these places for thousands of years."

Rock climbing seems more about taking than about giving. This makes me uncomfortable. Perhaps reciprocity begins with respect for land, its people, and, like Len said, its stories. Climbing doesn't have to be only conquering and taking. In my case, it led to a love, a desire to talk to people and to know a place better. This has given me more reverence for the place and a deeper respect for other people who also love it. I know climbing has encouraged the same in others. With a little more care, by encouraging reciprocity with the land, perhaps rock climbing can be less self-serving.

Just as the desert is different every day, so, too, is the status of Bears Ears National Monument. President Joe Biden took office in January 2021, and on his first day he signed an executive order that initiated yet another monument review. While Trump's review included twenty-seven large monuments, Biden's review specifically targeted the three monuments that President Trump had altered.

This policy seesaw reveals both the strengths and weaknesses of the Antiquities Act. The law is a useful tool when compromise cannot be reached. Action can be taken without the time-consuming work of reaching legislative consensus. Yet, it leaves land vulnerable to the political party in power. Monuments created by executive order can just as easily be removed by executive order, and then replaced again.

As the deadline for Biden's monument review approached, a delegation of senators and representatives from Utah—all Republican—sent the president a letter urging him to seek a permanent legislative solution for Bears Ears and Grand Staircase–Escalante. Perhaps they are weary of the ping-ponging boundaries and the decades of fighting about land use in Utah. Or perhaps they want to leave their fingerprints on the decision rather than letting Biden decide the outcome on his own.

Ignoring this plea for a legislative solution, on October 8, 2021, Joe Biden signed an executive order that restored the boundary of Bears Ears. This new proclamation also reestablished the Bears Ears Commission and Indigenous and federal comanagement of the monument.

Just as with all decisions made about this monument before, Biden's action made some people joyous and others livid. Passions have not dissipated. I suspect there is more to this story yet to come.

*

I tie in with a dirty rope, double-check my knot, fist-bump my belayer, and go. The first part of the climb is familiar: my hands flex and stretch to fill the crack, then shrink to a solid jam. I focus on staying relaxed, not over-gripping or expending extra energy. At the last rest I shake out the fatigue in my arms. Then I lunge and stack my fingers into the flared openings. The rock edges scrape my skin, my feet slip on smooth stone, and I feel my sweaty fingers slide. A bubble of fear rises in my chest.

Then I feel the landscape encompass me: red dirt, vibrant as crushed pastel crayons; delicate towers that rise under weathering clouds; hardy fairy shrimp that hide in potholes; rusty varnish that thickens and darkens with time. I think of oil rigs bobbing on the horizon and of mines spiraling underground. I think of ranchers sleeping in caves and cow hooves crushing hundred-year-old cryptobiotic soil. I think of the painted handprints of the past, of people who palmed rough rock, who let the desert form them. My body sways in the space above the ground. I cling to the side of this wall, tiny among uncountable cliffs. I reach to make my next move.

2. The Conflict of Dreams

KATAHDIN WOODS AND WATERS NATIONAL MONUMENT, MAINE

Dammit!" Jack hollered and kicked the back tire of the van where it had been spinning uselessly in thick snow. He continued to scream obscenities while I crept wordlessly from the passenger seat. With a torn and too-large sweatshirt hanging loosely off his thin, muscular frame, and unlaced snow boots dragging off his feet, he clawed at the snow behind the stuck rear tires. Jack and I had been friends for years, and after my last relationship ended, we decided to become something more. We were still sussing out if this relationship worked. I retrieved chains from the back of the van and brought them over to Jack, who ignored me and kept cussing. I felt as if his anger was directed at me, even though I hadn't been driving. But it had been my idea to come here. It was March 2018, and we were on a long, unpaved, and unplowed road to Bowlin Camp in the new Katahdin Woods and Waters National Monument.

"We shouldn't even be here! I mean look at this road! Why did you think the van would make it?" Jack yelled, gesturing at the deep white that surrounded us. I wasn't sure if the question was rhetorical, but

KATAHDIN WOODS AND WATERS
NATIONAL MONUMENT

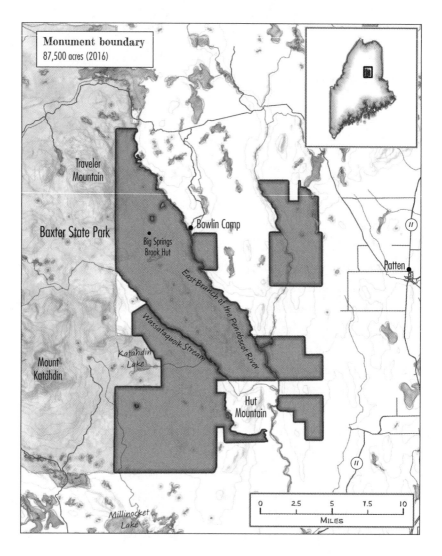

Monument boundary
87,500 acres (2016)

Traveler
Mountain

Baxter State Park

Bowlin Camp

Big Springs
Brook Hut

East Branch of the Penobscot River

Wassataquoik Stream

Katahdin
Lake

Mount
Katahdin

Hut
Mountain

Patten

Millinocket
Lake

0   2.5   5   7.5   10
MILES

I was sure that anything I said would ratchet up his anger further, so I kept quiet and sifted through my duffel to retrieve my gloves. We were on an ice-climbing trip and had spent a week exploring frozen waterfalls in New York and Vermont, but the past few days we had been cooped up during back-to-back nor'easter storms. Our moods were souring along with our damp clothes and gear.

Jack is tall with overgrown hair and eyes that are a marbled, stormy color that changes with his mood. When we were a new couple, I asked him what eye color was listed on his driver's license because I could not determine the hue. His eyes have looked at me in a lively blue, a cold gray, and even a mischievous pale green, but I cannot remember what color he believes his eyes are. Today they were the inhospitable color of roadside slush.

We bickered and got the chains wrapped around the rear tires. "Do you want to turn around?" I asked in exasperation once the van was moving again. I had spent weeks coordinating with a woman named Susan to reserve a night in a backcountry hut, but after the recent storms Susan wrote me a long email strongly discouraging us from going out in the deep, fresh snow. Perhaps it was better to abandon our plan altogether. Jack didn't respond but kept driving toward Bowlin Camp. In the parking lot we packed our bags in simmering silence. Before I was ready, Jack clicked into his cross-country skis and glided away.

I hurried to catch up. "Oh shoot, I left my headlamp in our climbing bag from yesterday. Did you get yours?" I asked.

"I have everything I need in my backpack," Jack responded icily.

Furious, I returned to the van, yanked my headlamp out of the bag, and was relocking the door when Jack skied over.

"Did you grab mine?" he asked, a little sheepishly.

I wonder if my headlamp will break if I throw it at him.

We collected our headlamps and skied through the parking lot, one after the other. The day was cold but sunny, a fresh break in stormy weather that felt cheerier than we did.

Our trail began by crossing a swinging bridge over the East Branch of the Penobscot River. Snow had sifted through the slats of the bridge and between them I could see glittering water rushing beneath. The river is named for the Penobscot people, "Penobscot" being a mispronunciation of their name for themselves: *Penawap-skewi*. It translates to "rocky part" or "descending ledges," a description of their home near the river. Today, the Penobscot people are one of four nations that together are called the Wabanaki, meaning "People of the Dawnland." They and their ancestors have been living in the region now known as Maine for at least twelve thousand years.

Along the river's opposite bank we entered a forest of birch and maple mixed with eastern pine and hemlock. The sharp green scent of needles jumped in my nose. We followed the trail steeply uphill and struggled on our slick skis. At first I approached the hill straight on but slid backwards into a messy tangle of poles and limbs, so I changed tactics and sidestepped up, breathing hard.

Normally a packed trail leads five miles through the monument to the Big Spring Brook Hut, but since there had been so much recent snow, the staff had been unable to groom the road. Perhaps Susan was right, and we shouldn't be out here. Navigation was easy since the road was a wide path cut through young trees and it was lined with blazes, but the snow was deep, and our pace was slow. There was a thin crust on top of the snow, formed when bright sun melted surface crystals that subsequently refroze overnight. This ice layer held our weight momentarily before our narrow skis punched through and sank into softness underneath. It was somehow better than wading. The sharp edges of the crust scraped against my rental boots, eroding the fabric seams. With every step, I felt cold air tingle my big toes, and I knew the boots were tearing where the upper met the sole. But I didn't want to bring it up. I hoped they would last the five miles to the hut.

We moved forward in jerks and hitches rather than a smooth glide. The woods were silent except for the crunch of our skis, just us and the forest. My legs burned with effort, my breath burst out in hot puffs, and my cheeks pinked in the chill air. Jack's back was rigid ahead of me. I pictured the miles ahead with some despair. To distract myself, I thought instead about this new monument and its origin story.

ROXANNE QUIMBY HAD A DREAM about a national park in the woods of Maine. As a live-off-the-land Mainer, she and her partner Burt Shavitz started making beeswax candles and selling them at farmers markets in 1984. This grew into the popular lip balm and lotion company Burt's Bees. In 2007 she sold the company and made $173 million in the deal. Soft-spoken and in love with the Maine woods, Quimby used her newfound wealth to purchase parcels of land from dying paper companies, most of which neighbored Baxter State Park and Mount Katahdin, Maine's highest peak. In total, she acquired 120,000 acres of forest and, in her zeal for preservation, outlawed logging, hunting, snowmobiling, and other forms of recreation that had previously been allowed on the land. She wanted to give this overused land a chance to breathe without people.

The paper mills had let visitors do whatever they wanted in the woods, and even leased portions for people to build cabins. Quimby evicted people from these long-held camps along the East Branch of the Penobscot and sealed off access to land that was cherished by many. The local backlash was widespread. No one likes being told that they can't visit their secret hunting spots or prized fishing holes. When word got out about her plans to turn the same land into a national park, even more people became even more upset.

Snowmobiling and hunting are not allowed in most national parks, and ways that people have enjoyed this land for years would likely be forbidden under a park's management. Maine residents felt excluded from land that had essentially been theirs for generations, and powerless to make decisions regarding this place they loved. Many were losing jobs as Maine's logging and paper mill industries collapsed, and now they were losing leisure activities as well. They had lost control of their future. The region's economy was in distress, and Quimby's privatization of land was, it seemed, further eroding the Mainer way of life. To locals, it appeared that acquiring, protecting, and accessing land was a luxury only for the wealthy.

For Quimby's plan for a national park to become a reality, she needed legislative action, but in 2011 all four of Maine's congressional members sided with the public in opposition to her idea. However, the need for state support and a legislative vote could be circumvented with an even more controversial idea: using a presidential proclamation to establish a national monument. On the surface, it seemed as though this would require convincing only one person: the president.

JACK AND I SKIED between thin fences of ghostly white paper birch, dark peeling yellow birch, and maple trunks speckled with pale lichen rings—a young forest. It had certainly been logged, because these spindly trees couldn't be much older than me at thirty-three. In its past life, this forest had been harvested and stripped, but now it was regrowing.

There were two things that I hoped to see here in Maine. First, I wanted to see a national monument in its infancy. When we were skiing through winter forest, Katahdin Woods and Waters was only a little over a year old. "Imagine if you got to visit Yellowstone or Yosemite before all the visitor infrastructure was built, when it wasn't swarmed with people," Friends of Katahdin Woods and Waters executive director Andrew Bossie said to me. Perhaps one day this place would be as popular as those iconic parks, but at the moment it was remote, rough, and natural. We were able to experience this place in the condition that prompted it to earn protection.

Second, I wanted to see the night sky. Humans consider electricity necessary for modern life, but a consequence is that we can't see the world the way we used to. Light pollution is temporary and reversible, yet illuminated cities feel increasingly permanent. True darkness has become rare, especially on the United States' heavily populated East Coast, but central Maine is a velvety exception. The National Park Service website claims, "with the night comes dazzling pinpoints of light and the Milky Way unfurled in luminous mystery. Nighttime views and environments are among the critical park features the National Park Service protects. Night sky protection enhances qualities of solitude and undeveloped wilderness character that animals depend on for survival, park visitors seek for connections, and many cultural-historical parks require for preservation." At the time of my visit, the monument's application was still under consideration, but in 2020 Katahdin Woods and Waters became the first International Dark Sky Sanctuary on the United States' Eastern Seaboard, a designation reserved for places around the world with a light pollution–free nocturnal environment. On a moonless night, the stars here would be exquisite.

"Did you see this?" Jack pointed with his ski pole to tracks in the snow. We leaned down to examine the delicate outline of soft feline pads. Unlike us wading through breakable crust and leaving a churned trail in our wake, the cat floated on the surface and left only gentle evidence of its passing. We guessed it was a bobcat. Like us, the bobcat had taken advantage of the easy, wide trail for travel rather than squeezing through tightly packed tree trunks. We followed the

tracks for some time, eventually finding a small hole where the bobcat had dug down to snap up a rodent that thought it was safe under a
haven of snow. Our mutual curiosity melted earlier frustrations, and
the silence between Jack and me warmed to comfortable.

IN MAINE, there is a pattern of private land donations to the public.
This started in the late 1800s with the Eliots, a family that summered
on Mount Desert Island. Charles W. Eliot, the father, was the president of Harvard University; Charles Eliot, his son, grew up with an
emotional attachment to Maine's coast and, as a result, aspired to
be a landscape architect. Of Maine he wrote, "It is the blackness of
these dwarf coniferous woods which, with the desolation of the surf-
beaten ledges and the frequent coming of the fog, impresses the trav-
eller with the fact that this is a really wild and sub-arctic shore."

He died in 1897 from spinal meningitis at the young age of thirty-
seven. His grieving father read through the younger Eliot's journals,
where he described the beauty of Maine as well as the ways in which
humanity was destroying it. In particular, he had been upset that
privately owned plots limited access to the woods and beaches. He
lamented, "Can nothing be done to preserve for the use and enjoyment of the great unorganized body of the common people some
fine parts, at least, of this seaside wilderness?"

Inspired by his son's wish, in 1901 Charles W. Eliot formed the
Hancock County Trustees of Public Reservations with the mission to purchase private land and make it accessible for public enjoyment. Headed by executive secretary George Dorr, another man
who grew up vacationing along Maine's shores, the organization acquired 5,000 acres. Dorr and Eliot decided to present this land as a

gift to the federal government. In 1916, President Woodrow Wilson accepted the gift and designated the area Sieur de Monts National Monument. Three years later Congress converted it to Lafayette National Park, the first national park east of the Mississippi. It has since been renamed Acadia.

WE TURNED OFF THE MAIN TRAIL toward Big Spring Brook Hut, and I mistook several snow-covered boulders for our cabin. Other backcountry huts I have stayed in are small, primitive shacks with just enough room for a woodstove and a few bunk beds. Instead, a palatial cabin waited for us, including a separate woodshed and an outhouse. The snow level was even with the deck of the covered porch, so I slid directly onto the wooden planks, released my broken boots from my skis, and opened the door.

Inside, bunk beds lined the walls of the first floor and, along with two separate lofts, provided enough space for sixteen people to sleep. Pipes connected to a propane cookstove and wall-mounted lanterns, a luxury almost as easy as electricity. Chairs were arranged in a communal arch around a huge black woodstove. I opened every cupboard and counted no less than three bottles of maple syrup left behind by past visitors. Jack rifled through the bookshelf and tallied the board games. "I can't believe we can stay here for free," he said, starting to seem enthusiastic.

We fell into an easy evening routine of partners: Jack skied to the woodshed and tossed logs into the back stairwell while I stacked them inside. He got a fire crackling in the woodstove while I cooked dinner. Jack spent almost an hour devising a way to fix my torn boots with supplies scrounged in the hut. We found a puzzle that depicted a fall landscape, and giggled and elbowed each other as we worked until we concluded several pieces were missing and gave up. We chose to spend the night in the loft, where the heat collected in the rafters, and curled together on the floor. I anxiously waited for stars to emerge while Jack slept.

LIKE THE YOUNGER CHARLES ELIOT, John D. Rockefeller Jr. fell in love with salty air and pink granite cliffs after purchasing a summer home on Maine's coast in 1910. But he cringed as he watched automobiles encroach on the rugged seaside. He dreamed up a plan to build car-free carriage roads for horses and people to access the cliffs and beaches in hopes that they would prevent the puttering, greasy automobile from altering the area's natural beauty. He, too, began buying land. Between 1913 and 1940, he supervised the building of a network of carriage roads. Instead of paved roads that dominate a landscape, he designed the roads to complement the scenery. Bridges were faced with intricately laid native stone, and large rough-hewn boulders called coping stones lined the gravel paths in place of guardrails.

Ultimately, Rockefeller Jr. spent $3.5 million and donated 10,000 acres of land to create forty-five miles of carriage roads in the new park. These roads still provide hiking and biking access for visitors. True to his vision, the carriage roads have kept cars out of Acadia.

While Rockefeller Jr. was building roads, Senator Percival Baxter was formulating a plan for the highest peak in Maine. In 1920, he joined a group of political figures to climb the 5,269-foot-tall Mount Katahdin. He squirmed across a knife-edge ridge to reach the summit and, with fear and adrenaline pumping in his veins, observed tiny trees and glistening lakes far below in a view unlike any he had seen before. Afterward Baxter declared, "I wouldn't do it again for a million, I wouldn't have missed it for a million." The following year, still under the spell of that adventure, he introduced a bill to the state legislature that proposed a 57,232-acre park encompassing Mount Katahdin and Katahdin Lake. It was rejected.

Baxter served as governor for four years but was unable to convince the legislature to designate his park. Still, he was determined to protect the peak that he viewed as the treasure of Maine. Between 1931 and 1962, like Quimby years later, he bought twenty-eight heavily logged parcels of land from timber companies. His first purchase was almost 6,000 acres from Great Northern Paper Company that included Mount Katahdin. He donated this parcel to the state under the condition that it remain wild and natural. Over the next thirty years he continued to add land parcels to this donation, along with an endowment of almost $7 million for its management. Baxter laid out specific plans for how he wanted the park to be run: 75 percent wildlife sanctuary and 25 percent open for hunting and trapping. Additionally, a portion of the park is a Scientific Forest Management Area, where logging and sustainable forestry practices are studied. He also issued a mandate that the land remain in control of the state and not be transferred to the federal government. This land became Baxter State Park, and it remains open to the public today.

MORE RECENTLY, amid protests against Roxanne Quimby's national park plan, her son, Lucas St. Clair, took over the family's campaign with the public. Like George Dorr before him, he met with the Department of the Interior about the idea of creating a national monument. Officials made it clear that there would be no monument unless the public supported it. The monument designation was far from a "federal land grab"; the Department of the Interior required extensive outreach and proof of public support before it would entertain even so generous an idea as a gifted monument. St. Clair had to convince Mainers they shared his mother's dream of protected land.

KATAHDIN WOODS AND WATERS

"The challenge was that people really didn't know what we were talking about," St. Clair told me. "I had to explain to people that no, the monument is not going to be a big statue of my mom."

Embracing an attitude of conservation rather than his mother's view of preservation, St. Clair reopened his family's land to recreation. He removed "no trespassing" signs, cleared snowmobile trails, and welcomed hunters back into the woods. Then he embarked on a statewide tour to arouse local support for the idea of a national monument. He made the campaign a dialogue and listened to residents' concerns, ideas, and protests.

"I spent a lot of time in high school gymnasiums and local libraries explaining what we were trying to do and saying that no, we don't want to destroy your economy or your town," he said. "Oh, and by the way, this is private land. We can do whatever we want with it because we own it. What we're trying to do is put it into the public trust so everybody owns it collectively and it becomes public, not private."

Over five years, St. Clair emphasized how tourism could help the economically depressed area where the timber industry had no hope of revitalizing. By making it an economic argument rather than a conservation argument, he got people's attention. He also proposed ways that the land could be shared between different user groups. People began to warm to his idea.

"We did a bunch of public polling, and we were able to show that to the White House and to our congressional delegation to get them on board," he said. "Our highest poll was 72 percent support. That's the type of support apple pie gets."

Just like Charles W. Eliot did one hundred years earlier, Roxanne Quimby donated 87,563 acres of her own land to the federal government in August 2016. The following day President Obama issued a proclamation designating it Katahdin Woods and Waters National Monument. Using the Antiquities Act to protect this part of Maine allowed the process to be quick. The Quimby family still hopes that one day Congress will convert this monument to a national park like it did with Acadia, but for now Quimby's vision of protected public land in Maine has been realized.

The eventual management plan for Katahdin Woods and Waters was a community effort of compromise that grew from St. Clair's public campaign: hunting is prohibited in certain areas but allowed in others; snowmobiling is permitted in some regions and banned in others to keep some wilderness quiet and remote. Similar compromises over fishing, biking, camping, and skiing access exist as well. The original opposition to the monument makes this compromise an even greater success.

"We went into the conversation trying to solve for yes," St. Clair told me. "If we try to solve for everyone's maximum benefit, the conversation becomes much more inclusive, much more calm, and much more thoughtful. More people enjoy it." This effort illustrates how conflict can evolve into richer solutions. Without an initial phase of unrest, there can be complacency rather than innovation and progress. Though uncomfortable and unpleasant, conflict itself is not a bad thing but can be the first step toward a more nuanced relationship.

Conflict is inevitable when unique, complicated, selfish, lovable people come together around any topic, whether that topic is skiing to a hut in fresh snow or the much broader question of how to use land. Of course, something as personal as access to place—which evokes emotional attachment and has potential for generating income—is sure to rile people up. Similar conflicts over land use are happening all over the country.

When Secretary of the Interior Ryan Zinke conducted his monument review a year after Katahdin Woods and Waters was established, he went to Maine to get a sense of the local sentiment about this new monument. "We went through a long, deliberative process to grow support and understand what this is, to create something that's unique to Maine with a ton of buy-in," St. Clair said. "When Zinke got here, he was expecting another fight, like he saw in Utah and other places. Instead everyone was like, 'Hey, thanks for coming! We love this place and we really recommend you leave it alone.' By the time he left, he loved it too."

Quimby, St. Clair, Baxter, Rockefeller Jr., Dorr, and both Eliots all had a personal love of place that was so big, it demanded sharing. Unrequited love is never complete, and since the land couldn't love back in a tangible way, their love could only reach full potential through giving, allowing others to experience similar profound moments and form deep connections to place themselves.

By the time this monument was created, many residents of Maine had grown to love the idea of legally protecting it. It hadn't really taken them long to change their minds. They already loved the place, but they learned to love and to share. I wonder what people in the future will think when they look back at this moment of decision. Perhaps this formerly logged and lumbered region will become as adored as national icons like Yosemite and Acadia. In hindsight, a monument designation will seem like an obvious choice.

AWAKE IN THE DELICIOUSLY WARM LOFT, I extracted myself from underneath Jack's arm, slipped my feet into his too-large boots, and skied toward the outhouse. The night sky sat there like a presence. It was dark but not the inky bottomless dark of a dry desert night. Instead the darkness echoed with color, like the difference between a true black, single-shade ink and a rich black composed of four color inks: cyan, black, yellow, and magenta. My skis glided over the packed track and wind tickled at the gaps between my leggings and my boots, sliding icy fingers around my calves. My body, still warm from the fire-heated cabin, didn't notice. Or maybe I didn't notice the cold because I had never really noticed a partly cloudy night sky before. A fuzzy, plum cloud obscured Orion. The other half of the sky brightened with sparks, like embers in a waning fire. Starlight illuminated the snow, painting the clearing and cabin in monochrome shades of shadow and gleam.

Something about this particular night sky, edged in bare branches, felt ancient and spectacular. It wasn't as vast as a treeless western night but felt weightier, more enigmatic and rare. My hair blew in tangles in front of my face as clouds seeped across the sky and stars disappeared behind indigo blots and reemerged in a spray of glitter.

Something primal is lost when we don't have night, when city lights bleed upwards and darkness becomes thin and weak and wobbling. Scientific evidence has revealed that too much artificial light interferes with the circadian rhythms of people and wildlife, such as migrating birds and baby sea turtles trying to find the ocean. Humans used to be able to navigate by the night sky, but now most of us use cell phones and glowing GPS maps. We aren't as directionless as a tiny turtle crawling toward dunes instead of waves, but our disconnection with the world is more like moths bouncing into porch lights in a puff of wing dust. We have lost our sense of place.

Lacking an anchored sense of place, we have also lost our understanding of how to relate to the earth. We no longer seem to know how to benefit from land without destroying it. Instead of working toward coexistence, we perceive a choice between protection or destruction. Paper companies tore through old-growth forest without much care for its regrowth. Roxanne Quimby and Lucas St. Clair wanted to protect and preserve. They dreamed of a quiet wilderness without whining snowmobiles and the pop of hunting rifles, and certainly without whirring chainsaws dropping trees with echoing thumps. Quimby didn't want people in the Maine woods at all.

KATAHDIN WOODS AND WATERS

But St. Clair recognized that is unrealistic. People want to be in the woods, and they want to be there in different ways. There must be creative consideration about access and land use because people aren't separate from the land around them. Just as the stars are inseparable from the sky, we are enmeshed with the land. In hindsight, perhaps this too will become obvious.

A YEAR AFTER OUR KATAHDIN TRIP got off to its miserable start, Jack spent two months climbing in Argentina. He trudged through snow and wind and spent a couple nights hunkered down in a cabin waiting for weather to clear. He sent me a message from a satellite phone:

> Rough day. Battered by blowing snow. Thankfully we are now cozy inside a plush refugio where living is easy. It feels like the Maine cabin here. That was so much fun!

3. The Meaning of Monuments

BERRYESSA SNOW MOUNTAIN NATIONAL
MONUMENT, CALIFORNIA

Fires raged all over California. It was July 22, 2017. On July 21, the Garza fire in Fresno County and the Long Valley fire in Lassen County had been announced as contained. The Detwiler fire in Mariposa County still burned.

Veronica and I ignored the flames and spent two days hiking up Snow Mountain in the northern region of Berryessa Snow Mountain National Monument. Descriptions I read of this hike said crampons might be required to ascend snowfields, even in summer. We left those behind.

We woke up in San Francisco to annoyed honks and the clang of garbage trucks rocketing into our friend's apartment window. We walked down a crowded street rumbling with cars to get breakfast, then drove a few hours through dead-grass hillsides and a paste of heat to the Deafy Glade trailhead, where it felt eerily deserted after the congestion of the city. We parked and saw no other cars, no other people. Sweating, we loaded our backpacks for an overnight, packing extra water since we were unsure where we could refill. The

45

BERRYESSA SNOW MOUNTAIN
NATIONAL MONUMENT

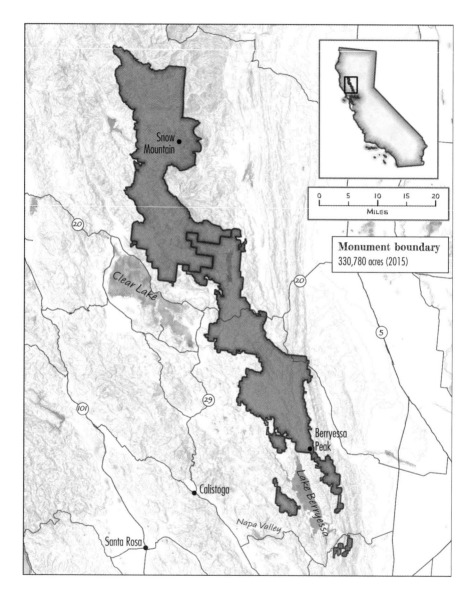

0   5   10   15   20
MILES

Monument boundary
330,780 acres (2015)

Snow
Mountain

Clear Lake

Berryessa
Peak

Calistoga

Napa Valley

Lake Berryessa

Santa Rosa

oppressive heat and silvery silence unsettled us, but neither of us mentioned it.

Hedged by Napa Valley and Sacramento, this monument connects Snow Mountain in the north to Berryessa Peak in the south and is refreshingly empty of both people and sound for an area so close to large populations. Like preserving dark night skies, preserving acoustic environments is an aim of protected land such as parks and monuments, and standing in woods absent of human-made clatter, I understood why. In *Protecting National Park Soundscapes*, Proctor Reid and Steve Olson write, "just as smog smudges the visual horizon, noise obscures the listening horizon for both visitors and wildlife." We hiked into quiet Jeffrey pine and incense cedar.

Veronica brought the wrong shoes, so she struggled behind me in the heat as we climbed a steep, manzanita-lined hill. The trail curved around a treed meadow where the evening light caught my eye, so I paused for a moment of solitude. Low, golden sunlight filtered through tree branches and shimmered off leaves. I had a sensation like peering into clear water on a sunny day when bright spots and speckles flicker and dance around your field of vision. Then I realized that the meadow was filled with dragonflies, hundreds of dragonflies, darting in and out of the light, flashes of brightness bouncing off their wings.

Veronica joined me in the meadow and we continued hiking above tree line. Smoke hazed the horizon. It blew north from the fire in Mariposa and ignited the sunset. Smooth hills undulated in front of rusty sky and misted into the distance. We set up our tent on a flat, sandy spot between boulders, took photos of the filmy sunset, and heated up an easy dinner. Then we sat together as the light faded, listening to the rattle of evening insects. We saw no stars through the murkiness.

The next morning, Veronica and I ambled up the summit of Snow

Mountain: wide, flat, brown, dirt. I usually envision mountain summits as sharp and rocky, but this one was a smooth, gentle walkway. There was one boulder on the summit, so we gravitated to it, lounging on its folds and edges as we enjoyed our accomplishment. It was still morning, but I ate my lunch anyway. Tame, conifer-coated mountains of the Snow Mountain Wilderness unfolded before me. There was not a single speck or flash of white on Snow Mountain this July.

The climate is warming, and this is not good news for fire-prone California. The Union of Concerned Scientists notes that "higher spring and summer temperatures and earlier spring snow-melt typically cause soils to be drier for longer, increasing the likelihood of drought and a longer wildfire season, particularly in the western United States. These hot, dry conditions also increase the likelihood that, once wildfires are started by lightning strikes or human error, they will be more intense and long-burning."

"THIS IS THE BEST PLACE IN THE WORLD to see plate tectonics," Bob Schneider told me. "You could go to the Marianas Trench, but you'd need a submarine. . . . So this is the best place." Bob was talking about the Berryessa Snow region in our shared state of California.

Like me, Bob is a climber. He came of age climbing granite in Yosemite and the Sierra in the 1960s and 1970s, the formative era of California rock climbing. Steve Schneider, Bob's younger brother by twelve years, is renowned for his first ascents of impressive routes. "I used to be known as Bob Schneider the climber, now I'm just known as Bob, Steve Schneider's brother," he joked. But Bob has an impressive climbing résumé too. He completed the twenty-first ascent of The Nose on El Capitan, a famous Yosemite route that has now been climbed thousands of times. In 1972, Bob made the twentieth aid-climbing ascent of the Salathé Wall on El Cap, ten years after that route's first ascent. In the 1990s Steve Schneider completed the first solo ascent of the Free Rider, a free-climbing version of the Salathé Wall, in less than twenty-four hours ("he used a rope, mind you.") Twenty years after that, Alex Honnold free-soloed the Free Rider, meaning he climbed it without a rope or any protection at all. "So in fifty years it went from the first ascent to Alex's free-solo ascent. That's just an incredible story of human potential and development," Bob marveled.

Doug Robinson, another influential climber from the same era, had put me in touch with Bob, saying, "you may like to know that an old climbing buddy of mine, Bob Schneider (brother of Steve), worked really hard to bring Berryessa Snow Mountain National Monument to fruition." I looked Bob up and learned that even though he doesn't have the name recognition his brother has in climbing, he has won awards for his land advocacy efforts. Now Bob and I were chatting about climbing and conservation.

"I started doing a lot more hiking in the Coast Range, and I just fell in love with this place. I mean, I'd always been about the Sierra and rock and ice and granite and pretty places. But this place was a lot more distinct in terms of biological diversity." The southern part of the monument, near Lake Berryessa, sits at sea level. Roughly one hundred miles north, Snow Mountain reaches to over seven thousand feet. It formed as an underwater mountain almost two hundred million years ago. Covering this wide range in elevation are wetlands, woodlands, grassland prairies, and chaparral habitats, which intersect and provide rich living space for wildlife such as black bears, bald eagles, tricolored blackbirds, creeping wild rye, and the endangered foothill yellow-legged frog.

"Because of the geology, you have a lot of serpentine soils," Bob said. Serpentine soil is a grayish-green degraded rock exposed through crustal movement. "[This soil] doesn't have many nutrients in terms of nitrogen or potassium and is very high in iron and magnesium. A lot of plants can't grow on it, but some plants have evolved to only grow in serpentine soils. There are a lot of special endemic and rare plants associated with the serpentine." These include Lake County stonecrop, a tiny red succulent with bell-shaped yellow flowers that grows within the monument, only in Lake County, California. There is also Brewer's jewelflower, Purdy's fringed onion, and Snow Mountain buckwheat.

In 2002, Bob and his friend Andrew Fulks decided that this area needed more trails so people could experience its uniqueness for themselves. They formed the nonprofit Tuleyome (a Lake Miwok word that means "deep home place") to work on access and preservation issues that they cared about.

"The first big project that we really worked on was getting Cache Creek established as a state Wild and Scenic River. And that was 2005. And then, I think, in 2006, we worked on Mike Thompson's North Coast Wilderness Wild Heritage bill. That established the Cedar Roughs Wilderness, the Cache Creek Wilderness, an addition to the Snow Mountain Wilderness . . . and a whole bunch else. After that, we realized this really is a special region, and we wanted to get it designated as a national conservation area, which is a congressional designation, but with the politics it just wasn't happening. So we moved to working toward a national monument."

THE SECOND TIME I VISITED Berryessa Snow Mountain National Monument, I went to the southern section with my entire family during Christmas. We spent a week camping in yurts outside Calistoga and divided our days between wine tasting and hiking. We purchased "Winter in the Wineries" passports that gave us access to seventeen different wineries. The first pages of the passport provided instructions for tasting wine:

1. Tilt and Look
2. Swirl and Smell
3. Sip and Taste
4. Repeat and Conclude

We tasted a lot of chardonnays, a Napa Valley specialty. I learned that the typical California-style chardonnay has a rich, buttery flavor that comes from being aged in oak barrels. A French-style chardonnay is cleaner, clearer, crisper. This slim flavor is achieved from aging in stainless steel barrels. As one of the winery employees explained, this style allows for more of the flavor of the actual fruit to come through since it is not obscured by the complex, woody essence of oak. As a current trend, many wineries in the region are steering away from oak and switching to this more natural, French-style chardonnay.

The inspiration for our family trip to Napa Valley was my youngest sister, Alex. She is enthusiastic about wine and wanted to share the tasting experience with all of us. When she goes tasting, she brings a wine journal and records notes about everything she tries. The journal has preprinted sections for each wine: color depth, hue, and clarity; aroma intensity and notes; body, balance, acidity; flavor intensity and notes; and a final prompt for a star rating. Alex is an engineer and likes to keep details tight and orderly. I am slightly embarrassed at the prospect of taking notes in front of winery employees, who serve us two-ounce pours with a practiced hand and talk fluently about wine, but I secretly love that Alex records everything. Her determination to work through the journal's questions involves the whole group. "What color would you say this is, brick or ruby?" she asks everyone, holding up her glass of cabernet. "What do you smell? I detect some citrus, maybe a hint of grass," she says with her nose in a glass of chardonnay. "What do you taste? I think a faint flavor of key lime and white flowers." Her insistence on asking these questions for every sip makes all of us think more closely about what we are tasting. If I were on my own, I might get swept up in the experience, talking and laughing as I drink. This way I pay attention.

Sip and Taste. I decide that I like the creamy, deep flavor that comes with oak. It is less sanitized than the stainless chardonnays and leaves a sunniness lingering on my tongue.

SINCE NATIONAL MONUMENTS ARE DESIGNATED by presidential proclamation rather than by vote, a monument is often the result of a specific public's vision rather than that of the public at large. Katahdin Woods and Waters was formed because of the interests of the Quimby and St. Clair family and the support of Maine residents that they worked hard to earn. Bears Ears was the result of years of research, lobbying, and partnership among Indigenous tribes, environmental groups, and others who cared for that place. It was clearly not the will of Utah as a whole but of that particular public.

"The range of possibilities allowed by the Antiquities Act has made the national monuments the focus of the attention of special-interest groups with agendas that differ from those of federal agencies," wrote Hal Rothman in his history of national monuments. The Antiquities Act remains relevant today because presidential orders can easily adapt to the changing values of society, even the changing values of a small cross section of society.

This is apparent here in Berryessa Snow. Bob Schneider and Tuleyome spearheaded a regional advocacy effort to create specific support for their monument idea. "This isn't just a few people. It's a long story of informing people, taking people out to the area, and

Morning light and manzanita along the hike up Snow Mountain, Berryessa Snow Mountain National Monument, California. Photograph by Veronica Palmer.

building support. Near the start of this campaign, we said, 'This has to be a very inclusive movement where we recognize everyone that cares about public lands and wants to be a part of this.' And that's what we did."

User groups commonly clash over land access issues. Off-roaders and ATVers often oppose environmental groups that advocate for wilderness designations since these designations forbid motorized access. Likewise, some environmental groups actively oppose off-road vehicle use. Tuleyome decided to confront this potential conflict at the start. "We met with Don Amador, he's an off-road vehicle guy, and I didn't really know him." Bob said. "Don said nobody had ever asked [for his participation] before. And that commitment that we made [to work together] then, it didn't end with the designation, it has continued into the present time." Tuleyome's effort to include a spectrum of user groups in their monument concept ensured that a diversity of access issues was incorporated in the plan, which encouraged more widespread support.

"In the end we had [the support of] thousands of individuals, two hundred and something businesses, sixty elected officials. We had community groups, conservation groups, off-road vehicle groups, mountain bike groups, and equestrian groups." It took over five years, but eventually this coalition of widely differing interests convinced President Obama to designate the monument in July 2015. The proclamation emphasized the biodiversity of this unique region as well as the numerous human uses that make the area significant to people.

"I think the fact that we made a conscious decision to pursue that [inclusive] goal was really important," said Bob. "I mean, it didn't just happen, it was part of our planning."

ON A DAY OFF FROM TASTING, we walked along the bathtub-ring shore of Lake Berryessa as a group of eight, four pairs of binoculars around necks. I had purchased a bird book in anticipation of this holiday trip, thinking that bird-watching would give us something fun to do together as we camped for the week. Like the winery passport, the front of the book offered tips to identify birds:

Pay attention to seasons
Look closely
Recognize patterns
Practice seeing details

BERRYESSA SNOW MOUNTAIN

Pay attention to seasons: It was December, and birds had been conspicuously absent. The open shoreline and large body of water gave us our first chance to really try bird-watching. New to this activity, the entire group paused and took turns sighting a black-and-white bird floating on the water.

Look closely: We listed the characteristics aloud to one another: black body, black head, a white face, and a long white neck with a narrow black stripe down the back. Someone pulled out a phone and typed in our observations. A grebe, perhaps? We looked at the photograph on the screen and then back at the bird on the water. Yes, a grebe, we all agreed.

We reached the end of our hike and sat at a picnic table on an exposed hill. The surface of the water was far below us, revealing a dead shadow of the lake's previous level.

As my family ate lunch, Jack and I decided to jog back to the cars and drive them closer so we could do something else with our day instead of walking back the way we came. We returned and sat down to our hummus wraps. "Oh!" my mom was excited, fidgeting and looking over her shoulder. "There was a hummingbird flying around us. His head is this intense ruby red. I want you to see it! He keeps coming back, I hope you get a chance to look at him." Seeing a hummingbird would be quite the evolution of our lackluster day of bird-watching. I had taken a seat and bitten into my sandwich when everyone got excited again. Veronica thrust binoculars into my hand and pointed straight ahead where a hummingbird hovered near a branch.

Practice seeing details: I focused the binoculars on his silhouette and saw the furious motion of his wings as he seemingly hung in the air. His body was a silvery gray-green, like lichen or Spanish moss. His head looked dark, but I didn't see any red. The bird pivoted and faced me. Feathers around his head caught the light and flashed a glowing garnet. Fascinated, I continued to watch. From the side, the bird looked dark and drab; only when he was at a certain angle, facing me head-on, could I see the brilliance around his face.

We flipped through the bird book and identified it as a male Anna's hummingbird, common in the oak-chaparral habitat of the Pacific coast. Even the illustration depicted the head as dark from the side and bright from the front, though it didn't quite do the illuminating feathers justice.

IN 1993, the director of the California office of the Bureau of Land Management, Ed Hastey, complained to the then secretary of the interior Bruce Babbitt that the government kept taking the BLM's best lands and giving them to other agencies to administer. Previously, the BLM focused primarily on managing mining and grazing leases. With the passage of the Federal Lands Policy and Management Act, the bureau was directed to consider conservation as part of its mission. But still, when a new monument was created on BLM land, it was transferred to the National Park Service to manage. Babbitt took this complaint to heart and later wrote, "How can you expect the BLM, with the largest land base of all, to get serious about conservation if you continually transfer its 'crown jewels' to other agencies?"

Grand Staircase–Escalante provided an opportunity to change this, and in 1996 when that monument was created, Babbitt and Clinton left its management to the BLM. After this, leaving monuments under the jurisdiction of their previous managing agency became common. In 2000, Babbitt created the National Conservation Lands as a unit within the BLM to give certain significant landscapes in its system a new conservation-focused mission. This new subagency sparked a radical change in the way the BLM operated:

BERRYESSA SNOW MOUNTAIN

in addition to regulating extractive leases, the organization began to focus on ways to conserve and preserve.

Conservation is an approach to land management that prioritizes interacting with land sustainably. It supports access and resource extraction but not too much or too destructively. The aim is to interact with land in a way beneficial to humans without causing great harm to land. Preservation, on the other hand, is a stricter approach that aims to keep places natural, without obvious human influence. Lasting human impacts such as roads, trails, mining, and grazing are considered intrusive and impermissible under this ethos. Wilderness designations, which are notoriously roadless, adhere to a preservation ethic.

Though these definitions seem clearly delineated and even in opposition, in practice this is never the case. Certain things are preserved and conserved in every landscape, and often these philosophies overlap in the same space. Efforts for preservation of an endangered species can take place in a conservation-focused landscape with widespread recreation. Even wilderness designations have some grazing exceptions.

Within Berryessa Snow Mountain there are three different wilderness areas managed for preservation and nonmotorized recreation. Other parts of the monument feature a world-class off-highway vehicle trail system, campgrounds, boat launches, and livestock grazing. After a long list of the plants and animals whose habitats the monument aims to preserve, the monument proclamation states, "Today, the area is important for ranching and also provides outdoor recreation opportunities . . . to a burgeoning population center." With a complex mission, the monument aims to protect these uses along with unique wildlife.

"The BLM and the Forest Service worked together. That was an interesting complexity of this," Bob told me. Berryessa Snow Mountain National Monument is managed not by one agency alone but jointly by the BLM and U.S. Forest Service. The monument boundary includes land originally administered by both agencies, so management was left to both, each with a slightly different approach to how the land should be cared for. In advocating for the monument, Tuleyome earned the support of people and agencies with different ideas about land use. Now constant compromise and cooperation are required.

MY FAMILY DROVE TO BLUE RIDGE to hike on a mountain that offered incredible views of a southern arm of Lake Berryessa. Lake Berryessa is not technically part of the monument. The border snakes along the shore and includes mountains that overlook the lake.

Recognize patterns: Wildfires haunted the region, just like when Veronica and I hiked Snow Mountain. Between October 8 and 9, 2017, twelve wildfires burned across California. The Atlas and Tubbs fires raged through Sonoma and Napa Counties, destroying over five thousand structures and killing around thirty people. We drove past pale skeletal house foundations lying on blank earth and car frames that rested on the ground with tires melted away.

As we walked out of the Blue Ridge parking lot, I glanced at a sign warning visitors that since this area burned in 2015, there is no shade on the hike. This wouldn't be a problem in the weak sun and cool air of December. We passed charred husks of trees that protruded from green manzanita with waxy red branches like twisting candlesticks. The chaparral shrubbery flourished even as the bones of trees reminded us how different this landscape was just a couple of years ago.

A small bird danced from bare branch to bare branch, and we

were able to get a close look. This was the first bird we had seen in days other than a raven near our campsite and turkey vultures circling over power lines, so we examined this one.

Look closely: small, like a sparrow, and a mottled brown. The back was a smooth dark brown and the belly was sand-colored. The wings and tail had subtle stripes. We paused on a rock for a break from the steep hike and I consulted the bird book. A wren. Pacific wren most likely, though very similar to a winter wren.

We hiked higher, and I noted the lake's remnant ring and the lowered surface of the water. After years of drought, Lake Berryessa was almost thirty feet below normal.

Tilt and Look. Some chardonnays have a rich golden hue, while others are so pale that they are almost clear. The wine journal lists these color options for a white wine: greenish, yellow, straw yellow, gold, amber.

From the top of Blue Ridge, we noticed that all the east-facing hillsides were green, covered in trees and manzanita, while the west-facing aspects were dry, yellowed grassland, fuel awaiting a spark.

Swirl and Smell. Taking time to smell wine is an essential step in the tasting process. Often the scent enhances and reinforces the flavor. Sometimes, remarkably, the aroma is completely different than the taste. Chardonnay can smell of honeysuckle, grass, and pear but then taste of vanilla and apricot. Cabernet sauvignon, another of California's specialty varietals, smells to me of fields of earth warming in the sunshine, fruit ripening on a vine, and sometimes, as we recorded in our journal, chocolate and cloves, raspberry jam, plum, clay, and blackberry.

The air blowing off the water was cool and felt good on our sweating faces. It carried with it a slight note of pine needles, the earthy scent of dried grass, an underlying tinge of smoke.

WHAT IS NATURAL? Wildfires are natural. In fact, chaparral ecosystems depend on them to remain healthy. But were the 2017 fires a natural disaster? Or an unnatural one, since they were likely caused by a warmer and drier climate resulting from human impacts? Change is natural. But the scale of change we are witnessing in the natural world does not seem to be moving at a natural pace.

It is easy to equate natural with good and unnatural with bad, but it is not really that simple. Years ago, grapes didn't naturally grow in California. Now California is renowned worldwide for the high-quality wines produced here. It is a thriving and much-loved industry.

National parks and monuments attempt to preserve many natural things: viewsheds, soundscapes, the darkness of the night sky, the biodiversity of a region. But what happens to the mission of saving the scenery and the stars when smoke obscures both? We say that we established this place to protect biodiversity, but human-influenced climate change is killing off the very creatures and habitats that we want to preserve.

What is more natural: a buttery, oaky chardonnay aged in real wood, or a stainless steel–aged, unobstructed–fruit flavor chardonnay?

THERE WAS NOT ALWAYS A LAKE HERE. It used to be a farmland valley housing the town of Monticello and before that was a Spanish settlement and before that was a Wintum village. In the 1950s, the Bureau of Reclamation developed a plan to dam Putah Creek and feed the water to Solano County. The residents of Monticello fiercely opposed this plan. However, a small town of around 250 people did not stand a chance against the thirsty thousands of Solano County. Eventually all Monticello businesses closed, houses were physically removed, and the cemetery was unearthed and relocated. Every last remnant of civilization was cleared away. The dam was finished in 1957, and the valley was filled up like a trough. Now it is occupied by a lake more than 15 miles long and 3 miles wide with 165 miles of shoreline.

Well before the dam, the Wintum, Yuki, Nomlaki, Patwin, Pomo, Huchnom, Wappo, and Lake Miwok people lived in and traveled through the Berryessa Snow Mountain region. These Indigenous peoples gathered acorns, hunted, quarried rock, crafted tools, hiked through mountains, and cultivated nut crops using careful and clever burning practices. For millennia, Indigenous people of this region set small, contained fires to renew the landscape. New growth flourishes after a fire. The practice of these burns was a way to keep the land healthy, a way of living with the land rather than merely taking from it. In 1850, intentional burns in California were outlawed, dismissing Indigenous knowledge in favor of protecting timber and its potential profits. It took more than a hundred years, but forest managers eventually noticed that no new giant sequoias had sprouted in the unburned forest: sequoia cones need a fire's heat to crack them open and release their seeds.

Today, out-of-control wildfires in California are attributed in part to a warming climate but also to more than a century of fire suppression. One hundred years with few fires have allowed more and different plants to grow and to grow closer to one another, which means more fuel. When fires do happen, the additional fuel means they are larger and more destructive than they would be if fires had been more frequent.

WHAT IS UNNATURAL? My family enjoyed the view of nature at Lake Berryessa, but the lake itself is not natural—it would not exist without human scheming. In the mid-nineteenth century prescribed burns were viewed as unnatural, a meddling, and were forbidden. Yet their suppression has resulted in fires that rampage with an unnatural ferocity, and plants have been prevented from growing in their natural cycle.

Is a flame ignited by lightning natural? Is extinguishing it to protect lives and property unnatural? In today's heated conditions, the line between a natural fire and an unnatural one is indistinguishable.

At Berryessa Snow Mountain, we have drawn an unnatural boundary around a complex landscape to preserve what naturally lives there. Without this imaginary line we might not have the restraint to let some things be as they are, natural or not.

TOWARD THE END OF OUR CONVERSATION, Bob and I discussed his legacy of conservation and ended up talking about how his work changed him. "When I was young, I was a climber. That's who I was and that's how I defined myself. Then I met Annie and she was a climber too, and we got married and had a family and I dabbled a lot more." Bob paused, getting a tiny bit choked up. "This is emotional," he said.

"When Annie died—she had ovarian cancer and died in 2010—I began to discover that half your brain, the lizard part of your brain, is where all your emotions are. And they are communicated through your amygdala to your forebrain. And I had spent all my life living in my forebrain and not paying attention to my emotional life. And then that changed."

Bob's recognition of the emotional connections he had not been paying attention to made me think about the complex human connections that made this area a monument: the determined people who forged relationships among hikers, four-wheelers, and horseback riders; two friends who started a small local nonprofit that partnered with two large government agencies; the devoted supporters who urged Secretary of the Interior Sally Jewell and her staff to convince President Obama to sign a proclamation.

Like these human relationships, entwined physical relationships make up this area, connections easily overlooked: the grand, rumbling shift of the earth's plates and the fragile, blooming life of serpentine sunflower; the California lilac's need for intense heat for its seeds to germinate and the wildfire that sometimes renews as it destroys; the foothill yellow-legged frog populations declining in part due to roads that lead into their territory, their protection ensured in part by the dusty tracks of four-wheelers that carry people to see the world's wonders. The delicate balance of preservation and conservation, protection and access. Each detail dependent upon the other. Every monument is built on similar gossamer threads of relationship.

Recognize patterns: Places evoke emotion. This is what inspires people to work so hard to protect them. Bob reminded me that details, when savored, and emotions, when openly felt, are what enrich a life.

"I feel a lot more vulnerable. I feel a lot more caring toward people. That has been an exploration in and of itself," he continued. "So while I used to think of myself as a climber, and still do, later I began to realize, oh, I actually am also a husband and a dad, and now a granddad, and a conservationist."

AT THE END OF CHRISTMAS WEEK, we chose our favorite from the numerous wines we had tasted and surprised ourselves by selecting an unexpected varietal: a 2014 Napa Valley zinfandel from Chateau Montelena. It was smoother and more delicate, less overtly alcoholic than other zinfandels. It smelled of fig and tasted of raspberries and tart pear. We purchased a bottle to share during our last dinner together.

Afterward, we sat around a campfire in a contemplative mood and reminisced about our week. Veronica's husband, Austin, blew on the fire to keep it going, and tendrils of fragrant smoke hung in the air. Veronica and my dad stuffed bananas with marshmallows and chocolate chips and rolled them in foil to heat over the flames. "I think we should always live life as if we are wine tasting," Jack said, leaning back in his camp chair. "It makes you appreciate the details around you."

Repeat and Conclude.

Part II. Rift

RIFT (noun)
: fissure, crevasse, fault

RIFT (verb)
: to burst open
: to cleave, divide

The gifts of the earth are to be shared, but gifts are not limitless.
The generosity of the earth is not an invitation to take it all.

ROBIN WALL KIMMERER
*Braiding Sweetgrass: Indigenous Wisdom, Scientific Knowledge,
and the Teachings of Plants*

4. Seeing

CASCADE-SISKIYOU NATIONAL MONUMENT, OREGON AND CALIFORNIA

My alarm buzzes in the early gray of morning. Condensation coats the inner walls of my tent and dampens the top of my sleeping bag. I roll over and feel around in the cold for my jacket, when a coyote howl erupts nearby. I freeze. It begins like a yipping bark and ends with a high-pitched whistling call. Rather than carrying one smooth note, it breaks and cracks. A faraway howl echoes this one. I wait until the howls drift farther away and then unzip the door to heat up water for coffee.

I am camped in Cascade-Siskiyou National Monument, the homeland of the Takelman, Athapaskan, Shastan, and Klamath peoples. My intention is to backpack solo along the Pacific Crest Trail for a couple of days. My interest in national monuments has spurred me to take more trips alone, and the political background of this monument on the California–Oregon border is interesting enough for me to set aside a weekend to visit. Cascade-Siskiyou was designated by President Clinton, expanded by President Obama, and put under review by President Trump: this seems like a lot of drama for a forest.

CASCADE-SISKIYOU
NATIONAL MONUMENT

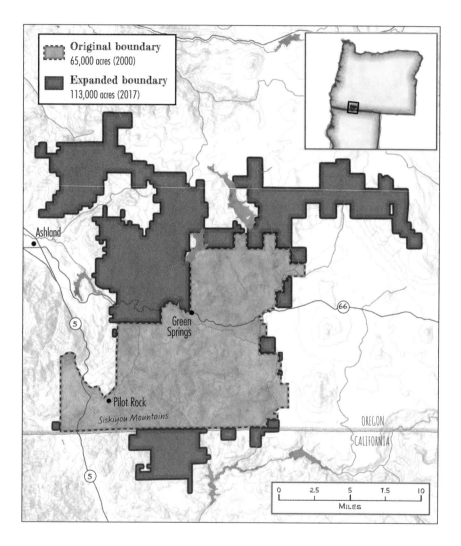

Original boundary
65,000 acres (2000)

Expanded boundary
113,000 acres (2017)

Ashland

Green
Springs

66

Pilot Rock

Siskiyou Mountains

OREGON
CALIFORNIA

0   2.5   5   7.5   10
MILES

The night before, as I set up camp in the darkness, a car crunched by just below me on the hillside. I hadn't realized a road was so close to the trail. I was camping during the collision of summer and winter, at the intersection of habitation and wilderness, and at the overlap of public land's seemingly irreconcilable goals of preservation and tourism.

Now, the morning light is chilled like the air. The sky pales, easing into a faint blue. I can't see much of the sunrise over the hillside, so I pack my damp sleeping bag and wet tent with cold hands and begin walking to warm up. After five minutes a red-and-gray coyote leaps over the trail in front of me and trots through a meadow. I stand still and watch as it lopes between manzanita and cinnamon bush.

BILL CLINTON USED THE ANTIQUITIES ACT to designate Cascade-Siskiyou as a 65,000-acre monument in 2000. The region is unique because it sits at the convergence of multiple ecosystems: the wet forests of the Cascade Range meet the unusually east–west-oriented Siskiyou Mountains, meet the old and round Klamath Mountains, meet the young and craggy Sierra Nevada, meet the dry and expansive Great Basin Desert. This intersection of environments allows for a commingling of species not seen anywhere else. The World Wildlife Fund counts this region among the two hundred "most outstanding and representative areas of biodiversity." Biodiversity, the variety of living organisms in a given area, is a measure used to indicate if an area is ecologically healthy. President Clinton's proclamation declared Cascade-Siskiyou National Monument "home to a spectacular variety of rare and beautiful species of plants and animals, whose survival in this region depends upon its continued ecological integrity." With these words, Cascade-Siskiyou became the first-ever national monument established to protect biodiversity.

In May 2015, a group of eighty-five scientists sent a letter to

President Obama encouraging him to expand Cascade-Siskiyou's boundary. Fifteen years after the monument was created, logging, climate change, and water diversion were endangering some of the species it was designed to protect. The scientists explained that to continue to preserve the incredible biodiversity of the area, the boundary needed to be enlarged to include complete watersheds, to protect habitat for plants and animals whose ranges were shifting due to a warming climate, and to prevent increased development near the borders.

During his final days as president, in January 2017, Obama signed a proclamation to expand the monument by 48,000 acres. Obama declared, "since 2000, scientific studies of the area have reinforced that the environmental processes supporting the biodiversity of the monument require habitat connectivity corridors for species migration and dispersal." The proclamation then lists many of the monument's inhabitants: birds such as the purple martin, golden eagle, and snowy egret; mammals like the black-tailed deer, big-eared bat, and gray wolf; and plants such as coffee cliffbrake, creamy stonecrop, and sugar pine.

I HIKE THROUGH FOREST where the air is green and damp. Pale rays of light filter through tall evergreen branches, leaving me in a dark and open understory. My footsteps are silent on a soft pad of needles. Fallen pine cones line the trail, and I pause to examine one. Protruding from behind each scale on the cone is a three-pointed bract, paler and flimsier than the stiff brown scales. These bracts look separate from the cone while being within it, like a thin bookmark saving a place in a thick text. I recall a story told to me by a friend, an anecdote meant to help people identify trees. In the story, field mice attempt to escape an oncoming wildfire by hiding within a Douglas fir. Douglas fir have thick, fire-resistant bark, and the mice, remembering this detail but confusing the specifics, end up cowering inside the cones. Since the cones are not resistant to fire, the mice meet a fiery end. As the story goes, the mice's error is memorialized in the cones by the bracts, which, with three points, resemble the hind legs and tail of a mouse. It does look as if teeny mice are diving inside the cones.

A Douglas fir isn't really a fir at all. More closely related to a larch, Douglas fir is in a genus all its own, *Pseudotsuga*, which means "false hemlock." It can grow up to two hundred feet tall and live for one thousand years. And because of its size, it is also one of the most common trees used for lumber in Oregon.

I stand at the base of a Douglas fir trunk three times my own width. Its shade tickles my face, rough bark ridges scratch my fingers, needle-sweet scent fills my nose, and I gaze into a canopy of branches that thread like lace across the sky.

ACCORDING TO THE AMERICAN FOREST RESOURCE COUNCIL, more than 80 percent of the land included in the 2017 Cascade-Siskiyou monument expansion was Oregon and California Railroad land, known as O&C land. Originally granted by the government to the Oregon and California Railroad Company in 1886, the land was intended to provide space for the completion of a railway connecting the two states. When the company committed fraud and violated the terms of the grant, Congress took back the title to 2.8 million acres in 1916. Then in 1937, Congress passed a law commonly known as the O&C Act, which put the land under the jurisdiction of the Department of the Interior and set it aside for permanent forest production. A percentage of the timber sales from this forest goes directly to the eighteen counties that contain O&C land. The act stipulated that timber must be harvested on a sustained yield basis, which means trees can be cut down but not clear-cut; the harvest must allow for regrowth and the health of the forest. Though this stipulation might sound pro-environment, the primary goal was to ensure productive timber harvest in the future and a continual source of revenue.

With Obama's proclamation, 40,000 acres of O&C land were re-established as part of Cascade-Siskiyou National Monument, where logging is prohibited. Understandably, timber companies objected. These 40,000 acres make up 3 percent of the over 2 million acres of O&C land in western Oregon still available for logging. In a lawsuit filed against the federal government in February 2017, the Murphy Timber Company contended that the monument expansion directly violates the 1937 O&C Act. The company complained that the Griffen Moon Timber Sale, which would have happened during the summer on land included in the monument expansion, would have generated four million board feet and more than $500,000 for Jackson County. A board foot, for those like me who don't count trees by volume, is one square foot of wood that is one inch thick. Murphy Timber claimed the trees labeled off-limits by the monument designation would reduce the Bureau of Land Management timber sales by four to six million board feet per year and jeopardize the jobs and livelihood of four hundred employees at their Oregon processing mills.

When President Trump issued his monument review in 2017, Cascade-Siskiyou and its expansion were included. A federal judge granted the Trump administration extra time to respond to the Murphy Timber Company lawsuit until the secretary of the interior completed the review.

This left everyone—the locals who lived near the tall forests, the Rogue River tribes who have close ties to the land, the lumber companies who itched to cut down the Douglas fir, and the BLM, which was responsible for managing the monument—in limbo as they waited to hear what would become of this place.

AROUND 135 BUTTERFLY SPECIES live in Cascade-Siskiyou National Monument. As I hike through old-growth forests and open meadows, I lament not visiting in spring when I could have seen some of them dancing among flowers. I pass a sign set among tall roadside grasses. "Mardon skipper Recovery Area," the sign announces. "To protect the Mardon skipper and the fragile meadow vegetation that the skipper depends on, please stay on trails and do not camp in meadows in this area."

The Mardon skipper is a small butterfly, less than an inch long, with a thick, hairy body fanned by persimmon wings. This butterfly lives in grassland meadows, completing one life cycle a year. Females lay eggs on native grasses in the fall, and the larvae hatch and munch on grass for three months before pupating and emerging as adults in summer.

Because of widespread loss of this specific grassland habitat, Mardon skipper populations are struggling. There are only thirty-seven sites where Mardon skippers are known to live, and many of those sites host fewer than fifty individuals. Open grasslands continue to disappear as development seeps across more and more land. This monument is one place where meadow habitat is being preserved.

Since it is well past summer, I walk through the meadow without seeing a single orange butterfly. But later in the day a flutter of wings catches my eye. A white butterfly startles as I pass, and it bobs around me, in search of a safe space to land. It is so small and so insignificant in color that if I didn't know this monument is a haven for butterflies, I would not have noticed it at all. It lands on a leaf covered in fine white bristles, and I creep forward to get a closer look. It sits with its white wings folded, which is how I know it is a butterfly instead of a moth. Using amateur identification skills, I determine that this butterfly is either a native margined white or a cabbage white, imported from Europe.

Knowing this detail changes my experience. Being able to identify the spiked cones of the Douglas fir forces me to recognize the specific place I am standing instead of labeling it as "forest." When "butterflies" are just a general concept in my mind, I don't stop to notice them. But because I know the golden Mardon skipper is here, and the transplanted cabbage white is here, and 133 other kinds of butterflies are here, this place forms a singular shape in my mind.

It seems obvious to me that selling off any remaining Mardon skipper habitat for $500,000 of lumber isn't worth it. But I can now tell you that the burnt orange butterflies that bounce through the meadow grasses in summer are Mardon skippers. I might not have cared if I couldn't name them.

I HIKE FARTHER, tall grasses grazing my legs, thinking that Veronica and her husband, Austin, may have hiked this same section of trail. When they were a new couple, they hiked the Appalachian Trail together, then for their honeymoon they hiked the Pacific Crest Trail. I imagine their footsteps falling on the exact patches of earth where my footsteps land.

The Pacific Crest Trail, or PCT, travels 2,650 miles from Mexico to Canada. Nineteen of those miles run through the original Cascade-Siskiyou National Monument, and with the expansion, the PCT crosses even more monument territory. The number of thruhikers who intend to walk the entire trail has been growing each year. People crave the types of experiences where they are forced to rise and face challenges, where they learn about themselves and can see beyond incredible vistas to larger truths about the world. In 2013,

View of Pilot Rock from the Pacific Crest Trail, Cascade-Siskiyou National Monument, Oregon. Photograph by Bob Wick/Bureau of Land Management.

1,041 PCT thru-hike permits were issued. Veronica and Austin hiked the trail in 2014, and that year 1,461 permits were issued. The number continued to grow each year, and by 2019 it exceeded 5,000. That means that more than 5,000 people intended to hike the entire PCT, and that number does not count people who, like myself on this trip, go out for shorter sections or day hikes. Five thousand people hiking this exact same path that I am on now. Five thousand people camping alongside the trail. Five thousand people pulling water from creeks, pooping in the woods, leaving footprints on ridges and mountaintops. Five thousand people who we hope are not trampling Mardon skipper meadow habitat.

This region is special because of the incredible number of plants

and animals that live here, but it is in danger of losing that uniqueness because humans—just another species that moves through the
area—are affecting the land. Once lost, extinct species cannot be recovered. Ecosystems can become unbalanced, and more plants and
animals suffer in a downward spiral. Cascade-Siskiyou was the first
monument designated with the express purpose of protecting biodiversity. If this is the goal, should I even be allowed here? Should
the PCT hikers?

When comparing the effects of logging on a landscape to the effects of recreation, recreation seems like the lesser evil, though it
does have a noticeable and often negative impact. Although recreation and conservation are generally seen as compatible, they start
to appear mutually exclusive when the fate of the Mardon skipper is
confronted with the crushing love of thousands of hikers. It seems
contradictory to protect habitat for a dying species but then usher
thousands of people right through that habitat. And yet, allowing
people access to the wild can inspire passion that ignites appreciation for the little Mardon skipper and advocacy for legal protection
of places like this.

WHEN PRESIDENTS ESTABLISH NATIONAL MONUMENTS, the debate
that follows is often centered around economics. The loss of revenue
from potential resource extraction is weighed against the revenue
that will come from attracting visitors to the new park. So while the
Murphy Timber Company bemoans the loss of $500,000 for Jack-
son County and the possible loss of four hundred local jobs, people
in favor of the monument counter that tourism will bring different
jobs and new wealth to the area.

Headwaters Economics, a nonpartisan independent research
center, performed a study evaluating the local economies around
seventeen national monuments in the West. Cascade-Siskiyou

was included in this study, and the most recent results indicate that Jackson County has experienced strong economic growth since the monument's creation in 2000. From 2001 to 2015, jobs grew by 14 percent. Travel and tourism specifically account for 13,067 jobs, which equates to 19 percent of private employment in Jackson County. In contrast, timber jobs account for 4.2 percent of private employment.

The study concluded that overall prosperity in the communities surrounding Cascade-Siskiyou increased by around 12 percent as well. This number is slightly skewed, however. Not all the growth is new prosperity; some of it is from wealthy people moving to the area. It is understandable that community members might be reluctant to welcome new wealth moving in and would not view this as a real improvement. Still, the monument seems to have made a positive economic impact on the region.

But this economic analysis is limited. It trades one form of moneymaking for another. Some economists and environmentalists have developed ways to understand the importance of nature by assigning an economic value to land and its natural processes. This is an attempt to translate intangible environmental benefits into the language of a profit-driven corporation or money-minded politician. When abstract things like "nature" are given a monetary value, statistics and mathematics can be used to argue for land's conservation. There are several common methods for doing this; all are somewhat flawed and imprecise, but they can be useful.

First, there is contingent valuation, which uses surveys that ask how much people would be willing to pay for things, such as a house on a lake or to hear songbirds in their backyard. There is hedonic pricing, where the sale prices of houses in proximity to environmental amenities, such as scenic vistas, are compared to ones without. The difference is then attributed to the value of the resource itself.

The travel-cost method measures how much people spend to experience a certain resource, tallying how much is spent to travel to a national park, rent a lakefront house, purchase hiking equipment, or pay for permits and campsites. The replacement cost method calculates how much it would cost to replace a certain resource. If you logged, developed, or polluted a forest, how much would it cost to build or regrow another? This ignores the wide-ranging effects that destruction would have on an ecosystem but assigns a concrete number to the resource itself. Finally, the marked evidence method is the simplest: how much could you sell the resource for? In the case of Cascade-Siskiyou, how much are the timber, soil, and water worth?

Numbers generated from these methods can be used to make a case for conserving some aspects of a landscape. If these numbers convince a person in power to leave the land as is, then the numbers have been useful even if they aren't entirely accurate. But I take issue with the idea that everything must be translated into money to be considered valuable. None of these methods represents the intrinsic value of nature or the land itself. They attempt to justify the existence of nature based on a limited capitalistic perspective, and for that reason, they all fall short. They don't tabulate the beauty and incredible height of the Douglas fir, the complex communication of the coyote, or the extraordinary convergence of species in this one unique place. Our society overall has accepted basic human rights on principle, and acknowledges life has value. Land is the same. Its innate value should be revered.

THE TURNAROUND POINT of my hike is Pilot Rock, a volcanic intrusion of columnar andesite. Just as Douglas fir is unique compared to other trees, the composition of Pilot Rock is unlike any of the stone that surrounds it. With an easy scramble to its craggy summit, Pilot Rock is one of the advertised attractions of the monument, and there are a road and a parking lot a mere mile from the buttress. After not passing another person all day, I suddenly hear voices through the trees.

I trudge up the steep trail, passing gossiping teenagers and harried families heading the opposite direction. The easiest way to the summit is up a low-angle fissure that cuts through the stone. The left wall is steep with the heads of hexagonal basalt columns visible like a tile pattern. On the right the rock slants away at an unworkable angle. What is left is a narrow hallway funneling visitors to the top. There are two moves that resemble climbing more than walking. I step into the crack and pull myself over the steepest part.

On the summit, I expect people but find no one. Walking across the flat top, I gaze at the cloud-encrusted volcanic cone of California's Mount Shasta to the south and the snowy dome of Oregon's Mount McLoughlin to the north. I fold myself into a gap in the stone and lounge, observing the waves of green and brown forest that stretch before me under gauzy clouds. I wonder how many board feet I can see from here. This is Cascade-Siskiyou, land set aside to protect biodiversity. What does "set aside" mean anyway? It is strange that we specify which land is off-limits for development and resource harvest rather than which land is open for it. It seems like it should be the other way around.

A cool breeze curls around my neck, and I consider the value of being allowed to come here. Perhaps this experience, the ability to visit this place, and even the experience of hiking the PCT are worth the cost of protecting it.

I take a few photographs and scramble back down, passing a dad and his two young kids on their way up, then hordes of people hiking to the base. My solitude on the summit feels miraculous.

I hike back the way I came, past thimbleberry and blue elderberry and western sword fern. I set up my tent by one of two springs along this twelve-mile section of the PCT. There is a flat spot pillowed with cedar needles for my tent, and it would be idyllic if it weren't for the dirt road only a few feet away. A truck is parked nearby, and I feel oddly violated by its presence.

Turning my back toward the road, I lean against the big cedar and pull out my notebook. My campsite is in a downhill-trending valley rimmed by trees. I cannot see the horizon or the sunset, so instead of meditating on the color and the power of the sky, I decide to write down every sound that I hear as the day dwindles to evening.

> Chip-chip-chip. The rapid, rhythmic calls of a dark-eyed junco.
>
> A deeper, more melodic warble.
>
> Thup-thup-thup. the beating of wings as a flock of birds takes flight in unison.
>
> A twig snaps from a tree with a sharp TAK and lands on the ground with a gentle thud.
>
> The chittering of birds fades and quiets as the evening progresses.
>
> I hear the crooning of an insect, the first to welcome darkness.
>
> A very quiet, slight hint of blades of grass rubbing together.

IN HIS FINAL REPORT about national monuments for President Trump, Secretary Ryan Zinke recommended removing all O&C land from Cascade-Siskiyou's boundary. He also suggested reducing the size of Bears Ears and Grand Staircase–Escalante, which the president did. Trump did not alter Cascade-Siskiyou and instead let the case move through the courts.

First, in April 2019, U.S. Magistrate Judge Mark Clarke wrote a report that stated President Obama acted legally when he created the monument and suggested the Murphy Timber Company case be dismissed. "If the BLM has the authority under the O&C Act to reserve lands from harvest, then the President reserving lands within the confines of the smallest area permitted under the Antiquities Act presents no irreconcilable conflict with the O&C Act," he wrote. "Land can be reserved from timber harvest under both Acts." This looked like a win for monument supporters.

But that following November, U.S. District Court Judge Richard Leon ruled the opposite way in a summary judgment. He found that Obama did not have the authority to include O&C land in the monument boundary and remove it from timber production because that violated the O&C Act. "The Congressional mandates to manage O&C timberland for 'permanent forest production' and to 'sell, cut, and remove timber in conformity with the principle of sustained yield . . .' cannot be rescinded by Presidential Proclamation," the ruling reads.

The dueling rulings set things up for continued legal action, and unsurprisingly environmental groups appealed Judge Leon's decision. Much more interesting is the fact that the Trump administration also appealed this decision—on the same side as the environmental groups. The reason for this: presidential power.

Judge Leon's ruling, which on the surface sides with an anti-monument administration, limits presidential action through proclamation. If his ruling stands, it could have implications for the cases concerning President Trump's reductions of Bears Ears and Grand Staircase–Escalante—implications that might reduce Trump's power to modify them.

THE NEXT MORNING, I hike to my car, toss my pack into the back, slide into the driver's seat, and realize that I am unsure what I learned from this visit. I drive a couple minutes into the town of Green Springs, park, and walk past a giant WE LOVE OUR MONU-MENT banner on the wooden deck of a restaurant, where a couple of old men lean on the railing, mugs in hand. I step into the steamy heat of a busy diner. All the tables are full, and dishes clang in the back kitchen. "You can sit here," the waitress motions to an empty chair at the bar as she swipes a used mug from the counter. "There's a lady sitting here," she points at a loose pile of newspaper in front of the neighboring seat. I order coffee.

The newspaper woman returns. She has short, graying hair and wears hiking boots and a puffy vest over a flannel shirt. After glancing at me over reading glasses, she nudges half of the newspaper in my direction. "You can read this if you want." I scan the local headlines as the waitress places a large plate of eggs and sausage in front of the woman. I order the chanterelle mushroom scramble special. "This place is just wonderful. I think they pick those mushrooms themselves," the woman comments.

We begin to chat, and she tells me she lives in a nearby valley. I ask her what people who live here think about the monument expansion and the suggested reduction. "Oh, they love the monument. Of course, there is always friction with ranchers and people who want to drive motorcycles and snowmobiles, but they need to look at it and figure that out. They certainly shouldn't do away with it." She eats as we talk and knocks a chunk of sausage off her plate and onto the floor. Still talking, she stands up and scoops the sausage into a napkin, folding it into her pocket. "For the dogs," she explains. "I come up here every weekend. I have two Australian shepherds, so I bring them on a walk, and they go for a swim, and I come here for breakfast, and then I get water from the spring. That is my Sunday church ritual."

Perhaps that is one of the not-quite-tangible values of a place like Cascade-Siskiyou: the almost religious experiences that people have in wildness. If religion brings joy to people's lives, draws them outside themselves to search for meaning, the natural world offers a similar shift in perception. I did not have an epic adventure on my journey to this monument. There was no teetering on the edge of life and death, no shivering trial of survival. My experience here was highlighted not by adrenaline but by my mind opening. Taking the time to identify trees, notice a butterfly, and listen to birds left me with a peace, an expanding love.

Even if we could not recreate on a plot of earth, could not pull a profit from its boundaries, could not even visit, land still retains value. The survival of the Mardon skipper does matter, even if I haven't seen one. A Douglas fir can still grow for one thousand years even if no one counts its rings. Biodiversity loss can happen while no one is paying attention. And the way we choose to value and care for and interact with landscapes still has an effect on the world, even if we are still searching for the right answer.

5. Digging

CASTLE MOUNTAINS NATIONAL MONUMENT, CALIFORNIA

We trespassed. I wanted to see the mine. We parked Jack's van by signs that read "Danger Open Pit—No Trespassing," and from there I could see the edge of a massive pink hole. We tiptoed up a loose mound of red- and rust-colored tailings to peek into the pit. At the crest of the pile, a bighorn sheep with glossy curled horns glared at us, then scampered off, bits of gravel clicking down the slope as he ran. He was trespassing too.

We still couldn't see the bottom of the pit, but we could see some infrastructure across the rim: a tower, bulldozers, trucks. We crept closer and aimed for a service road near the edge. Jack seemed nervous, but I was too excited to care. A truck drove along the opposite rim, kicking up a cloud of rosy dust. We were close enough to see people walking about. "We need to go back now," Jack said with finality. He was right, of course. We turned around mere feet from a good view into the pit mine.

From a recreation standpoint, there isn't much to do at Castle Mountains National Monument. There are no trails, campgrounds,

CASTLE MOUNTAINS
NATIONAL MONUMENT

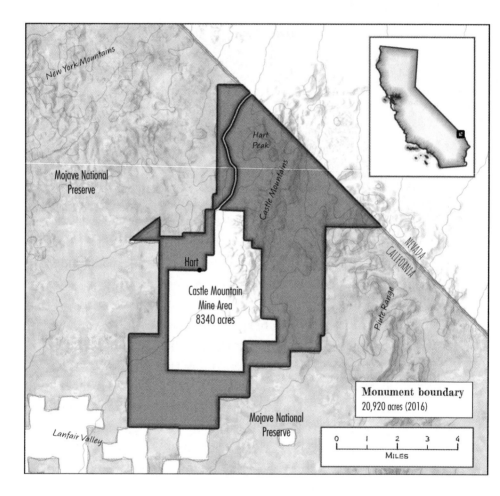

New York Mountains

Hart Peak

Mojave National Preserve

Castle Mountains

NEVADA
CALIFORNIA

Hart

Castle Mountain Mine Area 8340 acres

Piute Range

Monument boundary
20,920 acres (2016)

Mojave National Preserve

Lanfair Valley

0 1 2 3 4
MILES

or scenic sites. It is a 20,920-acre parcel of Mojave desert, and its largest feature is a pit mine. Almost half of the monument map is a hatch-marked block labeled "Castle Mountain Mine Area," and these 8,340 acres are leased by a private company and excluded from the monument's total. A separation of the gold from the slag, as some would say. But which part is gold, and which is slag?

This monument is the final, tiny corner in a much larger corridor of protected California desert that includes the Mojave National Preserve, Mojave Trails National Monument, Joshua Tree National Park, and Sand to Snow National Monument. Castle Mountains, Mojave Trails, and Sand to Snow were all designated by President Obama on February 12, 2016. Surrounded on three sides by the preserve, Castle Mountains links wildlife habitats for animals such as mountain lions and bighorn sheep. Desert bighorn populations have been declining since the colonization and settlement of the West. In 1998, as few as 280 bighorns were left in Southern California. A herd of desert bighorn is known to reside in Castle Mountains, and these animals are listed as protected in the monument proclamation. Seeing one up close was a rare and special sight—perhaps more special than the view into the mine that I was aiming for.

Castle Mountains also completes the protection of the Lanfair groundwater basin, a closed system. The monument sits above a large aquifer that feeds nearby Piute Spring, which is essential to the rich desert ecosystem. The water in the aquifer is believed to be nearly seven thousand years old. It never occurred to me to date water, but this nugget of information is illuminating. The water in that aquifer is about two thousand years older than the pyramids in Egypt. When water first trickled into that aquifer, the Sahara was a grassland. While that water has hidden underground, all written languages have been developed.

This region is home to at least twenty-eight rare native grasses,

89

such as burro grass. The sandy, gravelly plains are ideal habitat for buckhorn cholla, the most common cactus found in the Mojave and Sonoran Deserts. The Tohono O'odham people are known to pit-roast the flower buds and eat them. I have heard they taste like asparagus tips. Castle Mountains is also home to some of the most exceptional Joshua tree forest in the Mojave. Joshua trees look like cartoon impersonations of trees, or like yucca plants attempting yoga. With dense and extensive root systems, they grow spaced well apart, forming a forest that does not look like a forest at all. There is no canopy, no understory, just shaggy characters with arms akimbo, each with their own yoga mat's worth of personal space.

It is rumored that the whimsical Joshua tree was the inspiration for Dr. Seuss's famous Truffula trees in his book *The Lorax*. A parable about the near-total destruction of trees for commercial use and featuring a character who "speaks for the trees," this book is a child's lesson in environmentalism. *"UNLESS someone like you cares a whole awful lot, nothing is going to get better. It's not."*

Mining has taken place here since at least 1907. The Castle Mountain Mine is an open-pit gold mine, a hole dug into the ground and left open for the duration of the mine's life. This is a common technique for mining hard metals, such as copper, gold, iron, and aluminum. Stepped benches and access roads lead into the bottom, where active mining takes place. To unearth ore, large quantities of waste rock are removed, processed, and relocated into piles called tailings. The Castle Mountain Mine is a giant, terraced, pink chasm.

The proclamation that established the monument states that if either all mining has ceased or no commercial mining occurs for another ten years, then the land reverts to the ownership and management of the National Park Service, an interesting plan for reclaiming looted land.

In 2016, when the monument was designated, the latest iteration

CASTLE MOUNTAINS

of this gold mine had been closed for twelve years. The Castle Mountain Mine, owned by Viceroy Gold Corporation, produced one million ounces of gold between 1992 and 2004, then it shut down because of low gold prices. In 2012, the Canadian-owned NewCastle Gold acquired the lease. Amid rumors that NewCastle Gold wanted to renew its hunt for underground treasure, it was speculated that the monument designation was the Obama administration's way of preventing the mine's reopening. This strategy, if it was in fact a strategy, did not pan out.

NewCastle Gold was purchased by Trek Mining in 2017, now renamed Equinox Gold. In 2018, Equinox completed a pre-feasibility study for a two-phase, low-cost mining operation and began the first phase in mid-2019. The mine has been reopened, and new technology is being used to extract ore as well as reprocess tailings from previous eras. Since commercial mining restarted before the proclamation's ten-year time limit lapsed, the land will not revert to the control of the National Park Service, and the company will maintain ownership of the mine lease.

Though not one of the large monuments reviewed by the Trump administration in 2017, Castle Mountains still garnered opposition. NewCastle Gold, supported by California representative Paul Cook, requested that the Trump administration shrink this already small monument to make room for the reopened mine.

To visit this place, Jack and I made a detour on the way home from a climbing trip in Joshua Tree National Park. We drove down gravel roads for hours into remote desert. Far away from civilization, as evening fell, we parked the van on an open expanse of sand encircled by Joshua trees. We stacked boxes of firewood to form a table for our Coleman camp stove and stir-fried vegetables as the sky darkened and the air cooled. In the distance, two gigantic floodlights near the mine haloed the desert. As we ate and prepared to sleep, the

Hart Peak, Castle Mountains National Monument, California. Photograph by Matthew Dillon.

glowing lights watched us like the observant eyes of a dragon guarding its hoard.

This mine got its start in December 1907, when Jim Hart and brothers Bert and Clark Hitt struck gold in Castle Mountains. According to the General Mining Law of 1872, any U.S. citizen has the right to locate a mineral lode on federal land, stake that claim, and open it to mining. That person then has the right to all the ore removed from the land. Improbably, this law remains in effect today. Hoping for a Midas touch, Hart and the Hitt brothers staked claims in this sunny desert that became the Big Chief and Oro Belle mines.

CASTLE MOUNTAINS

News of glittering gold veins running through the Mojave spread in a rush. Prospectors thought Castle Mountains could be the next Comstock, so they rushed to that corner of California. People packed in a rush, loaded their families in a rush, smacked the back of their horses, urging them to rush. When they arrived, they rushed to erect phone lines, rushed in a mail service, and so rushed to build a stamp mill that the first foundation was faulty and had to be rebuilt. They built five hotels, eight saloons, two lumberyards, a flophouse, and a candy store, creating the boomtown of Hart, which produced a weekly newspaper but lacked a single church or school. Within two months, six hundred to seven hundred folk had settled in the gilded camp, hoping for a bonanza.

In May 1908 the first child was born under the lopsided mountain they dubbed Hart Peak, and the boy's family was promised a "golden loving cup" cast from Hart's own gleaming gold. Later that year Hart and the Hitt brothers cashed in their golden ticket and sold their claims to a man from Philadelphia, which turned out to be prescient because the pockets of promise were shallow; the mine was never profitable in the days of Hart.

Though in the mine's original days the dream was to strike it rich, gold is valuable for uses other than currency. In modern American society, almost every person owns something that contains gold. Because gold is an excellent conductor that will not tarnish, small amounts of it are found in almost every cell phone and computer. Every spacecraft launched by NASA contains bits of gold, and satellites that provide the world with internet signals use gold-plated components. It is nonallergenic and has been commonly used in dentistry for fillings, crowns, and bridges. For the same reasons, it is used in lifesaving devices such as defibrillators and pacemakers. Its value and durability make gold ideal for wedding rings. Gold unearthed from Castle Mountains could become everyday objects in the everyday lives of people who have never come near the Mojave Desert.

After our trespassing shenanigans, we stopped near a lonely bronze plaque installed in 1984 by the Clampers, a raucous society dedicated to drinking and preserving mining history. The plaque memorialized the town of Hart and told us that the nearest rail connection was three and a half miles away. I looked in every direction and saw mine tailings, Joshua trees, and a single standing stone structure. We walked toward it, weaving around creosote bushes and stepping over shallow arroyos. It is remote here even now, and it must have felt even more so back in the town's heyday before cars and cell phones. Glass and rusty metal littered the ground amid thriving cactus. One tall chimney stood, with the edges of wooden beams still visible in the base, the stones around the hearth blackened with soot.

In December 1910, sparks from a chimney ignited a blaze that consumed most of the town. Perhaps because it was already obvious that the mine would not produce much, the buildings were never rebuilt. Ten years after it opened, the mine was played out, and by 1917 tumbleweeds blew down the boulevards of a ghost town. Today, the desert has mostly reclaimed the town; all that remains of Hart is a chimney standing amid creosote—a sad symbol of the town's destruction.

After Hart was abandoned, the claim changed hands numerous times, and mining continued on and off as new technologies attempted to extract ore by different methods. The newest plan for this mine will use heap leaching on newly mined ore and discarded backfill leftover from the last time the mine was in operation. Heap leaching is a process in which ore is ground up into small pieces, piled onto a plastic- or clay-lined pad, and covered with a chemical solution that dissolves the precious metal or mineral. The Castle Mountain mine will use a combination of quicklime and then dilute sodium cyanide.

CASTLE MOUNTAINS

The solution containing the dissolved metals is then collected and treated to recover the metal. The recovered gold will then be smelted.

Equinox Gold plans to reprocess as much as 51 million tons of tailings from Castle Mountain Mine's previous operations and estimates that the mine could produce as much as 2.8 million ounces of gold, earning up to $865 million in sixteen years. It is thought that over 77 percent of the earth's gold supply has already been extracted and that within twenty years all recoverable reserves will be depleted. This fact makes the gold left within Castle Mountains rare and valuable, like the resident bighorn and surrounding native grasses. But unlike grass, whose rarity is often honored by leaving it undisturbed, the rarity of gold triggers the need to possess it.

This premium, precious gold exists in this desert alongside one-of-a-kind plants, endangered animals, and an ancient perennial spring. Pit mining is destructive, but if our society requires this mineral and it sometimes saves lives, perhaps its extraction is necessary. After seeing craggy Hart Peak and the sculpted rim of the mine, I wondered if mining is part of our partnership with this planet, a way that Earth provides for people, or if it is an example of our exploitation of it.

The State of California has a department titled the Office of Mine Reclamation; its job is to ensure mine operators clean up their messes when they leave. The department defines *mine reclamation* as "the combined process by which adverse environmental effects of surface mining are minimized and mined lands are returned to a beneficial end use." The dictionary gives two definitions for *reclamation*: 1. the reclaiming of desert, marshy, or submerged areas or other wasteland for cultivation or other use; 2. the process or industry of deriving usable materials from waste, by-products, etc. Both definitions take for granted that the thing being reclaimed is waste. Desert is directly called out as a "wasteland." Under this definition, reclamation would be mining itself: "deriving usable materials" from the desert "wasteland," not the other way around. At Castle Mountains, Equinox Gold is reclaiming the mine by reopening it.

Or perhaps the desert can reclaim the gold claim. Maybe a monument's protection can rewild a pit mine. Deserts used to be considered wastelands; today they are more often recognized as precious and dwindling, like the gold chipped from beneath. Monumental last-ditch efforts are being made to acquire every last flake of gold in places like Castle Mountains. Similar effort and technology should be put toward conserving what is left of the Mojave, what remains of precious places.

Two hundred years ago this desert was inhabited by the Tudinu people, desert tortoises in cool, sandy burrows, and hillsides of buckhorn cholla and contorting Joshua trees. One hundred years ago there was a feverish town and a huge hole in the ground. Today the town has disappeared, the hole deepened.

Perhaps the next century will still see that bold, solitary chimney hearth, the solid silhouette of the peak named Hart—or maybe the only remnant of today will be that giant hole we carved, aiming downward toward the earth's molten heart.

6. Shifting

SAND TO SNOW NATIONAL MONUMENT, CALIFORNIA

Hi, I am looking for . . ." I glanced at the Sand to Snow National Monument visitor center countertop, which featured a map pinned underneath Plexiglas. "This! This map, please."

"San Gorgonio Wilderness, all right." A gray-haired man in a forest-green polo bent to leaf through a box behind the counter.

Sand to Snow was designated a national monument in February 2016 by President Obama along with Castle Mountains and Mojave Trails. Outside the metropolis of San Bernardino, these three monuments stitch together sections of the Mojave and Sonoran Deserts on either side of Joshua Tree National Park, creating a U-shaped corridor of protected desert filled with sand dunes, cactus, and grainy granite. Along its southern edge, Sand to Snow is separated from the congressionally designated Santa Rosa and San Jacinto Mountains National Monument by a wind farm on San Gorgonio pass.

"Where is the nearest camping?" I asked.

"Oh, far away. The closest campgrounds are about a forty-minute drive from here."

SAND TO SNOW
NATIONAL MONUMENT

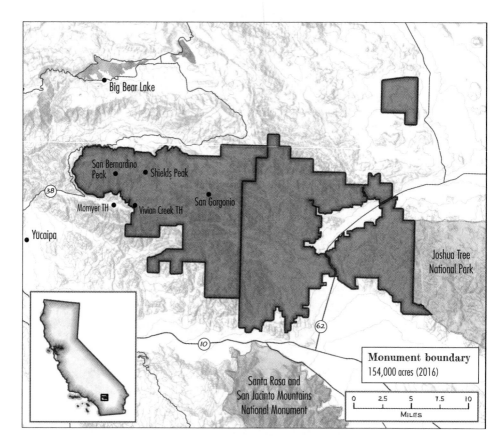

Big Bear Lake

San Bernardino Peak   Shields Peak

38

Momyer TH   Vivian Creek TH   San Gorgonio

Yucaipa

Joshua Tree National Park

62

10

Monument boundary
154,000 acres (2016)

Santa Rosa and San Jacinto Mountains National Monument

0   2.5   5   7.5   10
MILES

"There is not camping out toward Vivian Creek?"

"Nope, not unless you hike to it. The closest is Vivian Creek Camp, which is about one and a half miles straight up." The man looked me up and down, openly assessing my capability. His salt-and-pepper mustache twitched. "And steep, I mean steep." I noticed that his eyes were slightly out of alignment. "You'll see. If you trip, you fall up, straight up. It is that steep. Just you wait, you will get there and you will see what I mean about falling up."

I had devised a plan to enable a self-shuttle as I attempted a solo linkup of nine summits, known as the Nine Peak Challenge. In total this adventure would be 26.5 miles, like a marathon but without the food stations. I wanted to hike it in a single day, starting the next morning.

Another man in work clothes walked in and suggested an alternate camping option.

"Oh, no, that's not what she wants, she wants a regular campground," said the volunteer, assuming he knew exactly what I wanted. He looked back at me. "There is a campground over in Yucaipa," he waved his hand dismissively, "but I have no idea how much they charge or anything."

The other man requested a day-hike permit. Then he addressed me: "If I had your kind of time, I would head up to the Sierra."

"That's where I live, I just drove down from the Sierra. I came here to see something different." It had been cool and bright when I left my house; here it was tepid and muggy.

"Well, you are going to be disappointed," he said, laughing. I smiled, unconvinced.

I turned to the volunteer and pointed to my planned descent trail on the map, which was listed as unmaintained. "What is this Momyer Trail like? Is the junction easy to find?"

"Oh, you aren't going to want to go there! It is overgrown with lots of bushes and stuff. If you wear nice clothes, they will get ripped and everything." He tugged on his shirt and looked pointedly at my tank top. "No, you want to stay over here." He tapped the map. "I mean, just going to the summit of San Gorgonio is nine miles one way, and that is a huge day, let me tell you, a *huge* day. And like I said, steep. No, you don't need to worry about over there, you will have a big day over here."

I decided not to tell this man what I had planned.

I nodded to the other visitor and went to find the campground in Yucaipa. It was less than ten minutes away. I erected my tent near a field illuminated by floodlights, set my alarm for 3:45 a.m., lay down in the heat of the afternoon, and tried to sleep.

The quiet part of my mind wondered if a physical-limit-pushing challenge was the best way to experience this landscape. I felt contradictory urges: the athlete in me wanted to prove my capability with a tangible, difficult goal, while the thoughtful part of me yearned for still moments to listen to wind and watch birds.

I AM GRATEFUL that others have taken time to carefully watch California's desert birds. In the early 1900s, field biologist Joseph Grinnell worried about the impact of human development on wildlife. He conducted rigorous surveys throughout California to create a detailed record of plant and animal species and their distribution. His studies indicated that wildlife was disappearing because of human influence. Today, with an increasing human population and the climate changing, there is even more reason to believe that people are hurting wildlife.

For the later part of his career, Grinnell served as the first director of the Museum of Vertebrate Zoology (MVZ) at the University of

California, Berkeley. He stated that the value of his flora and fauna cataloging would not be "realized until the lapse of many years, possibly a century . . . [when] the student of the future will have access to the original record of faunal conditions in California and the West." Exactly a century later, those future students, biologists at UC Berkeley and scientists from the San Diego Museum of Natural History, revisited Grinnell's transects to compare data.

Lori Hargrove and Phil Unitt from the San Diego Museum of Natural History resurveyed Grinnell's sites just south of what is now Sand to Snow National Monument in 2008, on the one-hundredth anniversary of Grinnell's survey of the San Jacinto Mountains. "We had two goals," Hargrove told me. "One was to retrace his steps, replicate what he did as best we could to look at changes over a hundred years. Our second goal was to establish a new baseline for the student of the future, one hundred years from now." One of their first observations was that summer high temperatures had risen seven to nine degrees on the desert floor.

I AWOKE BEFORE MY ALARM and packed my tent. On the drive to the Momyer trailhead I guzzled a bottle of cold brew coffee and choked down an oatmeal bar. I parked where my hike would end, wiggled my mountain bike out of the back hatch, and pedaled off toward the starting trailhead by 4:15 a.m.

The road rose steeply in front of my wheel. I breathed hard in the cold morning air, my legs spun the pedals on the lowest gear, and the bike inched upward at a painful pace. There were no flat sections on this road to recover. My backpack was loaded with five liters of water and dragged me backward. Phlegm collected in my throat. I contemplated quitting, and I hadn't even really started.

After what felt like hours, I made it to Vivian Creek trailhead and locked my bike to a tree. I began hiking at 4:45. The trail was steep. I did think about falling up. Then I thought about the condescending volunteer and hiked faster.

Sand to Snow got its name because of the elevation gradient that stretches from sand on the Mojave and Sonoran Deserts' floors to snow line on the highest peak in southern California, the 11,503-foot San Gorgonio. This was the peak I was hiking first.

Sweat dampened my clothes, and I sucked down water, grateful to be hiking the steepest section of trail in the cool darkness of morning. As I walked, I plotted turnaround points in case I moved too slow. If I made it up four peaks by noon, I would be happy with my progress.

I passed two women in early darkness and a man pumping water at High Creek Camp, then nobody else for hours. Eventually, the trail emerged from shade into sunshine on the ridge before San Gorgonio's top, and, ravenous and shaky, I had to stop. I balanced on a boulder next to the trail and scarfed down food, worried that I hadn't brought enough. Feeling depleted before even the first summit, it occurred to me I might not make it to all nine. But I needed to top out at least one.

San Gorgonio was named by Spanish missionaries after Saint Gorgonius, a Christian martyr who was tortured and killed for his religion. Before that, this peak was known to the Cahuilla people as Kwiria-Kaich, meaning "bald or smooth." For years people in Southern California have referred to it as "Old Grayback." It did, in fact, look like a bald, gray lump.

Just after nine, I reached the gray granite summit with mixed feelings of accomplishment and wariness. I still had a long way to go. I looked out at the green and brown hills surrounding the summit and wondered what wildlife lived along San Gorgonio's flanks. I ate another snack, signed the summit register, consulted the map, and carried on.

IN GRINNELL'S posthumously published 1944 California bird survey, he noted that black-tailed gnatcatchers were common in the Mojave and Sonoran Deserts and bred mostly below 1,000 feet in elevation. The highest observation of a black-tailed gnatcatcher then was 2,590 feet above sea level.

The black-tailed gnatcatcher is one of the smallest songbirds in North America. It weighs about as much as a nickel. Both males and females are soft gray with flashy black tails, and unlike most songbirds, they mate for life. Males wear a black cap in summer. They do not migrate, and they defend their homes in mesquite and creosote bushes with rapid scolds. Like me, they love the desert. They prefer sun, sand, and places with very little water. When winter comes, they cannot survive if temperatures dip below 36 degrees F regularly.

During Hargrove and Unitt's resurvey in 2008, they recorded black-tailed gnatcatchers at 3,850 feet and 4,860 feet, and noted that this bird is now considered common at 5,000 feet. Rising temperatures have allowed the desert-dwelling, cold-sensitive gnatcatcher to shift upslope.

I WALKED UNDER GLARING SUN along the ridge toward Jepson Peak, the second summit of the day, and was surprised to find the trail empty. San Gorgonio is the highest peak in densely populated Southern California; I expected more people would be climbing it. Physical feats and checking off summits are popular among hikers and climbers; someone is always trying to do something faster, bigger, and longer. Sometimes it seems as if being outdoors is all about achievement: speed records, linkups, and firsts. The fastest known time for a woman to hike the 211-mile John Muir Trail, for example, is three days, seven hours, and fifty-seven minutes. The men's record is two days, nineteen hours, and twenty-six minutes. Similarly specific records exist for numerous obscure accomplishments. Here in Southern California, the Nine Peak Challenge is a common undertaking, at least according to the internet. And if that challenge seems too easy, there is the SoCal Triple Crown, which climbs the three tallest "Sans" in one day: San Gorgonio, San Jacinto, and San Antonio. That challenge is nearly 40 miles of hiking and requires driving between trailheads. But today I was the only one attempting a challenge. Actually, the only one up here at all.

It took me some time to get used to identifying the mountains from the map. Small rises in the ridge were deceiving, and the rounded peaks weren't all that distinctive, but I got the hang of it. Off-trail navigation kept my mind occupied, and I worried less about how much farther I had to go.

Jepson Peak lay not far off the main trail. I headed up a sandy, low-angle slope to reach the second summit, a point that rose above a sea of other rounded peaks.

HARGROVE AND UNITT HYPOTHESIZED that a warming climate would have caused many birds to shift their habitat ranges northward and upslope, like the black-tailed gnatcatcher, in order to continue living in consistent temperatures with similar foliage. Unexpectedly, they found that many birds were not contracting their range but were expanding their range in the opposite direction: southward and downslope.

One such bird is the white-crowned sparrow, a brown and gray speckled bird with a bright-yellow beak and black-and-white racing stripes along its head. The males sing a distinctive song—one of the most studied sounds in animal behavior. It has been evaluated for its dialect variations among populations. The song is a sweet, rich whistle that starts low and long, rises and curls, and finishes with a buzz.

Grinnell hiked through the San Bernardino Mountains, including up to the summit of San Gorgonio, at least six times and never saw a white-crowned sparrow. He recorded that it lived in California's northern peaks—Mount Shasta, Lassen Peak, the White Mountains—and bred as far south as in what is now Sequoia and Kings Canyon National Parks. But in 1956 the white-crowned sparrow was found nesting about two hundred miles south of there, on the northern flank of San Gorgonio, and has been seen there ever since.

I STOMPED DOWN THE SANDY FLANK of Jepson in big sliding steps toward the trail, which then curved around a small peaklet and met a saddle on the ridge below Little Charlton. I sipped bland, lukewarm water. It was hot. This was Southern California after all, not the chilled alpine air and devious sun that I am used to. Instead, it was hot in an obvious way, dry and puddling and thorny.

I ascended the hillside, picking my footing between boulders, bushes, and trees. The trees had bark like golden scales and grew widely spaced. Most were wind sculpted and gnarled, life-size bonsai trees. The pairs of clumped needles and cornflake bark indicated lodgepole pine.

The summit of Little Charlton was a nondescript blob, even on the map, and there was no summit register, so I didn't pause for a break.

THE LODGEPOLE CHIPMUNK is a small rodent that lives in subalpine forest like the kind I was hiking through on Little Charlton, between 3,000 and 10,000 feet in elevation.

In Grinnell's 1908 surveys, the lodgepole chipmunk was the most commonly trapped at the two highest elevation sites in the San

Jacinto Mountains. By the time Hargrove and Unitt conducted surveys one hundred years later, other scientists had already reported that they could not find the lodgepole chipmunk in these regions. They expended extra effort to find this rodent, both by duplicating Grinnell's trapping methods and by devising some of their own. They found none.

Many plants and animals live in isolated habitat on mountain peaks like these. If the climate warms and it becomes too hot for these creatures to survive on their mountaintops, they have nowhere to go. There is no shifting farther up when up is only sky. Called sky island species, these creatures are stranded on mountains by an ocean of desert and a sea of suburbs. Certain birds can fly to higher peaks, but other birds, some plants, small mammals, and reptiles are unable to move. They cannot travel lower through oppressive heat and neighborhood mazes. So they die.

The lodgepole chipmunk continues to live on sky islands elsewhere in the Sierra but is no longer as far south as the San Jacinto Mountains. Instead, chaparral and Merriam's chipmunks, species known to prefer warmer weather and lower elevations, have shifted upslope and are now the common chipmunks on these peaks.

FROM LITTLE CHARLTON it was an easy walk across a broad, skylined saddle and then a short climb to reach the summit of Charlton Peak. Breathing hard, I arrived at a flat area scattered with stones the color of blush and steel, baby powder and pine boards. A bolt chained a rusted olive-green ammo can to a boulder.

The time was 10:40 a.m., plenty ahead of my noon goal for peak number four. I dropped my pack on the ground and enjoyed the luxury of sitting. My phone had an excellent signal, so I sent quick text updates to friends and received encouraging messages in return.

Around me waves of cobalt sky gradated to a foamy white stripe at the horizon. Tan peaks wrinkled the ground's surface like seaside sand dunes, the folds soft and shadowy.

Was I missing something by moving so quickly? Would I have a more profound experience if I spent the night here, seeing the mixed palette of sunset and starlight and sunrise? Warm sun reminded me I needed sunscreen, so I smeared some on my sweaty face and pulled myself up and out of the dirt to keep moving.

EARLIER THAT SPRING, I stood in a pre-dawn meadow with binoculars and a bird book. The meadow was typical montane chaparral—open fields of sagebrush with a small stand of aspen trees lining a creek. A bird perched on a branch and trilled to the morning. I stooped and focused. It was small and somewhat nondescript, but it did have one notable feature: a rusty cap. It fluffed out its feathers, settled more comfortably on the branch, and unleashed a sputtering melodic song.

What was it? I paged through *The Sibley Guide* and typed its colors into a phone app but couldn't find a match. It was definitely not a rufous-crowned sparrow, which has spots and speckles. This one was smooth, with a pale white throat fading to a gray belly. Finally, the bird fluttered onto a fence post, flashing me its electric green tail. Ah, a green-tailed towhee.

Like the white-crowned sparrow, the green-tailed towhee has expanded its range southward. In 1908 Grinnell found it in the San Jacintos but not on Santa Rosa Mountain. It was first seen there in the 1970s. In 1978 it was recorded farther south, in San Diego County. Now it is seen regularly in Baja. Scientists speculate this southward expansion could be partially due to the importation of water. Formerly arid regions of California now house golf courses, lawns, and reservoirs. "Down on the valley floors, there are now a lot of trees in people's yards where it used to be mostly scrubland," Hargrove observed. "We're seeing forest birds in these urban areas, attracted by the trees, of course."

UNLIKE THE OBVIOUS FRONT FLANK, the backside of Charlton Peak was steep, loose, and tricky to navigate. I surfed down sand and bounced over spongy trees rotting into the soil. Dollar Lake Saddle was my goal in the distance and also marked my escape route. My legs felt floppy, I was sweating through my shirt, and I was hungry. At the saddle, I paused and looked wistfully down the trail that led to my car. *If I'm tired at the next summit, I can still backtrack to here.* Comforted by this thought, I continued. The trail ascended through reddish stone outcrops and the skeletal remains of a burn, then flattened on the top of the ridge. Remarkably, I still hadn't seen a single person since low on San Gorgonio.

I relished this solitude. Instead of craving the adrenaline and risk that comes with climbing, lately I had been delighting in mindful attention to my surroundings: slow camping trips, waking at first light, identifying trees. My friends teased me about my newfound interest in birds. Perhaps I'm transitioning from a goal-oriented climber to a meditative naturalist. Is that how I want to evolve?

According to the map, Alto Diablo Peak lies right off the trail. In my eagerness, I veered off-trail too early and found myself in steep talus. I agonized over wasted energy and diagonaled back to the flat path. When I did reach Alto Diablo, it was only a one-hundred-foot detour from the trail to the dark rock summit. About an hour had passed since the last peak, but it was still before noon. I signed the register and observed peaks undulating below with a hazy glimmer of San Bernardino and Los Angeles in the distance.

One hundred years ago, the American robin lived in just three mountain ranges in Southern California: the San Bernardino Mountains, the San Gabriel Mountains, and Mount Pinos. Today

San Gorgonio Wilderness, Sand to Snow National Monument, California.
Photograph by Bureau of Land Management.

the robin has made a widespread and impressive expansion, more
than doubling its range to live along the entire Southern California
coast. The robin lives in orchards, irrigated farms, cultivated lawns,
and forests where it did not live before. Though the robin had a small
and specific habitat in the past, it has become a generalist.

The robin is cheerful, recognizable, and ubiquitous. It has a gray
back, a black head, and a trademark ruddy belly. Its song is a familiar rising, dipping, and rolling of notes that sounds like spring. It is
common enough to see a robin yanking earthworms out of a moist
front yard, and spotting one isn't cause for celebration.

This bird began its takeover of the California coast around 1930, fifteen years behind human colonization of the Bay Area and the Central Valley. Its range expansion has paralleled human expansion. Like humans, the robin found ways to live in places previously thought to be unlivable.

SHIELDS PEAK WAS GUARDED by talus, the only talus I was required to negotiate all day. After Alto Diablo I marched across Shields Flat, then hopped up granite boulders toward the rocky summit. It didn't require much gain in elevation, and I reached the top quickly.

I removed my pack, took a few panoramic photographs of blue sky above an ocean of hillsides, and nestled between two boulders to let them hold me as I ate a sandwich. I was tired. I was hot. It really hit me then. But this point was the middle of the traverse. Quitting from here was almost impossible; it was a long way back in either direction.

I pulled out headphones and played some bubbly music to lift my spirits.

SOME POPULATIONS that Hargrove expected to be in decline were actually doing just fine. The Lincoln's sparrow is a sky island species at the southern tip of its range in the San Jacinto Mountains. These brown speckled birds nest in skunk cabbage that grows in montane meadows. They sing a trilling, repetitive song, and the male's mahogany-striped crown is often peaked like a mohawk. In 1908, Grinnell observed the Lincoln's sparrow nesting at the two highest elevation sites in his survey.

In a warming climate, no one was sure of the Lincoln's sparrow's status at these high elevations. Perhaps temperatures had risen to the point where these mountaintop birds were forced from their island. Hargrove was happy to find thriving populations in the same places. "I like to tell the good stories too," she said.

I ANGLED DOWN THE TALUS of Shields Peak and regained the trail. Shields Peak and Anderson Peak were separated by a blessedly easy stretch called Anderson Flat. I kept my pace quick on the level trail then ascended toward Anderson's summit. It felt difficult.

The final two peaks were a long distance from Anderson, and to reach them I would have to pass the junction with the descent trail, hike up to the last two summits, and then backtrack. I was exhausted. With how I was feeling now, it occurred to me that walking past the descent was going to require monumental self-discipline.

I assessed my remaining water, took a conservative gulp, then ate some espresso-infused gel and hoped the caffeine would kick in soon.

LIKE ROBINS EXPANDING into urban and rural environments, ravens are experiencing a similar renaissance. Ravens thrive on urbanization. Large and shiny as oil slicks, they feast on garbage near houses and campgrounds, enjoy effortless roadkill buffets, and slurp from decorative fountains, golf course ponds, and irrigation ditches. These birds are smart enough to unzip backpacks left alone for short periods of time and remove snacks stored inside, which has happened to me more than once.

Natural springs throughout the Mojave Desert have begun to dry up due to groundwater pumping. Disappearing springs have been partially responsible for the decline of species that rely on them for drinking sources, such as bighorn sheep and desert tortoises. People have begun to install guzzlers to help these species, but these fake springs have also aided ravens, allowing them to expand into desert regions they used to avoid. Ravens then kill and eat the endangered desert tortoise.

SINCE THE MOMYER TRAIL IS UNMAINTAINED, and the man in the visitor's center would not give me any information about it, I worried it would be difficult to locate. I stumbled onto a cairn and wasted time trying to find a path nearby, but found only a tangled blanket of manzanita. Dispirited, I kept walking toward San Bernardino East until I came across an obvious signed junction with an easy to follow trail. What a relief.

I hesitated. My comfortable car felt so close. I sipped water and examined my fatigue. Quitting wouldn't feel too good; I decided to continue.

The final two peaks were some of the easiest to climb but the greatest distance apart. It was over a mile to San Bernardino East. The busted ammo can on the summit lacked a register, so I didn't take a break, just a photograph, and kept moving.

ANOTHER SKY ISLAND SPECIES in this region, the San Bernardino flying squirrel, is a small gray rodent with weblike membranes that connect forelegs to back legs to allow them to coast between trees. From a 60-foot perch, they can glide over 160 feet horizontally. Wing suits designed for base jumping were modeled after these animals, allowing people to leap off cliffs and soar for miles before deploying a parachute.

Grinnell caught one flying squirrel in a trap during his 1908 survey of the San Jacintos, which was then the southern tip of the squirrels' range. "While camped here July four to fifteen, we heard almost every night the chuckling of *Sciuropterus* in the black oaks and yellow pines around our beds," he wrote.

Hargrove and Unitt could not find flying squirrels in the San

Jacintos during their repeat surveys. Rather than declare them extirpated from the region, they continue to employ several different methods to try and locate them. The U.S. Forest Service collected hundreds of owl pellets from the same area during a spotted owl study and donated them to the Grinnell resurvey. Hargrove and Unitt's team dissected hundreds of pellets in search of flying squirrel bones. They found none.

The mammalogy team at the San Diego Natural History Museum developed a system of camera traps that broadcast flying squirrel calls and photograph responding animals. In the San Bernardino Mountains, where the rodents are still common, these traps captured many images of flying squirrels. Knowing that these devices work, they are now deploying them in the San Jacintos with the hope that some will be found living in the remote parts of that range. "We haven't given up on the flying squirrel yet," Hargrove said.

For now, the San Bernardino flying squirrel is believed to live only in the San Bernardino Mountains, in Sand to Snow National Monument. I wondered whether this sky island squirrel would eventually be eliminated from this small and specific range too.

I HIKED THE FINAL MILE to San Bernardino Peak, which was particularly painful knowing that I would have to rewalk that same distance, but the buzz of victory propelled me forward. At 1:50 p.m., I finished the short uphill to the 10,649-foot summit, elated. I basked in success and the shade of a stunted lodgepole pine as I sipped water and worried whether there was enough left for the return hike. I was glad not to have backpacked this route; there had not been a single water source since low on the first incline.

Another solo hiker walked up and, after a few awkward attempts at selfies, asked me to take a photo of him with the summit sign. I did, and he took a couple of me. We were both proud, filled with the sense of accomplishment that comes with a summit and a met goal.

Did I need these kinds of achievements to feel good about myself? The man in the visitor's center had doubted me, then I had doubted myself, and there was a deep satisfaction in proving these doubts wrong.

But the celebration was still premature. It was a long way to reach my car: two miles back to the junction, then seven more to the parking lot. I steeled myself for the descent from peak to desert.

THE FUTURE SUMMIT of San Bernardino could look like Grinnell's desert floor. The climate is changing. This slow simmering pushes animals into different territory or eliminates them altogether. In 2018, Kelly Iknayan and Steve Beissinger, scientists at UC Berkeley, published a study that found a 43 percent reduction in the number of bird species in the Mojave Desert since Grinnell's time. This loss of biodiversity is tragic and nonlinear. What about the robin? Is it invasive or resilient?

Some creatures shift, some disappear. Humans have tried to facilitate adaptation and shifting, such as by moving the desert tortoise to more temperate areas. We could vigorously work to keep everything the same as it was. But in that case, do we choose Grinnell's time period to mimic, or select a different one? We could let creatures adapt on their own and see how many Lincoln's sparrows thrive in defiance of human-caused environmental change. Meddling, even in an attempt at conservation, has wide-ranging effects. In California, we manufactured watering holes to replace the ones we drained dry, but now we must decide what to do with ravens that have proliferated as a result.

The Grinnell resurvey illustrated exactly what is being lost and what is changing. Our alteration of the planet has challenged the world's creatures to move or adapt, and they are responding as best they can, but most are losing. Like the robin, we adapt and spread, and this dispersion has displaced many other creatures. As Rachel Carson wrote in *Silent Spring,* "man is a part of nature, and his war against nature is inevitably a war against himself." We need to rise to the challenge of this warming planet ourselves.

It is all too easy and common to conceptualize nature and humans as distinctly different, as two independent islands separated by a great sea. But the warming climate and the unintended effects of conservation efforts reveal that no one thing on this planet exists in isolation. That great sea unites the islands and everything on them. Ecological philosopher Timothy Morton describes the interconnectedness of the planet as a great mesh, a concept that recognizes "the utter singularity and uniqueness of every life-form" while at the same time noting how each life-form and process lack a distinct and definite start and end. "The whole is a mesh, a very curious, radically open form without center or edge." If one strand of the mesh is pulled or moved or eliminated, the rest of the mesh becomes distorted and misshapen.

Morton has also developed a concept to help discuss and understand something as large, impactful, and intangible as global warming: *hyperobjects.* Hyperobjects are things that exist in massive scale across a spread of space and time. "Thinking ecologically about global warming requires a kind of mental upgrade, to cope with something that is so big and so powerful that until now we had no real word for it," Morton writes. The term is one way to understand the massive scale of a changing climate and all its effects, and one that, in turn, directs responsibility back to us. "If you can understand global warming, you have to do something about it."

We know the globe is warming, and we can see that this is forcing change. But so far, the steps taken to combat global warming have been small, short, and incremental. Now we need to contract our violent impact and expand awareness and understanding of our role in natural systems. Without a change in human behavior, one hundred years from now a student will come to this desert and find only empty sand and lifeless wind. Perhaps protected spaces such as national monuments can serve as a part of a solution. Sand to Snow provides room for plants and animals to shift, either up or downslope, and allows some space, however small, for creatures to exist undisturbed. Protecting this desert has also allowed for studies like the Grinnell resurveys to be conducted, so we can know with certainty what changes are taking place and with evidence begin to imagine solutions.

THE TOP HALF OF THE MOMYER TRAIL was unmaintained but easy to follow. Manzanita overhung the narrow path, which was interrupted by downed trees. I marched in a tired trance, ignoring my aching knees and growing thirst.

I am changing. This feels threatening, but I cannot remain static. Bob Schneider described how his definition of self had changed, that he had evolved from a goal-oriented climber to someone more vulnerable and caring, and that translated to his conservation work. Perhaps, like him, I can evolve into someone less selfish and more capable and, like the ranges of birds, contract in one direction and expand in another. I, too, am enmeshed with the world, and every action, every footstep brushes against other strands of this entangled planet.

Miles later, near the car, I almost stepped on a dark, hairy tarantula. It was just sitting in the middle of the sandy trail. My foot loomed above it, but I hopped backward at the last moment. It was tarantula migration season, so it must have been a male in search of a female still hiding in her burrow. The spider did not move. I squatted and examined it. Like me, this spider was traveling across the desert. Unlike my journey, his hike to find a mate might be the great challenge of his life. He dared me to try and pass. I surrendered to the tarantula and gingerly tiptoed around.

I arrived at my car thirteen hours after I left it. I had hiked 26.43 miles and tagged all nine peaks. The statistics tabulate but don't encapsulate my journey. I guzzled water and drove to collect my bike. Then I drove past the visitor center toward Los Angeles and the challenge ahead.

7. Expanding

PAPAHĀNAUMOKUĀKEA MARINE
NATIONAL MONUMENT, HAWAII

Fish darted between rust-colored coral in slightly cloudy water: small, yellow-and-black-striped convict tangs, orange-and-black triggerfish, and a couple of Moorish idols with tall trailing fins. Cold soaked the neoprene of my wet suit as I stretched my limbs in an easy float, buoyed by the salt. I scanned the sand below and pulled in my breaths through a snorkel tube, the rhythm of my breathing the only sound. My finned feet fluttered, and my arms lazily pulled water to propel me forward. Ahead a large shape swayed perpendicular to the water's surface. I jerked, startled, and back-paddled. What was that? It had a hard shell and two large appendages. At first my brain interpreted the shape as a giant crab with two humongous claws. Then it swiveled, and I saw it was a Hawaiian green sea turtle, or *honu* in Hawaiian.

The *honu* is a subpopulation of sea turtles that lives around the Hawaiian archipelago and was listed as endangered in 1978. At that time, the *honu* population had faded due to human harvesting, pollution, and accidental encounters with boats and fishing nets. Since

PAPAHĀNAUMOKUĀKEA MARINE
NATIONAL MONUMENT

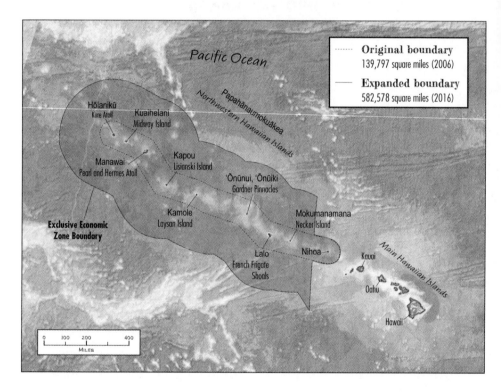

Pacific Ocean

Papahānaumokuākea
Northwestern Hawaiian Islands

.... **Original boundary**
139,797 square miles (2006)

——— **Expanded boundary**
582,578 square miles (2016)

Hōlanikū
Kure Atoll

Kuaihelani
Midway Island

Manawai
Pearl and Hermes Atoll

Kapou
Lisianski Island

ʻŌnūnui, ʻŌnūiki
Gardner Pinnacles

Kamole
Laysan Island

Mokumanamana
Necker Island

**Exclusive Economic
Zone Boundary**

Lalo
French Frigate
Shoals

Nihoa

Kauai

Main Hawaiian Islands

Oahu

Hawaii

0   100   200   400
MILES

then, the population has begun to recover, and turtles are once again commonly seen around Hawaii, though they have not yet been removed from the endangered species list.

I had come early to Kaiona Beach. As the Hawaiian island of Oahu brightened and saturated with blues and greens and yellows, I waded into waves, excited to see a rainbow of fish. I had not expected a turtle. I followed it in fascination. Its shell was smooth, its head a mottled brown and white, and its flippers fanned the water like blades. It peeked its little head above water for a sip of air and then nibbled coral. The hard-shelled body rocked with the waves. The same waves began to tug on me and slammed my shin into the sharp reef. Reluctantly, I retreated toward shore.

I am not a strong swimmer and regretted not having a buddy. The water was shallow, but I worried about currents. The strong pull of waves meant it was time for me to stop.

I surfaced to face a man standing waist deep in water and wearing a snorkel. "There was a turtle!" I exclaimed, too excited to keep it to myself.

"I know. I swim here every day," he said. "There are always turtles."

NINETY PERCENT of Hawaiian green sea turtles nest on the French Frigate Shoals, an atoll in the Northwestern Hawaiian Islands about 500 nautical miles northwest of Oahu. The small, unpopulated, rocky outcrops that form the northern arc of the Hawaiian archipelago are included in a 583,000-square-mile protected area called Papahānaumokuākea Marine National Monument. These islands barely breach the ocean's surface, and there is no fresh water found on any of them. Evidence of early native Hawaiians exists on some, especially Nihoa, the island closest to Kauai, but it is believed that people stayed there only temporarily or visited for ceremonial reasons.

Because humans and their influence are absent, the Northwestern Hawaiian Islands have become important breeding areas for marine wildlife, such as monk seals, humpback whales, albatross, and Hawaiian green sea turtles.

The public is not allowed to visit Papahānaumokuākea. Tourism is the source of 21 percent of jobs in the state of Hawaii, so it feels significant that not far from travel brochure paradise there is public land that does not encourage tourism at all. Papahānaumokuākea is unlike every other monument I visited. Most monuments attempt to balance conservation, resource extraction, and visitation under a multiple-use philosophy, but Papahānaumokuākea has only one apparent goal: preservation of the marine environment. Drilling and dredging are forbidden, fishing is outlawed, and no visitation is allowed without a special permit. The area is also remote: it can take nearly three months by boat to circumnavigate the Northwestern Hawaiian Islands and return to Oahu.

Recreation can have negative impact on places. I saw this firsthand in Bears Ears and Cascade-Siskiyou, where visitors overwhelmed beautiful areas. This monument in Hawaii was designed to protect pristine ecosystems; accepting the consequences of recreation does not fit within that mission. Expending resources to visit a place that is supposed to be shielded from my presence runs counter to my motivations for researching national monuments in the first place, so instead of visiting the monument, I went to Oahu to learn as much about it and Hawaiian wildlife as I could from afar.

Hawaii is the most isolated archipelago in the world. A quarter of all its life is unique and not found anywhere else. The Northwestern Hawaiian Islands have been protected in some form since 1909, fifty years before Hawaii became a state. In the late 1800s and early 1900s, feather hunters decimated seabird populations in search of decorations for women's hats. In response, President Theodore

PAPAHĀNAUMOKUĀKEA

Roosevelt reserved "the extreme western extension of the Hawaiian Archipelago," from Cure Island (known as Kure Atoll) to Bird Island (also known as Nihoa) "as a preserve and breeding ground for native birds." This action stopped short of creating a national monument, a new presidential possibility, but initiated some wildlife protection with the establishment of the Hawaiian Islands Bird Reservation.

As Hawaiian wildlife continued to suffer due to human exploitation, subsequent presidents and legislators expanded on Roosevelt's initial action. Franklin D. Roosevelt converted the bird reservation into the Hawaiian Islands Wildlife Refuge, with the aim to protect more than just birds. By the 1970s, overfishing had devastated populations of whales, fish, seals, sea turtles, and other creatures so much that numerous Hawaiian animals were added to the endangered species list that decade.

Coral reefs are biodiversity epicenters that are also declining. Twenty-five percent of the ocean's fish species depend on coral reefs; without them many sea organisms die. Coral reefs an oceanic organisms are also believed to produce about half of the world's oxygen. In 1996, the first large-scale coral bleaching in Hawaii occurred in Kaneohe Bay, off the eastern shore of Oahu. Coral bleaching happens when sea surface temperatures rise and kill the photosynthetic pigments in algae that live in symbiosis with coral. As a result, the coral loses its color and the companion organism that provides it with oxygen. This can lead to the coral's death.

Global warming is raising ocean temperatures, causing bleaching, and destroying the world's coral reefs. An El Niño event in 1997–98 caused such widespread coral bleaching that 16 percent of the world's coral was lost. President Bill Clinton issued two executive orders, in 2000 and 2001, that established the Northwestern Hawaiian Islands Coral Reef Ecosystem Reserve. Notably, he did not use the Antiquities Act to make this region a monument; instead, his action was intended to be reevaluated through the legislative process for establishing marine sanctuaries. In 2002 and again in 2004, as global and ocean temperatures continued to climb, mass coral bleaching occurred in the Northwestern Hawaiian Islands despite the reserve, which on its own can't do much to combat global warming.

When the idea of protecting the Northwestern Hawaiian Islands began in the early 1900s, birds were noticeably disappearing, and whales were already in decline. But at that time, it was difficult to imagine warming oceans, industrial fishing, and depleting the seemingly limitless fish in the sea.

NORMALLY, I hate preorganized tours and expensive, cookie-cutter experiences; however, I was in Oahu during peak whale migration season. After spying some faint white blows from shore, I decided seeing them up close would feel miraculous. I signed up for a whale watch tour.

I drove to the north shore of the island and boarded a catamaran with two couples, a photographer, the round and relaxed male captain, and two young, female employees with deep tans and sun-bleached hair. The catamaran motored slowly out of the harbor passing *honu* swimming in calm waters. I shaded my face with sunglasses and a ball cap and dangled my bare feet over the edge of the boat.

North Pacific humpback whales—*kohola*—spend summers feeding in cold, krill-rich waters around Alaska and eastern Russia. When winter comes, they head to warm waters around Hawaii and Mexico to breed. Ten thousand whales come to Hawaii between November and May, many of them in the mostly boat-free water of the monument. Our boat was cruising through whale-filled water off the north shore of Oahu, not a far swim to the monument for a whale.

Around two hundred thousand humpback whales were harvested

in the twentieth century, reducing the global population by 90 percent. Commercial hunting for blue and humpback whales was globally banned in 1966, when only five thousand humpbacks remained. This ban is still in effect, and humpback numbers have increased but not completely recovered. Now whale watch tours, like the one I was on, contribute around $20 million per year to Hawaii's economy.

A shiny black hump crested the ocean's surface in the distance, so the captain aimed the catamaran toward it. A tail fluke rose on the horizon. The two young girls shrieked and jumped up and down. I couldn't decide if their excitement was a show for the customers or if they were really that thrilled. Someone spied another pod off the boat's opposite side, so we anchored between the two, hoping one pod would swim closer.

"Let's swim!" one of the girls cried. They stripped to bikinis and backflipped off the rear deck as the customers watched awkwardly. I decided I might as well join them.

One of the girls climbed back in the boat, dripping, to grab a mask and fins and saw me preparing to get in the water. "Do you want a mask and fins too? With a snorkel or without?" she asked as she rummaged through a bin of equipment.

"With a snorkel," I said. "Do you see a lot of stuff out there?"

"No, the deep ocean is mostly a desert," she handed me a mask.

I pulled it on, jumped in with a cool splash, and opened my eyes to immense blue. I have swum in the ocean plenty but rarely with a mask that allowed me to see. There was nothing in the water at all, just endless blue striped with rays of sunlight. I didn't see a whale but felt like I was a whale. I kicked around in the silent, sparkling blue and stared into turquoise. I felt minuscule and part of a larger whole all at once. It was the same feeling that summiting a mountain evokes: the startling realization of your own insignificance in a vast, intricate world that doesn't care about you at all. Something about being forced to confront the triviality of my own life made the world feel colossal and powerful.

I basked in cool, salty blue until the captain called us back to the boat. Without a towel, I dripped on deck, warm wind drying me as the catamaran chased whales. Suddenly a dark and glistening hump about the same size as the catamaran surfaced right next to the boat. The girls screamed with joy. After that satisfying sighting, the captain turned toward harbor.

When the tour ended, it was still early in the day, so I decided to hike to Ka'ena Point, the northwest tip of the island. Ka'ena Point is a nature preserve with no roads; the three-mile hike out to the far end is the wildest part of Oahu.

I pulled hiking clothes on over my damp bathing suit, wrangled my salt-crusted hair into a ponytail, and started down a sandy path that threaded above the shore. Waves crashed violently on rocks, and beyond, in deep cobalt water, whales swam. White sprays of water erupted just past the rolling waves, and dark whale backs breached the surface. Amazed, I pulled out binoculars. The whales rolled on their sides and slapped the surface with their fins. They dove and hung tail flukes in the air. A small baby whale mimicked the side rolls and fin flaps of the adults. This pod was playing. They popped up for breath and hovered near the water's surface not far from shore. I sat in the sand with elbows propped on my knees and watched. Seeing this joyful family of *kohola* was even better than the sightings from the tour boat.

WHALES ARE GLOBAL CITIZENS that migrate to Hawaii seasonally. Fish, coral, and other sea creatures that live more localized lives populate Hawaii from ecological hotbeds elsewhere on the planet.

"There's a biodiversity gradient across the Pacific in what's called the Coral Triangle, which is between the Philippines, New Guinea,

PAPAHĀNAUMOKUĀKEA

and Indonesia. It is the pinnacle of marine biodiversity," said Brian Bowen, a genetic biologist at the Hawai'i Institute of Marine Biology (HIMB). "There's about 3,000 fish species in the Coral Triangle. By the time you get to Hawaii, it's 630. And by the time you get all the way over to Easter Island, the last outpost of the Indo-Pacific, it's only 130."

I was standing in a lab where people sat at desks and peered through microscopes. Brian, a large, soft-spoken man wearing plastic-rimmed glasses, a T-shirt, and sandals, stood in front of a map posted on the wall and circled the Coral Triangle with his finger. He leaped his finger to a tiny island halfway between the Triangle and Hawaii: Johnston Atoll.

"Things get to Johnston Atoll, and then from there it's pretty easy to get to here. It's only like six hundred kilometers. Once they're here, there's all sorts of great habitat, lots of yummy things to eat," Brian explained. He offered me a Coke Zero from a mini-fridge in the corner and we walked down the hall to a library where we could talk more.

I had taken a shuttle boat across Kaneohe Bay to the small, leafy island where Brian's office is located. Closed to the public, Coconut Island was privately owned by a string of wealthy businessmen and for a time was the rumored retreat of Marilyn Monroe. Now it is owned by the state and inhabited by HIMB facilities. Brian had met me on the dock and, in his enthusiasm about fish, had immediately begun talking about marine species dispersal.

"The receiving zone is French Frigate Shoals. That's where they arrive. And we have good genetic data to demonstrate that. The other route, when they come from Japan, the arrival point is Midway and Kure. So it's a really important aspect of the monument. Both of the entry points for reef organisms to colonize Hawaii are in the monument."

Humans first inhabited the Hawaiian Islands through movements similar to reef fish. Ancient Polynesians traveled across long stretches of ocean in double-hulled canoes, navigating by using careful observation of their surroundings: the movement of the sun and stars, wind patterns, ocean currents, and the flight of seabirds. Through long-distance travel, a single culture that originated in the South Pacific touched nearly every island between New Zealand, Easter Island, Samoa, and Hawaii.

"It's hard for fish," Brian said. "Even though they have larvae that drift around for thirty or forty days, it's hard for them to move more than about a thousand kilometers." That is why Hawaii has only 630 species of fish compared to 3,000 in the Philippines. Larvae float on waves; people sailed in canoes with no visible landforms for reference. I marveled at their confidence that they would find land. Fear of floating in endless ocean would be enough to keep me beach bound.

The people who eventually made Hawaii their home believed that land was immortal and had divine status similar to gods'. Therefore, land could not be owned. A caste system emerged, with the chiefs of the highest class, the *Ali'i*, serving as managers of the land while the people in lower castes worked the land. Land was divided among *Ali'i* in triangular units from ocean to mountain, like three-dimensional pizza slices. This way each group could access fresh water from the mountains and fish from the sea.

AFTER WATCHING WHALES for a good while, I hiked the rest of the way to Ka'ena Point. Surrounding the tip of the island is a tall metal fence that blocks furry predators from reaching the shore; I opened the gate and passed through. This nature preserve is one of few protected coastal dune ecosystems and is known for nesting seabirds and critically endangered monk seals. Monk seals, or *ilio-holo-i-ka-uaua*, traditionally lived in the Northwestern Hawaiian Islands, where females would emerge onto rocky atolls and sandy shores to give birth, but they are starting to appear more on the main Hawaiian Islands. Ka'ena Point, shielded by a fence, is one respite for them.

I walked down sandy paths between vines flecked with dainty, lavender beach morning glory flowers, *pōhuehue*, which bloom only for a single day. Sweating and sand-powdered, I reached the island's end, where frothy white waves crashed on slick brown rocks. I leaned against a boulder, ate a snack, and watched the ocean probe the cracks and spaces in between smooth stones with cold, salty fingers. Then one of the rocks sighed. Bubbles gurgled in the water around the shiny stone. The rock rose and fell, just slightly. That dark rock was a monk seal.

I had asked Brian to describe some interesting species that live in the monument and was surprised when this fish expert referenced a mammal. "The Hawaiian monk seal was basically thought to be extinct because of whalers, but a small population was found in the Northwestern Hawaiian Islands," he told me in the HIMB library. "They came back and rebounded. And then about thirty years ago they started declining again by about 5 percent a year. Mostly when the little ones are weaned, they don't make it, they starve. So it's a huge mystery here. Why, in a totally pristine habitat, could they undergo a century of unaided recovery and then start going down?"

I took a sip of cold, sweet Coke.

"Meanwhile, there's a very small population of them, about two hundred, in the main Hawaiian Islands," he continued. "The small population here is going up. In the pristine habitat, they're going down; in the heavily impacted habitat, they're doing great."

He laid his hands on the table between us.

"Now we're the conservation genetics lab for the university. So we check this out. Monk seals have extremely low genetic diversity, but we concluded that inbreeding depression is not what's getting them. We've pretty much ruled that out. So my favorite theory—and keep in mind I'm not a seal biologist—my favorite theory is that in the Northwestern Hawaiian Islands, when they roll stones over in search of food, there's some jacks and other fish that are smart enough to follow them, and when something comes out, they dart in and grab it."

"The fish does?" I ask.

"Yeah. That doesn't happen here because there's not as many fish. We fished out the competition." I understood then why Brian found the monk seals interesting: he believed they were being outsmarted by fish.

When Papahānaumokuākea Marine National Monument was established in 2006, fishing was phased out within the monument's new boundary. The Northwestern Hawaiian Islands became a place free from people for wildlife to thrive. But the monk seal wasn't thriving.

Those islands are not as free from human influence as it appears. Perhaps detritus from the Pacific Garbage Patch (a floating heap of the world's discarded plastic) washes up on shore, and seal pups get tangled in it, eat it, and suffer. Perhaps warming waters and rising sea levels are eliminating rocky resting places on the already small atolls. Or maybe, like Brian suggested, fish populations are thriving, and those fish create more intense competition for food. Is that a sign of a disturbed ecosystem or a healthy one? Overfishing, pollution, climate change, and other human activities have so disrupted animal populations that it is no longer clear what these systems would be like without our influence, even in a place that has recently been left alone.

PAPAHĀNAUMOKUĀKEA

SOME PEOPLE ARE SURPRISED when they hear that Republican president George W. Bush, often perceived as anti-environment, was responsible for reserving a large swath of Hawaiian ocean as a national monument. In the story of Papahānaumokuākea's designation, Jean-Michel Cousteau, son of the famed ocean explorer Jacques Cousteau, filmed a documentary about the Northwestern Hawaiian Islands and their wildlife called *Voyage to Kure*. This film was screened for George W. and Laura Bush at the White House, and the president was moved by the depictions of sea life and the ways it was being destroyed. The island of Laysan, for example, was devastated by guano mining and the introduction of rabbits, which ate all the native plants; an invasive weed from the Midwest is taking over Pearl and Hermes Atoll, home to the largest population of fish in the Northwestern Hawaiian Islands; and floating bits of plastic and lost fishing nets are killing seabirds that nest on Midway, which also houses the remains of a U.S. military base.

In 2006 Bush invoked the Antiquities Act to designate 140,000 square miles of ocean, islands, and atolls as a national monument, upending an effort to create a marine sanctuary that had been ongoing since Clinton created the Coral Reef Ecosystem Reserve five years earlier. Some people have argued that a legislative marine sanctuary would have given the area more robust protection than a monument. Considering that President Trump reduced and modified several monuments, they could be correct. Others argued that creating a sanctuary through congressional action takes too long— evidenced by the number years it had been in process—and the Antiquities Act allowed the area to be protected immediately, which may be better for wildlife in the long term.

Applying the Antiquities Act to the ocean is an unusual use of the law. The act states that it can be applied to "lands owned or

Schooling convict tangs, Papahānaumokuākea Marine National Monument, Hawaii. Photograph by John Burns/NOAA.

controlled by the Government of the United States." But who controls the seas? Oceans are typically thought of as a lawless, worldwide commons, something owned by everyone on the planet and not divided into possession by nations. This generous view of ownership makes ocean conservation problematic. How does one institute protections for a place that no one owns or regulates?

The original American colonies had a generally accepted rule that a nation controlled as far from shore as a cannon could shoot, giving some amount of sovereignty over shoreline. Today the internationally accepted rules for marine governance state that each nation has full ownership and control of its "territorial sea," which extends twelve nautical miles from shore. Nations can impose regulations to protect their territorial seas for a full twenty-four nautical miles from shore, considered the "contiguous zone." Extending two hundred nautical miles from shore is the Exclusive Economic Zone (EEZ), the area where a nation has the right to explore and exploit resources or conserve and manage them.

Papahānaumokuākea was not the first time the Antiquities Act was used to protect an ocean environment. President Franklin D. Roosevelt designated Channel Islands National Monument off the coast of California in 1938, and Santa Rosa Island National Monument off the coast of Florida the following year. President Clinton, though he did not apply the Antiquities Act to Hawaiian waters, did designate California Coastal National Monument in 2000, which encompasses all islands, rocks, and exposed reefs within the territorial sea boundary for the entire length of California. Because of a growing understanding of the importance of marine protected areas, after Bush designated Papahānaumokuākea, he established three more marine monuments in 2009: Marianas Trench, Pacific Remote Islands, and Rose Atoll, protecting around 254,000 square miles of ocean in total.

In 2016, President Obama expanded Papahānaumokuākea by roughly four times, extending the boundary to the edge of the EEZ. At the time, this expansion made Papahānaumokuākea the largest protected area in the world. At 583,000 square miles, it remains the largest contiguous conservation area in the United States, larger than all the rest of the country's national parks combined. This massive expansion banned resource extraction, the dumping of waste, and all commercial fishing within monument boundaries.

A month after Obama expanded Papahānaumokuākea, he established Northeast Canyons and Seamounts Marine National Monument southeast of Cape Cod, the first U.S. marine monument in the Atlantic Ocean. This region includes four undersea mountains and three underwater canyons and is home to endangered right whales and deep-sea corals that do not live anywhere else. As with the Hawaiian monument, commercial fishing was banned within the new 5,000-square-mile boundary. Fishing for red crab and American lobster was slated to be phased out over the subsequent seven years. At the time of this designation, numerous marine monuments already existed, but five commercial fishing industries challenged the monument with a lawsuit, alleging that the president did not have the authority to protect ocean under the Antiquities Act. The case, *Massachusetts Lobsterman's Association v. Ross*, was dismissed in 2018. Judge James E. Boasberg determined that the "lands" referred to in the Antiquities Act apply to submerged ocean floor and that the United States does control the land within the EEZ boundary for the purposes of the act. This ruling legitimizes Northeast Canyons and Seamounts, Papahānaumokuākea, and all other U.S. marine monuments.

PAPAHĀNAUMOKUĀKEA

In addition to wildlife preservation, an important aspect of Papahānaumokuākea is its recognition of Native Hawaiian culture. Public visitation is not allowed, but Native Hawaiians can visit and fish within the monument with a special permit. "There's two things that we're balancing," said Papahānaumokuākea's former superintendent Matthew Brown. "We're balancing the cultural heritage component, that need for cultural connection. And then the conservation piece."

Unlike many other Indigenous communities in the United States, Native Hawaiians do not have their own sovereign government. In the last two decades of the 1700s, Kamehameha, a member of the ruling class on the big island of Hawaii, overthrew the rulers of each Hawaiian island one by one and united the archipelago under a monarchy. Kamehameha became Hawaii's first king. In 1820, American missionaries arrived in Hawaii with the goal of colonizing and educating Hawaiians. After seventy years of an uneasy cohabitation and a sharp decline in the Native Hawaiian population, descendants of missionaries overthrew Hawaii's last monarch, Queen Lili'uokalani, in 1893. The United States annexed Hawaii five years later without any input from the recently overthrown Hawaiians. In 1978 Hawaii created the Office of Hawaiian Affairs, an organization independent of the state government designed to oversee Native Hawaiian interests, though Native Hawaiians still do not have a formally recognized government with rights of self-determination.

Papahānaumokuākea aims to honor Native Hawaiians and their connection to the land and water around Hawaii through its management. The monument is managed by four cotrustees: National Oceanic and Atmospheric Administration (NOAA), U.S. Fish and Wildlife Service, the State of Hawaii's Department of Land and Natural Resources, and the Office of Hawaiian Affairs. President Bush's proclamation states that "this area has great cultural significance to the Native Hawaiian community and a connection to early Polynesian culture worthy of protection and understanding." President Obama's expansion proclamation reinforces this idea, stating, "the ocean will always be seen as an integral part of cultural identity for the Native Hawaiian community. The deep sea, the ocean surface, the sky, and all the living things in the area adjacent to the Monument are important to this culture and are deeply rooted in creation and settlement stories."

It wasn't until a year after Bush's initial designation that the monument was named Papahānaumokuākea, at the recommendation of several Hawaiians. In Hawaiian legend, Papahānaumoku is Mother represented by Earth. Wākea is Father embodied in the sky. The union of the two resulted in the birth of the Hawaiian archipelago, and these islands are still considered sacred by many.

"The monument has a goal of allowing both traditional science using traditional knowledge as well as more Western science," Matthew Brown told me. Scientists and researchers with permits "can count and measure and document and photograph and fly LIDAR and deep sea dive, but then there's also something about just bringing cultural practitioners to a place where their ancestors have been for eight hundred-plus years. For them to taste the same food and drink the same water and smell the same smells. Perpetuating that connection is really important."

I spoke also with Mililani Trask, a Native Hawaiian woman involved in the Hawaiian sovereignty movement who opposed the monument. She felt the monument regulations made it more difficult for Hawaiians to access their sacred territory and disrupted many people's fishing income. Even more than the American national monument designation, Mililani opposed a UNESCO World Heritage Site designation, which was given to the same area in 2010. She pointed out that UNESCO and Papahānaumokuākea recognized this region has international appeal and significance, but nothing was being done to clean up the Pacific Garbage Patch, to prevent coral bleaching, or to halt global warming—all things directly harming this area that the designations claimed as special. Trask wanted more action.

ON OAHU, Hanauma Bay is legendary for snorkeling. It is a volcanic crater where the side facing the ocean has collapsed, forming a round, calm bay for coral and fish. This bay is managed as a nature preserve where fishing is prohibited. Tourism, on the other hand, is promoted. Snorkeling here is so popular that now there is a three-thousand-person daily limit, down from ten thousand in the past. Once that limit is reached, people are turned away. So I arrived early, before the front gate even opened, and waited in my car in the dark behind another vehicle.

When an employee opened the gate, I parked, gathered my snorkel gear, and joined the end of a line forming in front of the ticket kiosk. Each entrant must pay a fee and watch a ten-minute video about reef safety before being allowed on the beach. A gray-haired employee in a puffy jacket surveyed the line and told us that because we were early, we could skip all that and head to the beach for free. I flip-flopped down a steep, paved hill behind the rest of the early risers and made my way to an empty end of the beach. It was not even 7:00 a.m. and still completely dark. I spread my towel on cold, gray sand and sipped coffee from a thermos while black waves nosed the shore. A sliver of moon hung just above the outer edges of the crater. The sky slowly pinked, like cheeks warming from a morning walk. I could not believe I was spending a solitary morning watching the sunrise on a beach famous for being flooded with tourists. It was still early twilight when I waded into the water for my first foray at snorkeling.

I dipped my face into chilly water. A prickling, fizzing sound

137

hissed in my ears behind the rasp of my breath through the snorkel. I willed my body to relax as I drifted above the coral. Fish swam around me in a colorful cloud. Schools of striped convict tangs swam as one amorphous being, and bright-orange and black reef triggerfish—*humuhumunukunukuapua'a*—wiggled out of my way as I floated toward them. Iridescent, multicolored parrotfish, *uhu*, hovered near the pale sand. Parrotfish are a bright baby blue with pink stripes cascading along their bodies, yellow-edged fins, and tails accented with orange. No two of them seem to be the same, but they shimmer through the water in a rainbow flash. They get their name from their hard, birdlike beaks they use to scrape algae from coral.

I stayed at Hanauma Bay through the morning, taking breaks on the beach and swimming for increasingly longer times. The fish flashed brighter in stronger sunlight. With my face underwater, things were quiet, colorful, and serene. When I poked my head above water to get my bearings, the screams and splashes of families accosted me. On the beach, my solitary towel was overtaken by groups as they packed into any open slot of sand. I waited until I could no longer find any open spaces to swim, and then left.

Later that afternoon, I sat in the HIMB library with Brian Bowen discussing fish. "Did you see some big parrotfish?" he asked about Hanauma Bay.

"Yeah, I did. Those are the blue and pink fish? They were my favorite."

"You won't find any big parrotfish out there," he gestured out the window to Kaneohe Bay. "They're all gone. You can find juveniles and maybe some young, young adults, but I don't think I've seen one in this bay in five years."

"Really?"

"That is direct evidence in support of marine protected areas," he said.

PAPAHĀNAUMOKUĀKEA

"Because Hanauma Bay is a preserve?"

"Right. They are fished out here." He paused for a moment, thinking, then continued. "Parrotfish have a very cool method of sleeping. They get kind of comatose, but they secrete a bubble of mucus around them so that if anything disturbs the mucus, they wake up. That makes them tragically vulnerable to people spear-gunning at night because they can just shoot from outside the bubble. And that's why there're no big parrotfish in this bay. You literally saw the importance of protecting marine areas with your own eyes."

ONE OF THE MOST VOCAL ARGUMENTS against Obama's monument expansion came from the fishing industry. Unlike the monuments that allow grazing and other types of resource extraction, Papahānaumokuākea prohibits commercial fishing within its boundaries. The expansion quadrupled the area where fishing was outlawed. The fishing industry argued this would reduce their annual income by $10 million.

In 2020, four years after the expansion, two different studies on the effect of the monument on fisheries were published. Interestingly, they seemed to reach contradictory conclusions. The first study, by Hing Ling Chan, compared vessels from the Hawaiian longline tuna fleet that had previously fished within the monument to vessels that had not. Ten percent of tuna fleet vessels had fished in waters that became the national monument—a total of forty boats. Relative to other boats in the fleet, the profits for these boats declined by $3.5 million, which suggests that the monument had a negative economic impact on the fishery.

The second study, by John Lynham and colleagues, differed in its unit of study. Lynham compared the Hawaiian longline tuna fleet, which had previously fished within the monument's boundaries, to the Hawaiian longline swordfish fleet, which had not. After comparing the rise and fall of profits for both fleets, they found no negative effect on the tuna fleet after the monument expansion. Revenue did not decrease for the tuna fishery as a whole. In fact, Lynham noted that "revenue, catch, and catch-per-unit-effort have all increased since the expansion." This means that fishermen who expended the same amount of effort caught *more* fish than before. When these studies are taken together, it can be inferred that the $3.5 million lost by some tuna fleet vessels seems to have gone to other boats rather than been lost entirely.

Many scientists maintain that marine protected areas actually help fisheries. Studies have found that areas with partial fishing bans have three times the variety and abundance of fish than unprotected areas, and areas with complete commercial fishing bans have six times the number and diversity of fish. This abundance spills over into adjacent waters where fishing is allowed. Lynham references this in the conclusion of his study. "Protected areas provide a sufficiently large refuge to recover and maintain mobile stocks, which can still be targeted when they swim beyond the borders of the protected area." A safe place for tuna to live means more tuna in the ocean, which translates to more tuna that can be harvested.

The Atlantic fishing industries lost the court case that challenged the legality of Northeast Canyons and Seamounts National Monument; however, President Trump chose not to leave it at that. In June 2020 he issued a proclamation that removed the ban on commercial fishing within that monument. He did not reduce the size of the monument like he did for Bears Ears and Grand Staircase–Escalante, but he removed the regulation that arguably provides the most protection for the whales and corals that live there and nowhere else. The removal of this protection posed a risk to the fundamental benefits of marine monuments.

PAPAHĀNAUMOKUĀKEA

FROM KA'ENA POINT, I turned back to hike the way I had come, following a path that threaded through the low, waxy green bushes of beach cabbage, or *naupaka kahakai*. Hawaii is full of color: tangy green plants, warm golden sand, rosy reef rocks, blue and turquoise water that changes hue with its depth. A flash of white caught my eye, and I skidded to a stop. Right next to the trail, less than three feet away, a Laysan albatross—*moli*—sat on a nest shaded by a *naupaka's* canopy. Her face was tucked underneath her wing, so all I could see was a ball of brilliant-white feathers. I stood there and gawked. Almost all (99.7 percent) of Laysan albatross populations nest in the monument on Laysan, the island that gives them their name, and Midway, the site of a decisive battle between the United States and Japan in World War II. I had spotted one of the 0.3 percent of Laysan albatross that nest elsewhere. The albatross lifted her face and clicked her long, peach beak. This was the animal that had prompted the first efforts to protect the Northwestern Hawaiian Islands more than a century ago.

Before Theodore Roosevelt attempted to prevent the slaughtering of seabirds on these islands, people perceived the birds to be so numerous that killing them was inconsequential. In previous eras, an attitude of limitless abundance allowed for overzealous hunting and poaching. The first Polynesians who settled in Hawaii hunted some animals, such as the goose-like *moa-nalo*, to extinction. It is the same tragic story of many species now gone, such as the passenger pigeon, which used to be so numerous that its flocks blocked out the sun. I can't imagine living with this idea of perpetual, bountiful life. Limitless abundance is no longer a pervasive concept; instead, beauty in this world is more often seen as scarce, precarious, and fleeting.

In 2020 the NOAA Coral Reef Conservation Program released

a national status report for U.S. coral reefs. On a scale from good to impaired, U.S. reefs ranked as fair but declining, with reefs around Oahu—where I had been snorkeling—ranked impaired. Reefs adjacent to humans are much more impacted than remote reefs, yet the largest threat affects them all: climate change and its consequences of increased sea surface temperature, ocean acidification, and sea level rise. Global efforts to combat greenhouse gas emissions and the warming of the planet are crucial to protecting these marine biodiversity centers.

Here in Papahānaumokuākea, through the actions of several presidents and the work of many more citizen advocates, the United States has declared the ocean around the Northwestern Hawaiian Islands a national monument. This designation is particular to the United States, fraught with this nation's own conflicts and clashes. Yet this ocean isn't the distinct property of one nation; it is woven into the greater mesh of the world. Bluefin tuna swim into the monument and swim out of it, into seas where a boat from any nation can catch them. Whales breed here, and then swim to Russia. Reefs host fish that populate other reefs miles and countries away. Phytoplankton that grow in oceans produce much of the world's oxygen. The phytoplankton feed clouds, which repel the sun's heat and then provide rain and fresh water to the rest of the planet.

Because everything is enmeshed, localized destruction can have worldwide consequences. The ocean makes this obvious because a marine protected area's boundary is literally fluid. It cannot be fenced off like land; it cannot keep harm out with steel bars like at the Ka'ena Point preserve. Overfishing in one place reduces fish populations elsewhere. Garbage from around the world floats and collects onto a raft of trash in the Pacific. This mound holds bits from all of us. Perhaps a water bottle I used lies next to a discarded sole from your worn-out shoe. Climate change's effects are felt everywhere.

PAPAHĀNAUMOKUĀKEA

Warming and acidifying oceans bleach coral reefs, regardless of their location. Glaciers that melt in the Arctic will raise sea levels and one day swallow a tropical shoreline. When Hawaiian green sea turtles lay eggs, the temperature of the nest determines the sex of the babies: warmer nests produce females, and cooler nests produce males. If China, India, the United States, and other countries continue to pump harmful emissions into the atmosphere, fewer male Hawaiian sea turtles will hatch.

Just as localized destruction affects more than one place, preservation efforts that happen on a local scale can be world-felt. Fish, seals, corals, birds, whales, and turtles that benefit from a protected area contribute to the health of the ocean overall, which makes for a healthier planet. As one of the largest protected marine areas in the world, Papahānaumokuākea represents a unique and forward-thinking approach to environmental protection that reaches beyond America's borders. On the same day in 2021 that he restored the boundaries of Bears Ears and Grand Staircase–Escalante, President Biden reinstated the commercial fishing restriction to Northeast Canyons and Seamounts. The hope is that more protected marine areas will equal more fish in the sea.

Mililani Trask was not impressed with Papahānaumokuākea's designation because tangible steps were not being taken to fix global problems. She is correct that more needs to be done; small steps, such as reserving spaces free from tourists and commercial fishing, are a start.

Like fish species that migrate from the Coral Triangle to elsewhere in the sea, humans have a migratory history. Polynesians pushed offshore in canoes, and their deep understanding of the world around them allowed for long-distance, oversea navigation. The motion of the sun, stars, waves, and wind all held clues. They looked beyond the bow toward planetary signs. When it comes to preservation, it is also important to think beyond the boundary, to see past what is directly in front of us to the ways that everything and everyone in the world are entwined. This planet is the biological hotspot where all of us originated, and it is where we hope to continue to live and move and thrive, if only we can prevent it from being depleted entirely.

PAPAHĀNAUMOKUĀKEA

8. Layering

GRAND STAIRCASE–ESCALANTE
NATIONAL MONUMENT, UTAH

U tah sandstone swirls in candy-cane stripes of cream and strawberry sherbet and plum purple. In the 1870s, geologist Clarence Dutton described these rock layers that stair-step upward from the Grand Canyon as a Grand Staircase—like a colorful, expansive entryway to a blue sky palace. Dutton identified five prominent layers, starting at the Grand Canyon. The oldest and lowest layer is the Chocolate Cliffs; around the Utah–Arizona border lie the Vermilion Cliffs; then come the White Cliffs, the Gray Cliffs, and finally the Pink Cliffs—the youngest and uppermost layer exemplified by powdery hoodoos in Bryce Canyon National Park. Today geologists divide Dutton's five general layers into twenty-four distinct rock formations. Grand Staircase–Escalante National Monument, which features this vivid candy-striped stairway, was named in part for this geology.

I visited this monument many times, once with Veronica, once with Jack, and several times with other friends, in hope that each visit would clarify my understanding of what this place is. I wanted

GRAND STAIRCASE-ESCALANTE
NATIONAL MONUMENT

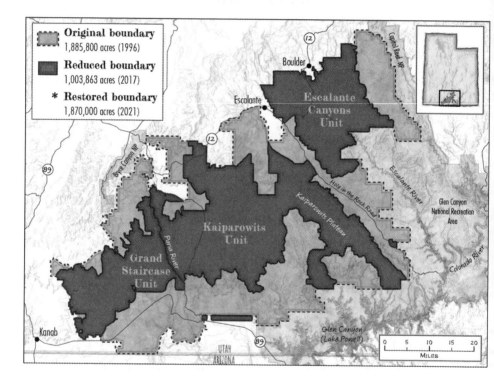

Original boundary
1,885,800 acres (1996)

Reduced boundary
1,003,863 acres (2017)

* Restored boundary
1,870,000 acres (2021)

Escalante Canyons Unit

Kaiparowits Unit

Grand Staircase Unit

Boulder

Escalante

Kanab

Bryce Canyon NP

Paria River

Kaiparowits Plateau

Hole in the Rock Road

Escalante River

Glen Canyon National Recreation Area

Colorado River

Capitol Reef NP

Glen Canyon (Lake Powell)

UTAH
ARIZONA

0   5   10   15   20
MILES

to know why the monument was mired in controversy, what the land means to people, and to connect those points in a straight and clear line. Instead, the more I learned, the more my thoughts curved and twisted. And the more affection I felt for this desert. I spiraled, Escher-like, through chocolate and truffle and red velvet icing steps, never reaching a landing.

Grand Staircase–Escalante is as layered and complex as the stone.

TINY SNOWFLAKES WHIRRED around our heads despite the spring sunshine. Veronica hiked with her curly hair tucked underneath a wide-brimmed sunhat, and I wore a fleece underneath my loaded backpack. We followed a dry riverbed of smooth stones as walls on either side funneled us toward a fissure in the ground. We stopped when a crack sliced into the earth at our feet and spread into the distance. The stone's surface was flat and dull tan, but the inside was soft and round, like juicy cinnamon apples tucked inside a buttery crust.

"We go down that?" Veronica asked, peering at the smooth-sided, thirty-foot drop. "There will be no coming back up once we get down there!"

We plopped our packs on the ground and exchanged nervous, excited glances.

"If you go first, I can lower the packs to you with the cord," I said.

"I have to go first?"

"Do you want to go last?"

The stone here contains many surprises: fossils, coal seams, slinky slot canyons. We were in the center of Grand Staircase–Escalante National Monument, along Cottonwood Road, which marks the western edge of the fifty-mile-long Kaiparowits Plateau, a name that means "mountain home of the people" in Paiute language. Seventy-five million years ago, a 1.3 ton *Kosmoceratops* with a frilled fin adorning its neck lumbered through a tangle of vines where today there is desert. It munched green shoots with its triangular snout and nudged aside giant ferns with its horns. Back in this creature's time, rivers threaded through the jungle and occasionally flooded, releasing piles of colorful sand along their banks. These alluvial floodplains hardened into the striped stone seen in Grand Staircase–Escalante today, preserving enormous dinosaur skeletons and delicate lacy leaves in the process. A *Kosmoceratops* skeleton was discovered in Kaiparowits Formation sandstone not far from where Veronica and I stood.

As years passed, water wormed its way through the solidified sand and cracked the stone into canyons. Southern Utah's landscape is incised with canyons that cannot be seen until you are right at their edges, unlike mountains, with obvious summits that can be seen and referenced from a distance. When looking toward the horizon, it is impossible to tell how many canyons ribbon their way through the ground. The desert of Grand Staircase–Escalante is so full of hidden canyons and labyrinthine twists and turns that it was the last place in the continental United States to be mapped.

The Navajo Sandstone at our feet split in a ripple pattern that evoked movement even as it stood still. We were about to see one of these stone slots from the inside. Veronica wriggled into the narrow opening, pressed hands and feet against soft walls, and eased herself to the bottom. Once her feet hit the sand, she looked up at me with a grin. Her pink jacket glowed in the bottom of the crevice. I lowered our packs to her one at a time on a small rope, then scooted to the edge so my feet dangled into the slot. I couldn't have told you then what we were heading toward, but the moment held the rift of beginning. I climbed down, sliding into the cupping caress of the canyon and headed toward the unknown.

GRAND STAIRCASE–ESCALANTE

IN 1990S AMERICA, many of the most obvious and majestic natural places had been protected as national parks, state parks, monuments, or recreation areas. The Antiquities Act hadn't been used since the late 1970s when President Jimmy Carter established fifteen enormous monuments in Alaska. But the 1990s were also a time when appreciation of the natural world began extending beyond the obvious. Ecosystems such as sage-steppe, desert, ocean, and grassland were receiving greater attention from conservationists.

President Bill Clinton's first term was wrapping up, and he was mounting his reelection campaign. Polls indicated that he needed to champion environmental policies to gain more votes from the Left. In Arizona it seemed as if Clinton had a fighting chance, but he would have to do something drastic. Utah was a lost cause; he would never win the staunchly red state. Senators Orrin Hatch and Bob Bennett and Governor Mike Leavitt were all Republican and all members of the Church of Jesus Christ of Latter-day Saints, which heavily influenced state politics. Clinton weighed his options and decided to make that drastic move to please environmentalists at the risk of angering some Utahans. On September 18, 1996, he stood on the edge of the Grand Canyon in Arizona and declared Grand Staircase–Escalante a national monument located entirely in Utah. "A Bold Stroke: Clinton Takes a 1.7 Million-Acre Stand in Utah," read the *High Country News* headline.

The way in which Clinton designated the monument—from Arizona, as a surprise, killing a long-hoped-for coal mine in the process—infuriated many Utah residents and politicians. Just like the Bears Ears designation twenty years later, the establishment of the monument was widely portrayed as an outsider telling Utahans what to do with their own land. "This is the mother of all land grabs," said Senator Hatch at the time.

149

Utah ranks third in the nation for concentration of public land, behind Alaska and Nevada. Seventy-five percent of Utah's land—around 35 million acres—belongs to the public. Utah politicians complained, even before Grand Staircase–Escalante became a monument, that too much of Utah was locked up in federal land and the state required more open land for development and progress. Though the area that became Grand Staircase–Escalante National Monument was already public under the jurisdiction of the BLM, that agency had granted leases to the Dutch mining company Andalex Resources Inc. to remove coal from the Kaiparowits Plateau. Thousands of jobs and thousands of tax dollars were expected for Utah. According to the state's Geological Survey, the Kaiparowits contained 11.375 billion tons of recoverable coal, the largest untapped coalfield in the country.

Clinton's 1996 monument proclamation was timed to halt these mining plans. It withdrew this area from any new mining claims or leases and made things so difficult for plans to move forward that Andalex withdrew its mining application the following year. This was an affront that Utah politicians could not forgive, even as decades passed. When President Trump took office in 2017, Utah's Governor Gary Herbert and Senator Hatch, still in office twenty years later, pleaded with him for a change.

"I'm approving the Bears Ears and Grand Staircase recommendations for you, Orrin," President Trump is reported to have said to Hatch in October, two months before signing an executive order that redrew the boundaries of both monuments to make them much, much smaller. He made it sounds as if two buddies were shaking hands over the sale of a car.

Trump reconfigured Grand Staircase–Escalante's boundary into three smaller parcels: the Escalante Canyons Unit in the northeast, the Kaiparowits Unit in the center, and the Grand Staircase Unit in the west. All had been scissored and shrunk around the edges. Notable tourist sites protected under the original monument proclamation, such as Grosvenor Arch, the historic Paria Townsite, and Dance Hall Rock, were just barely included by a boundary line. The redrawn map features pale strips of removed land wedged between the remaining monument units. In total, the monument was reduced by 45 percent, withdrawing over 876,000 acres. This withdrawn land would remain under the management of the BLM but was opened to the possibility of new mining leases and increased grazing permits.

President Clinton's original Grand Staircase–Escalante proclamation established wide-ranging protection for over 1.8 million acres of red and pink desert and declared it a science monument dedicated to the study of geology, paleontology, biology, archaeology, and history. President Trump's reduction proclamation devotes several pages to explaining why the regions removed are not important to protect. It claims that since similar geologic features and cultural sites are found across the Four Corners region, they are not unique. It rationalizes that in the past twenty years of the monument's existence research identified the locations of rare fossils and cultural sites, so the remaining areas are not important for science. The Trump administration justifies these decisions with the Antiquities Act itself, stating that the original monument boundary was not the smallest area compatible with proper care of the listed objects.

So which view is true? The one that finds this place to be unique, beautiful, and full of secrets of the past, or the one that claims it is bland, barren space, ideal for wrenching coal from its depths?

MY BACKPACK HIT THE SANDSTONE SLAB with a thunk and I rummaged through the top compartment for my binoculars. Our packs were heavy, loaded with five liters of water each, because Jack and I had hiked into the desert with no certainty about where we might find water. We had circled a few springs on our map, but since the Utah backcountry is mostly sand, stone, and pinyon pine, we weren't sure if these springs would be wet or dry.

We were not following a trail, just wandering across a mesa, when we stumbled over a black hose snaking through sagebrush. Realizing that this hose was laid out to fill cattle troughs and irrigate pasture, we followed it in hopes it would lead to a water source. Eventually the hose plunged over a cliff below. We perched on a rock outcrop overlooking a creamsicle-colored canyon and debated where to go next. Jack examined the map and I scanned the canyon's opposite rim.

On this trip to Grand Staircase–Escalante, I wanted to explore the remote interior of the monument on the coal-rich Kaiparowits Plateau, an area not easily accessed by roads. Remoteness and wilderness character are protected aspects of the monument. To really get a sense of this place, I had to get far into the backcountry. I had shown Jack a map of the monument with red and green dots indicating cultural and paleontological sites, and we selected an area with a high density of Ancestral Pueblo ruins. Hopi, Zuni, Diné, Ute, Ute Mountain Ute, San Juan Southern Paiute, Kaibab Paiute, and Acoma communities have current and historic connections to the Grand Staircase region. Long before these cultures, ancient communities lived in the arid deserts of what is now Utah, Colorado, Arizona, and New Mexico from roughly 750 CE until a peak in population around 1250 CE. These people built dwellings and kivas on cliffsides and in alcoves; they hunted, foraged, and farmed; they crafted baskets and pottery and weapons; and they observed complex religious customs. For five hundred years people lived and roamed here, but around 1300 CE, according to the archaeological record, they mysteriously disappeared. The leading theory is that extreme drought forced the Ancestral Puebloans to migrate to areas with more reliable water, such as the Rio Grande Basin, where they merged with other Puebloan people, the ancestors to Puebloan cultures of today.

Jack and I were captivated by the mystery of people who built elaborate structures high on cliffs and then vanished. So while Jack pondered our route options, I searched for history.

"I think I see a dwelling," I said. "Or a granary."

"Already? No way!" I passed the binoculars to Jack and pointed to an alcove at the terminus of the canyon. There was a small geometric shape on the ledge, which looked too straight and square to be a natural block.

"Hmmm. Maybe. It's hard to tell."

The bottom of the canyon was lined with aspen trunks, naked white pillars that promised water. This, coupled with the potential sighting of a ruin, convinced us to head down the steep, vegetated slope. We shouldered our packs and traversed the canyon rim until we found a break in the cliffside where we scrambled down sandy ledges and slipped down dead Gambel oak leaves. Eventually we reached a small trickle of water at the canyon bottom. We followed it downstream, away from the ruin at the head of the canyon, and the trickle grew wider and deeper. Relieved to have found a drinkable source, we made camp in the flattest spot we could find along the creek. It was not comfortable or scenic, but we were elated to have found water in the desert.

The next morning we packed camp and continued down canyon. The creek deepened and then disappeared underground altogether. We ducked under juniper branches and continued walking down the rocky riverbed until our drainage merged with another at a wide, flat confluence.

"Let's leave our packs here and explore a little more, then we can come back and camp for the night," Jack suggested. We hung our packs on low branches to thwart scavenging rodents, then noticed a peculiar stack of rocks underneath an overhang above us. The rocks looked intentionally piled.

"Look at that!" Jack said. "We have to get a closer look." Feeling freer with nothing on our backs, we hiked up the slope and climbed over some lichen-coated slabs below the overhang. Surrounded by heaps of bat guano were the remains of three granaries. Originally they were cylinders constructed from tight piles of flat stones packed with red clay mortar. They were built so that the overhang formed a ceiling, protecting the containers from sun and rain. Each of them was busted open, either by looters or time, and the front sides of the cylinders were missing. Jack and I sat on a flat rock near the structures and looked back down at the confluence. The intersecting canyons were a good landmark. It made sense to me why people would store food here, at a place that was easy to remember and describe. The canyon still felt wild, with little evidence of modern society. We were alone out here, and it could have been any place in time. It felt as though the people who built these granaries could walk around the bend any minute.

We returned to the riverbed and continued hiking down canyon. After another hour, I climbed over a stack of boulders and found myself on a large, flat platform at the end of the drainage. A huge red basin stretched out far below, its vibrance dramatically different from the peach-and-cream canyon we had been walking in. We peered westward from the edge of the Gray Cliffs to the radiant Vermilion Cliffs. A teal corner of the Lake Powell reservoir glinted in the sun, out of place amid all the rosy sand.

"Wow," Jack stood next to me, surveying the basin below.

"Whoa, look at those petroglyphs!" I pointed down and to our right. On the varnished canyon wall below us were huge, detailed carvings that depicted people in what appeared to be a family portrait.

Or maybe two families. A group on the left included three full-sized figures and one figure that was half-sized, like a child. Below them was a small drawing of a bighorn sheep, though it seemed more like a dog or pet. The group on the right consisted of two full-sized figures, one three-quarter-sized figure—a teenager perhaps—a half-sized figure, and then three tiny figures below, possibly babies or small children. There was another small bighorn sheep below this group.

Jack and I hiked around, picking our way over large rocks to descend to the lower level. The platform that we had been standing on formed a large overhang that shaded crumbled ruins mostly buried by sand. The drawings were carved on a side wall and were half my height. Each torso was an upside-down triangle topped with a distinctive hairstyle and elaborate necklaces, but it had no eyes or limbs.

Perhaps these drawings were a way of labeling who lived in this canyon, like a nameplate on a house or one of those stickers people paste on minivans that label every adult, child, and pet in a family. Or maybe they told a different story. How long were these people here? Did they build the granaries we saw up canyon? Did they live their lives here, or did drought force them to leave? I looked at their portraits and yearned to know them.

VERONICA AND I CONTINUED HIKING down the slot canyon. In some places it narrowed so that we had to pass each other our backpacks, turn to the side, and wriggle through with our bodies squeezed by walls. Gradually the walls grew taller and the passage widened until we walked in a flat, dry canyon bottom, our calves screaming as we struggled through deep sand. We zigzagged down this skeleton of a riverbed in search of the most solid ground. Route finding was easy; the varnished cherry-red walls directed us down canyon.

After eleven arid miles, thirsty green cottonwoods interrupted the red, and the sand became firm and damp. As improbable as a

Layered sandstone in Zebra Canyon, Grand Staircase–Escalante National Monument, Utah. Photograph by the author.

canoe traveling thousands of miles across open ocean to land on a tiny island, a spring emerged in the desert's dry heat. We followed the clear trickle until it welled into a creek, and decided to camp where the flow became deep enough for us to collect. Others before us had this same idea: hoof prints and cow patties littered the sand. In the flat spots clear of vegetation we found old fire rings filled with rusted tin cans. An old cowboy camp. Herds often grazed on grassy mesa tops, and ranchers would drive the cows into canyon bottoms to drink and rest for the night at springs like this.

We searched for the perfect place to pitch our tent but did not find an idyllic spot. We were hungry and tired of walking, so we settled on a spit of sand next to a soft-pink wall and a rusty spade abandoned in the bushes. The lumpy ground was covered with manure, so I took the spade and cleared a place for our tent and stove, irritated that this pristine spring was so contaminated. Veronica searched for the section of the stream with the least cow patties and filtered water for our dinner.

Some environmentalists claim that grazing destroys public land—land that belongs to all of us—so that a few people can profit. In Grand Staircase–Escalante, juniper and pinyon forest has been bulldozed and reseeded with non-native species such as alfalfa and flax to provide better pasture. Once cows have trampled long-growing cryptobiotic soil and eaten up the native basin wildrye, bluebunch wheatgrass, and desert needlegrass, invasive species like cheatgrass, Russian olive, and tamarisk move in and take over. Even before the Trump administration reduced the size of Grand Staircase–Escalante, 96 percent of the 1.8-million-acre monument was open to grazing, leaving only 64,000 acres closed to cows.

The rights to graze on public land are sold cheap, and in March 2019 the fees were lowered by 5 percent to the minimum lease price allowable under the Public Rangelands Improvement Act of 1978. Ranchers are charged a mere $1.35 per Animal Unit Month, which is the amount of forage consumed by one cow and her calf for one month. For comparison, private grazing rights on state land sell for $6.10 to $10.64 per AUM.

Though Grand Staircase–Escalante prohibits new mining, the monument proclamation states that "existing grazing uses shall continue to be governed by applicable laws and regulations." Grazing is allowed largely because of the BLM's multiple-use mission. Grand Staircase–Escalante was the first national monument to be administered by this agency. Since the 1930s, the management of newly created monuments had been transferred to the National Park Service. In 1978, Jimmy Carter broke with this pattern and directed the U.S. Forest Service to manage two new national monuments in Alaska. Grand Staircase–Escalante started a trend where new monuments are administered by their lands' previous managing agencies, in this case the BLM. Managing lands with different goals forced the BLM and Forest Service to incorporate conservation into their missions. Previously, the BLM dealt primarily with extractive leases, earning it the nickname "Bureau of Livestock and Mining." Today the BLM includes a conservation-focused subagency known as National Conservation Lands, which manages 35 million acres, including monuments like Grand Staircase–Escalante.

When Grand Staircase–Escalante was first designated, it was widely believed that the NPS would manage the new monument. At the time, many worried that large-scale tourism, like that of a park, would degrade the wild feel of the area. "Which is worse—a coal mine on the Kaiparowits Plateau, or a visitor center, large overcrowded campgrounds, RV dumps, millions of visitors . . . at Calf

Creek Falls?" wrote Utah resident Ron Hamblin in a 1996 letter to the editor in *Southern Utah News*. Though recreation in the area has greatly increased since the formation of the monument, leaving Grand Staircase–Escalante under the jurisdiction of the BLM made it less likely that the Escalante region would take on the feel of an amusement park, and allowed the management of certain activities, like livestock grazing, to continue seamlessly.

Many ranchers would argue that their families have been working this land for generations and it is part of their heritage, deserving of commemoration along with Indigenous histories of the landscape. Over one hundred years ago Mormon settlers who viewed Utah as their promised land proudly began ranching on rough desert; some have continued to do so. Today, with encroaching development and a recreation industry largely opposed to ranching, they feel their inherited way of life is being threatened.

Our backs against the wall, Veronica and I hungrily started in on bowls of macaroni and cheese when we noticed carvings in the stone, well above our heads, revealing that the sandy ground has eroded away over years. Names and dates were scrawled in angular handwriting—not petroglyphs but cowboy impressions. Above us read, "Art Chynoweth Dec. 19. 1900." Ranchers had been bringing their cows here for a very long time: long before this place became a monument, when backpacking was work rather than recreation, even before the Antiquities Act became law. Their names in the sandstone form another layer in this place's story, one that overlays cliff dwellings and petroglyphs, slot canyons and fossils.

IN MARCH 2018, I woke up in my apartment in California, made coffee, and read that public meetings were being held for the management plan of the reduced Grand Staircase–Escalante monument. I looked at my calendar. The meeting was the next day. I felt a rush of adrenaline that had nothing to do with caffeine: I had to be there. I tossed camping gear into the back of my car and began the eight-hour drive to Kanab, Utah, early the next morning.

Kanab is a red town surrounded by what Dutton labeled the Vermilion Cliffs, and it is the gateway to the southwestern part of the monument. My first stop was the BLM visitor center. A sand-colored industrial building with bathrooms and a water spigot outside, it squats on the road out of town like it is trying to camouflage with the desert around it. I poked around the small office, glancing at interpretive displays until I summoned enough courage to ask about free places to camp. The woman behind the counter pulled out a map and circled locations with a highlighter.

"Am I allowed to ask what you think about recent changes to the monument?" I asked.

The woman looked up and pulled back her shoulders. "I am only a volunteer. They can't fire me, so I can say whatever I want," she announced. "I'm against it. I can't even look over there." Keeping her eyes on me, she motioned to where a photograph of President Donald Trump hung between two doors. I mentioned that I was in town for the public meeting, and we discussed monument politics for a short while.

Before leaving, I flipped through the maps available in the gift shop. A man with a graying goatee and a long, thin ponytail, and wearing a BLM uniform sidled up to me. He was short and stood just a little too close. He must have overheard my conversation with the volunteer and wanted to talk. Russell Beesley told me that he had been a BLM ranger since 2000 and, in his opinion, the monument has been a good thing for the area, specifically the town of Kanab. The economy was doing well. He and his wife owned a bed-and-breakfast, and it was busy. "Look around," he said. "New hotels are being constructed here in town, but meanwhile the coal plant is shutting down." To him, it did not make economic sense to reduce this monument in favor of mining and resource extraction. "It's up to young people like you now, us baby boomers messed it all up."

I left the visitor center and drove to Kanab Middle School, where the meeting was being held. I emerged from my stuffy car into warm sunshine and sharp air and walked into the school, anticipating a town hall–style meeting with a large crowd and people speaking their minds. Instead, I walked into an echoing gymnasium with cardboard stations arranged around the perimeter like a public land science fair, complete with vague posters and an awkward, semi-interested crowd.

Each of the stations addressed a different planning issue: the planning process, the new national monument boundaries, travel management and roads, recreation, grazing, minerals, and cultural and paleontological resources. I wandered toward the planning process station, and a woman standing next to a map greeted me. She was young with reddish hair and seemed well caffeinated. She spoke fast.

"Hi, my name is Allison, and I coordinate the National Conservation Lands program statewide. If you have questions about the national monument policies or other special designations such as wilderness study areas, definitely let me know. I'd be happy to answer them."

"How did they decide . . . how did the new division come about?" I stumbled over my words, not having a great question prepared.

"The modified boundaries?" Allison asked, tucking a strand of hair behind her ear.

"Yeah."

"So what I can tell you is at the state office we presented hundreds of pages of maps and responses to information, all of which I presume actually influenced the final recommendation for the boundaries. I can't tell you why this line, why not this line. Most of the proclamation includes a lot of the justification that they had for the boundaries being where they are, but it doesn't give a lot of detail about specific areas."

"How do you feel about the changes?" I ventured.

"I can't talk about my personal opinion, but we are committed to moving forward with this planning process, and these are the boundaries that we are moving forward with. There certainly is going to be a high level of complexity in this planning process, and I do think it's really important for people to come tonight and throughout this process and share the concerns that they have and provide us with information that will help us write a good draft plan."

"So if what I'm concerned about is I don't want there to be mining anywhere that was in the previous boundary, what would I do about that?"

"There are areas on the Kaiparowits with high coal potential that are not currently part of the monument or a wilderness study area. If you want to submit a comment, you would need to provide information about other resources that are present that we need to consider."

"So just saying 'I really love the monument' isn't going to help?"

"If we get a hundred thousand comments that all say, 'we think the boundaries should be the old boundaries,' that counts as one comment. And it also doesn't count in the scope of this planning effort. It will get written down, and we will respond to it, but the more specific you can be, the better."

Allison interrupted her almost automated flow of information and looked at me more closely. "A really good comment letter, I'll just be frank with you, requires a lot of research. It requires looking at a lot of our current management decisions and very thoughtfully picking out specifically where you would like to see changes from the status quo." In the lobby outside the gymnasium I had walked past a station where volunteers recorded oral comments for people unable or unwilling to submit a comment online. It was difficult to imagine that these oral responses would go far beyond personal opinion and include the management specifics Allison said were required.

During Secretary Zinke's national monument review, over 2.8 million comments were submitted to the government in response to the review and about the status of monuments in general. According to an analysis performed by Key-Log Economics, of the 1.3 million comments that were posted before the end of the comment period, 93.5 percent opposed any alteration to monument boundaries. Much of the public involved in comment-gathering campaigns hoped this decisive majority opinion would make a difference.

Unfortunately, public comments are not votes. "Many who voice their opinion on the management of their public lands expect that if public opinion opposes a proposed action by the government, it will be abandoned or at least modified to meet the majority's concerns. This is not the case," writes environmental historian Michael W. Childers. The public comment process is designed to help government agencies collect as much information as possible. If people submit "substantive" comments, as Allison described, they could help decision makers understand the consequences of certain actions.

A substantive comment questions the accuracy of information or assumptions presented in a draft plan and presents new information to support a proposed course of action, such as citing scientific studies about the effects of mining on endangered sage grouse populations and suggesting ways the plan could be altered to accommodate the sage grouse. There have been some cases where a citizen's comment changed the course of a draft plan. In 2009, a retired pilot uncovered a math error in a fifteen-hundred-page draft that dramatically underestimated the impacts of introducing non-native oysters into Chesapeake Bay. As a result, the action was not approved.

But more often, even a detailed and documented list of negative environmental impacts does not change the agency's eventual management decision. "While public comments often reflect the divergent views on public land management, they are not meant to empower citizens to affect policy. Instead, they are gathered simply to keep in compliance with federal law," writes Childers.

Disheartened after my talk with Allison, I continued around the gymnasium's stations and saw Russell again. Instead of his gray-green government uniform he was wearing a loud, red floral Hawaiian shirt. He smiled and walked over. "I'm incognito," he whispered, gesturing to his shirt.

I laughed. Then I looked around at the posters and asked where the local opposition to the monument was coming from.

He sighed deeply. "Well, it's Kane County going back forty or fifty years, dreaming about all the jobs that would be created if they mined the coal. But if it was mineable and economically feasible, they would have done it forty years ago. If you've ever been out on the Kaiparowits Plateau . . . there's just so many canyons and cliffs, and it is rugged. Just building a road out there will cost millions of dollars."

The pauses in our conversation stretched longer, so I thanked him and prepared to leave. Instead of saying goodbye, Russell continued. "They say locals are against the monument. My great-great-grandfather was a scout with Brigham Young. His name was Orson Pratt. My other great-great-grandfather wrote the hymns that are in the Mormon hymnal. His name was Ebenezer Beesley. His son married Orson Pratt's daughter. And I come from that lineage. So nobody goes back more local than I do, to Utah when it was settled. So Utahans don't want this? I want it. I want it, a lot. The only ones here before were the Native Americans, they were here. And they want it too."

The idea for Grand Staircase–Escalante did not originate as an Indigenous-led movement like Bears Ears, but in the monument's oral history project Harlan Featherhat of the Shivwits Band of Paiutes mentions that before its designation a group of different tribal members met in Capitol Reef for five days to discuss which areas were most important and most in need of protection. They drew boundaries on maps and gave them to government officials. Featherhat thought that information may have been used to help determine the original monument boundaries.

CAN DONALD TRUMP DO WHAT HE DID to Grand Staircase–Escalante? Some legal scholars say yes and some say no. The language of the Antiquities Act is unclear. What is clear is that the president has the authority to establish monuments, but the act itself does not explicitly grant power to abolish or modify an existing monument.

One argument in Trump's favor states that if the president has the authority to create a monument, of course he could remove one: the power to do both is implied. Conversely, if a president can dismantle a previous administration's designations, it opens monuments up to wild policy swings, which is what we have seen during the past few presidencies. Congress is usually the accepted authority for modifying or revoking the work of previous administrations.

Presidents can expand a monument created by another, which is what Obama did at Cascade-Siskiyou and Papahānaumokuākea. However, expanding a monument is similar in process and in theory to creating a new one.

There is some historical precedent for presidents altering or shrinking monuments, but what President Trump attempted to do was to set a new precedent. Once it becomes acceptable for a president to open previously protected federal land to private interests, it will be far easier for this to happen in the future. Once removing these kinds of protections is normalized, the public may be too subdued to be outraged.

The same day that President Trump signed the proclamation that reduced Grand Staircase–Escalante and Bears Ears, lawsuits were filed in Washington, D.C., that named Trump, Secretary of the Interior Ryan Zinke, and acting BLM director Brian Steed as defendants. For Grand Staircase–Escalante, several suits were consolidated into one: *The Wilderness Society v. Donald Trump*.

In February 2020, a new management plan for Grand Staircase–Escalante was approved and went into effect. Despite numerous public comments in support of the original monument boundaries and against increased resource extraction, the final plan opened hundreds of thousands of acres of land to new mining and drilling leases, allowed for the construction of more roads, and opened livestock-free canyons with delicate riparian habitats to grazing, all before the courts had a chance to rule if the reduction itself was legal.

Land management decisions typically leave existing rights in place and only prohibit or allow new leases. This is one reason why grazing continued after this monument's creation; existing rights were upheld. Once mining claims are released to companies, they can be difficult or impossible to revoke. New mining claims were staked in land removed from both Grand Staircase–Escalante and Bears Ears, though many of these claims were not considered serious and some were subsequently abandoned. President Biden restored Grand Staircase–Escalante's boundary to near its original size in 2021, but the new leases that had been granted in the interim remain valid. The land had already been sacrificed.

There is more at stake with this monument and this decision than simply the park's size. The fight here runs deeper than environmentalists versus miners, or federal authority versus states' rights. This is a battle between concepts about how humans relate to land. One view is that the land is there for us to use, to benefit from, to control. Others think some of the nation's land deserves to exist unscathed. Is it our right to use the land's richness for progress and prosperity and to harvest useful resources, or is it our duty to protect and preserve the land, its inhabitants, and its history? This monument puzzle asks people to look beyond their own personal interests. The question asked by Grand Staircase–Escalante is: what do we value?

JACK AND I, back on the mesa, tripped over dried cow patties and emerged from a juniper thicket to find a stone arch poised on a cliff's edge. The sun was sinking low, illuminating the underside of the arch's curve, forming a shining gateway that overlooked tangled crimson canyons below. We were standing on top of the Straight Cliffs, looking east toward the Hole in the Rock Road, painstakingly built by Mormon pioneers in the late 1800s. Reddening evening sun saturated the landscape and made the view feel strangely intimate, like noticing someone's flushed cheeks and the burst of feeling behind the blush.

I moved under the archway and nudged a shiny black obsidian chip with my foot. Widening my view, I noticed debitage scattered all over the ground: flakes of stone left over from ancient tool construction, chips of pottery, some with bumpy modeled ridges, others with textured brush marks along the surface. The sand was filled with scattered evidence that this had once been a popular place. I looked up to call Jack over and noticed the soft underbelly of the arch was tattooed with graffiti. Names and dates were etched into the sandstone from as long ago as 1919 to as recent as the year before. This was still a popular place. We waited with the arch until the light strained gray and the canyons below dimmed from copper and gold to lavender and charcoal. My time in Grand Staircase–Escalante did not answer any of the questions I started with. It only raised more. Each time I dug in to investigate, I unearthed another layer, which overlaid another.

Sand sifted to the ground and solidified into stripes of rock. Traces of time wrinkled the surface with fossils and petroglyphs. Dinosaurs plodded across the earth for 165 million years; ancient Puebloans and their modern descendants have lived here for more than 500 years; Mormon settlers have called this place home for 100 years; the area has been outlined as a protected monument for 20. The subsequent rescission and then restoration of almost half the monument and the effects of grazing, mining, roads, and recreation are the next layer being laid in the landscape's mortar. Like layers of brilliant sandstone, one atop another, history and human actions solidify and stair-step toward the sky.

Part III. Ripple

RIPPLE (noun)
: the ruffling of the surface of water
: a usually slight noticeable effect or reaction

RIPPLE (verb)
: to have or produce a ripple effect, to spread

At the intersection of landscape and culture, diversity and inclusion, patterns of cooperation emerge in the name of community. The power of what binds us together, rather than what tears us apart, becomes a shared priority.

TERRY TEMPEST WILLIAMS
The Hour of Land: A Personal Topography of America's National Parks

9. On Sharing

RIO GRANDE DEL NORTE NATIONAL MONUMENT, NEW MEXICO

After the bridge, we are going to eddy out river left." Jim, the blond-bearded river guide, called back to me where I floated in an inflatable kayak. "I want to discuss the next rapid with you before we go in." Jim, on a raft with two others, floated under a low, decrepit bridge. I drifted underneath the rotten wooden planks, feeling a moment of sweet shade, then paddled toward shore.

"We call this rapid Big Rock because there is a big rock right in the middle of the river," he said, all seriousness. "There will be some fairly large rocks in the way first, and you have to go around them to the left. This will direct you right at Big Rock. Head far left, then turn sharp right to get around Big Rock. But there is a rock shelf there, so you can't go too far right. You need to catch the flow between Big Rock and the shelf, go down it, and make another sharp left." Jim used his hands to demonstrate the location of the rocks and the path around them. As he talked, the raft slowly drifted out into the current. I gripped a handful of reeds on the bank to stay in place and felt a wave of nausea. Jim, sitting with feet dangling over the rear of the

RIO GRANDE DEL NORTE

NATIONAL MONUMENT

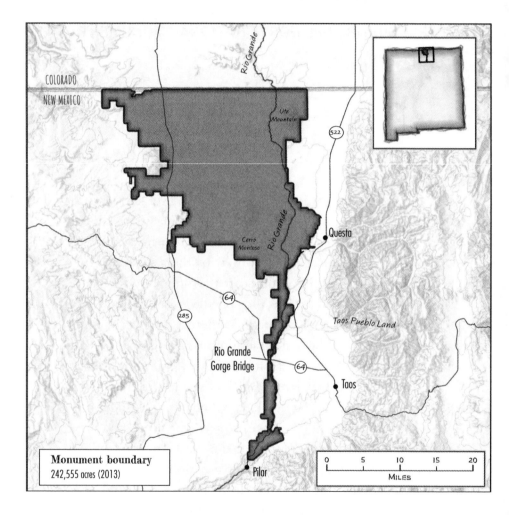

COLORADO
NEW MEXICO

Rio Grande

Ute Mountain

522

Rio Grande

Cerro Montoso

Questa

64

285

Taos Pueblo Land

Rio Grande
Gorge Bridge

64

Taos

Monument boundary
242,555 acres (2013)

Pilar

0   5   10   15   20
MILES

raft, paddled back to me and continued talking while his two passengers sat quietly in the front.

An image from the day before flashed in my mind: the front half of a neon-orange kayak lodged between boulders along the riverbank. The Rio Grande had ripped the thick plastic boat apart and spit its chunks back onto land. My knuckles whitened around the fistful of reeds. It was a mistake to think I could paddle this boat on my own.

"You don't want to hit Big Rock. Your boat will be pushed up onto it, and you will flip. This is really not a good place to swim. There is a hole under Big Rock, so if you swim, it is possible that you will be recirculating for a while. You need to get this right."

A FEW DAYS BEFORE MY FLOAT down the Rio Grande, I stood on a mesa and looked hundreds of feet down at a V of water that separated sage-covered hills at a confluence. At La Junta Point, the Red River and the Rio Grande merge at the deepest and widest part of the Rio Grande Gorge, forming one large river that continues south. From that vantage point, I could see two steel-colored ribbons thread past juniper trees far below the muscular cliffs that line the rim of the gorge.

Contrary to popular belief, the Rio Grande did not carve this gorge through the landscape by eroding layers one grain of sand at a time. Instead, it followed existing fault lines taking the path of least resistance southward. The Rio Grande—or *Río Bravo*—originates in Colorado from snowmelt in the San Juan Mountains, flows down the entire length of New Mexico, crosses into Mexico at Ciudad Juarez, and forms the boundary between Mexico and Texas until it empties into the Gulf of Mexico. The entire river is divided, partitioned, and regulated as if it was a chocolate bar broken on easy-to-snap lines and not an amorphous, moving, changing thing. Two

175

separate treaties between Mexico and Texas and Mexico and New Mexico determine the distribution of water, plus Colorado, New Mexico, and Texas have their own interstate agreement. In the north the United States is required to deliver a specified amount of water to Mexico, and in the south Mexico delivers to the United States.

There are also many small-scale diversions of the river, the most prominent of which are *acequias*. In Spanish, *acequia* means "canal"; in New Mexico, *acequia* refers to community-owned waterways used for irrigation. Many were built by Spanish colonists in the 1500s and 1600s. Today the rights to these canals and the water in them are managed by governing boards and committees.

The segments of the Rio Grande that course beneath La Junta Point and the part I paddled are still free flowing. Rio Grande del Norte National Monument protects a 240,000-acre triangle of land and a portion of the river at New Mexico's northern border that is part of the National Wild and Scenic Rivers System. Although there is some agricultural diversion in this section, there are no dams upstream. Farther downstream the river is so heavily regulated by dams that in southern New Mexico the river is completely dry for half of the year.

Northern New Mexico is shaped by cultures that have been colliding and intertwining for hundreds of years. The Pueblo people, or *Tiwa*, have been living here for an estimated two thousand years and maybe more, far longer than anyone else. The Taos Pueblo, located just outside the modern-day town of Taos, is thought to be the longest continuously inhabited pueblo in North America—lived in for more than one thousand years.

Spanish conquistadors and missionaries first arrived in the late 1500s, and for the next two hundred years the Spanish government "controlled" the land in present-day New Mexico and granted ownership of parcels to settlers there. When Mexico declared its independence from Spain, it took control of this huge northern Territorio de Nuevo Mexico. Later, to end the Mexican-American War, the two new countries signed the Treaty of Guadalupe Hidalgo, and Mexico ceded these northern territories to the United States in 1848. As part of the treaty, the United States agreed to respect the property rights of Mexican citizens who now found themselves living in America, and the U.S. government officially recognized Spanish land grants. Spanish descendants still hold these land grants today and sometimes refer to themselves as *norteños,* or northerners, which is a way of distinguishing themselves from their southern Mexican neighbors. People with Spanish or Mexican heritage, or a blend of both, constitute a large portion of New Mexico's modern population.

Then Anglo-American settlers came by way of the original colonies of the United States. With an expansionist concept of manifest destiny, they moved west in search of minerals, grazing pasture, and wealth. Many bullied their way into possession of land in New Mexico.

Rio Grande del Norte is a landscape dominated by opposing claims from these very different cultures. Despite this, the community found a way to come together for the sake of the land. The best way that I can tell this story is to share stories that were shared with me.

I MET ESTER GARCIA at the youth center in Questa, a low concrete building on a mostly empty road leading toward the Sangre de Cristo Mountains. I stepped out of the car onto rust-colored dirt at the same time Ester stepped out of hers.

Short, with close-cut hair and brown eyes, Ester Garcia is full of feistiness, willpower, and opinions. She is an eleventh-generation descendent from Spanish ancestors and an heir to the San Antonio del Rio Colorado Land Grant. She was born in Questa, grew up in Questa, and after a stint in Albuquerque became Questa's first female mayor, built the town's public library, and was one of Rio Grande del Norte National Monument's fiercest advocates. When President Obama designated the monument in 2013, Ester was standing there watching him sign the proclamation.

She led me inside to a bench in a common area. Her quilting group sewed around a long table at the other end of the room while she told me her story of the monument:

> When I first heard about the monument, it was in an article that was written in the *Albuquerque Journal*. And it was proposed as a conservation area at that time. So I read the article, and I decided, well, I'm going to call Washington, D.C., and find out what this is about. So I called Senator [Jeff] Bingaman's office, and they put me in touch with his staffer Jorge Silva-Bañuelos. I talked to him and I said: "How can you be proposing a conservation area that runs through a land grant without first letting land grant heirs know that this is going to happen within their land?"
>
> He asked: why were we opposing it? I said, "Well, it's concerning to us because all of these lands are common lands." The Spanish government gave the people the lands and included the waters. When the Forest Service and the BLM came into existence, they took over the lands and began managing those lands. But really, they don't own the lands. They just manage them. The lands belong to the people.
>
> The Land Grant Board said, "Well, if this [conservation area] bill is being proposed, we want to draft the bill ourselves. We want our cultural uses to remain in place." Our traditional uses are grazing and of course the water, wood cutting, herbs—because our people use a lot of herbs for medical reasons. And pinyon picking, which, my grandfather used to tell me, they picked the pinyon in the fall and it sustained them

in the winter. We don't want any of that taken away from us. So the Land Grant Board drafted the bill, and they went back to Washington, D.C.

Well then I got another call, and this time it was from the senator himself. And he said: "What would you think about it being proposed as a national monument instead of a conservation area?" And I said, that would be very helpful to our community, having the national monument in our backyard.

Ken Salazar was the secretary of interior, and every time he came to New Mexico, I would show up with a book about the history of New Mexico. Every time he showed up, I would show up. He was very familiar with me, cause I showed up everywhere. I went to testify before Congress twice. There was some opposition from a congressman from Utah. And I told him: "You know, like those trees in the forest, that's how deep our roots are in our small community. That's how deep my roots are. And we want to preserve what belongs to us. They are our common lands that were given to us. You don't have a warrant or deed for these common lands. So I think we have a lot of say in what happens here." Afterwards he came up to me and he said, "Well, I guess I kind of understand." And I said, "You wouldn't understand until you come and see what I'm talking about and why."

It was really my grandfather that instilled all of this in me. I was maybe twenty years old, we'd sit in the garage and wrap apples to store for the winter. So he'd tell me things. He was a very, very smart man. And he would tell me that water that flows through those *acequias*, it is going to be worth more than gold one day and there will be fights over it. He would tell me they're not making any more land, so if you don't take care of the land you have, you will be lost. As I got older, I understood what he was trying to tell me. And so I think that because of that, I got very involved in making sure that we protect our waters and we protect our lands, cause they aren't making any more land.

Well, they had a meeting at the Kachina Lodge in Taos, and more than two hundred people showed up in favor of it becoming a national monument. Ken Salazar was there. And so he saw that there was really an interest in doing it. And then all of a sudden, one day I get a call from the White House. And I thought, "Oh my goodness, the White House!" And they said: "Would you be able to come to Washington, D.C., on Monday?" This was, like, a Saturday. And I said, "Well, I guess I could if I can get a flight!"

Of course our Native American brothers and sisters, Taos Pueblo, were very supportive, and Sam Gomez was the war chief at the time, and he went to Washington, D.C., too. Sam and I were in the White House when the president signed the proclamation.

IT TOOK ME ALL MORNING to identify that my fear of paddling the inflatable kayak was because of several dramatic spills I took in one while floating through the Grand Canyon years before. That trip was twenty-one days long, and to break up the monotony of sitting on a raft, I took turns on the one inflatable kayak, called a ducky, that our group had with us. An inexperienced paddler and mediocre swimmer, I tipped over in fast-moving water, and both the boat and I had to be rescued by my friends. I hadn't been in a ducky since.

Here on the Rio Grande, the raft was big and sluggish, but my ducky was nimble and speedy. Jim directed me to follow behind him, so to keep from overtaking the raft and to practice steering the sensitive boat, I paddled back and forth across the width of the river and thought about the many ways this river impacts people's lives. It provides drinking water, irrigation, recreation, scenery. Before coming to this monument, I thought the story would be about water. Now, out on the water, I knew that a story about only water would be shallow and uninteresting. People and their relationship to it, how-ever, had a lot of depth.

I ARRANGED TO MEET GARRETT VENEKLASEN near Taos. He worked for New Mexico Wild, a nonprofit dedicated to the protection and restoration of land in the state. Garrett agreed to take me on a tour of special places in the monument. At our rendezvous spot, I pulled my shiny rental car onto grass beside muddy work trucks and rust-ing cars with for sale signs on the windshields. Cars zoomed past in the busy intersection behind me. I was assembling a backpack with water, snacks, my notebook, and camera, when a truck pulled in be-hind me. I smiled and climbed in. A big sandy-haired guy wearing flannel and work boots sat behind the wheel and a black dog panted from the backseat. As I buckled in, I realized that no one else knew where I was. I was a lone female in the vehicle of a complete stranger. Suddenly I felt very vulnerable.

I didn't have much to worry about, though. Without even a pause for hello or introductory small talk, Garrett launched into a wide-ranging discussion about public land that touched on ecological and social issues. Just as I had recognized in Bears Ears, my vulnerability echoed the vulnerability of the land and vulnerable people connected to it. Feeling exposed made it easier to understand what was at stake.

Garrett drove over the Rio Grande Gorge Bridge, where the river sparkled six hundred feet below in the bottom of a narrow canyon. We looked for the resident bighorn herd nearby but did not find them. Garret turned onto a dirt road, and we bounced through sage-brush and juniper while his dog ran alongside the truck and indie music played from his stereo.

When the road ended, we hiked to the top of a small, rocky hill. There was no trail; we just wandered toward the high point. At the

summit stood a small circle built of stones. I could tell it was old by the pale green lichen that grew over the cracks between the stacked maroon rocks. From this point, I could see for miles. Clouds hung in low puffs over hills that rolled toward the horizon in a patchwork of volcanic craters, dark-green juniper forest, and golden open land. The wind played with my hair, and Garrett talked about the monument:

> This is a great view. From here you can see the entire monument. This hill is called Cerro Viento, or Windy Mountain. I would love to know what the *Tiwa* word for it is.
>
> You know, these landscapes didn't look like this a hundred years ago. Pinyon, juniper, sage are all from overgrazing. This was a grassland five hundred years ago. Live water was everywhere. The water tables have dropped because of five hundred years of overgrazing. There was some sagebrush here, but it didn't look like this. It was grass, and it was belly-deep grass.
>
> Recently I took this young man, a first-generation Mexican American, took him elk hunting out on the Valles Caldera. He couldn't afford, as a boy, to go do this, and he harvested this elk, and now he has two hundred pounds of meat in his freezer. That's pretty cool, right? Someone of lesser means who has the ability to utilize these landscapes in a really meaningful way. I just thought that was such a beautiful idea. Anyone can do this. It doesn't cost thousands of dollars to go out on a public landscape and cut your firewood. I mean, I heat my home with wood from these landscapes. I pick pinyon, I put an elk in my freezer every year, you know, I feed my family with this stuff. But I'm a newcomer

here, right? I mean, I was born and raised here. But who cares? My last name is VeneKlasen. How white European can you get?

Once upon a time I was an ATV-riding redneck idiot. I mean, I'd call myself a reformed OHV outlaw. I had this sense of entitlement. Like, "It's mine to use, I'm a taxpayer!" and that's so short-sighted and selfish and greedy. The question really is: how do we develop this place correctly so that it doesn't get ruined? The land needs to maintain its integrity a hundred years from now.

More often than not, Native Americans are left out of the [land management] conversation, which is bullshit. At the end of the day, we're talking about a massive societal and political power shift from white western settlers to Native Americans. That's what Bears Ears is all about. That's what Standing Rock was all about, giving true sovereignty and true policy-making, decision-making, law-making power to Native American communities. It is a huge threat to the traditional white status quo because they've been able to exploit these resources forever. These are sovereign nations, right? We are not respecting their sovereignness, if that's a word. But we are, more than ever before, doing that in New Mexico. There are social justice movements throughout New Mexico where we're recognizing communities of color in a really precedent-setting and, what I believe, very necessary way. The cultural identity is the true identity of this place. The first sentence in the story was there was wilderness and then the second sentence was the Native American community came here. That's our story. That's the core of our identity.

[Before the monument] Secretary of Interior Salazar came here— they always have a public meeting to take the community's temperature. There were three hundred people in the room. There were land grant heirs, *acequia parciantes*, Picuris Pueblo, Taos Pueblo, sportsmen and women, environmentalists, grazing permittees. There was every type of stakeholder you could imagine. Three hundred people in the room, right? Very, very different interests. Secretary Salazar said:

RIO GRANDE DEL NORTE

"Is there anyone in this room that opposes this designation?" Three hundred people. Not one person in the room raised their hand. And so that's the power of community. Congressman Richardson introduced the original legislation twenty-five years ago. It took twenty-five years to find community consensus. You come together as a respectful community and of course you're going to disagree, right? But we can all come together and plan fifty years out, seventy-five years out. At the end of the day, the glass of water in the middle of the table is the fact that we all love our public lands and that it's the center of our identity as a community. Whether you're Nick Straight who owns Taos fly shop, the governor of Taos Pueblo, Ester Garcia, or grazing permittee Elio Romero. Western communities, they argue. But we came together.

If we can find consensus here, where we have extreme religious and racial tensions, then consensus can be reached anywhere. Anyone can fucking figure it out. I mean, it's such a great metaphor for community. It's so American in its essence, this whole idea about having differing opinions but coalescing around common values. That's a pretty special thing. That's sacrosanct.

AT THE START OF THE FLOAT TRIP, I stood sweating on shore in my bulky life jacket and helmet while Jim rigged the raft. Slate-blue water rushed past curtains of green, invasive salt cedar on the banks. Jim began a safety talk, but one of the rafters interrupted and pointed across the water. Along the opposite bank a river otter ambled along a stretch of gravel. Wet fir glistened in the sun as the long, snakelike body moved awkwardly on land. It stumbled for a few steps, dipped into the water and swam gracefully for a few feet, then hopped back out on shore. "Wow, that's a special sight," Jim said. "You know, river otters used to be extinct here. They were reintroduced about ten years ago."

185

After his safety talk, I dragged my ducky to the river's edge and climbed aboard. Cool water lapped over my legs. After days of talking about the monument and looking down at threads of river in canyon bottoms, I felt the need to feel the river between my fingers, to sense the power of this water that is life for so many. I pointed the boat toward gentle riffles and let the Rio Grande carry me along. The river meandered slowly past banks lined with juniper, red willow, and cottonwood trees. A great blue heron stood regally on shore, but when it saw us, it squawked and flew over steely water. It landed among grasses just out of sight. Our boats curved with the current around a slight bend, and we saw the heron again, with two others perched nearby. "Do you see all three?" Jim called excitedly from the back of the raft.

AFTER OUR HIKE, Garret and I visited Taos Pueblo. We parked in a dirt lot outside a garage filled with machinery on one side and offices on the other. Garrett and I took seats at a long table in the center of the open garage. A man with a long, graying ponytail wearing a thick, white button-down work shirt walked out of an office in back and greeted us. Cameron Martinez is a member of the Taos Pueblo and the director of the Pueblo's Department of Natural Resources. His department works on conservation projects for the tribe and comments on projects initiated by the BLM or U.S. Forest Service to make the opinions of his tribe known.

Before he sat down, Cameron spoke with one of his employees, a younger man in a black cotton hoody. The young man looked at us questioningly. Cameron explained that I was researching national monuments and wanted to learn about Rio Grande del Norte. "So she realized she needed to talk to us," the young man said with an ironic laugh that I took to mean: "This is our land and our story. If you are going to talk about it all, you have to talk to us."

RIO GRANDE DEL NORTE

Cameron sat down and told me about his land:

Our history is verbal and is still really strong here, we don't write anything down. It's what everybody knows. It's a living language, living culture, and we strive to keep that going.

This has always been the home of the Red Willow people. If you've seen the Rio Grande, there's red willows down there. Our people have lived here more than one thousand years, and we have not moved far from where the village is now. Our ancestors stayed in Taos, and that's where our culture is strongest. This whole area provided everything for us to live. It is our world. Our people would use everything north on the Rio Grande, all the way up into Colorado and the San Juan Mountains. We would go east to hunt buffalo. The men would spend a couple of months out hunting and dry everything and then bring back meat and hides. Our people have been up and down the Rio Grande trading with the various Pueblo tribes.

We lived in buildings that Spanish explorers were familiar with, and when they got here, they said, "Oh, this is a city." And so they gave us five leagues north, south, east, and west from the church. And that was the amount of land that they thought we should have. We told them, "No, we go all over this valley!"

When the United States came in, they didn't dispute the boundaries established by the Spanish. At that moment. They said, "Everything around your Pueblo, that's going to be national forest." And so right then and there we started to say that the Blue Lake area, the high country lakes up below Wheeler Peak, is one of our most sacred sites. That is one of the reasons why we're here. We've been here for many centuries, and we want this land as our own, and we don't want to share it with everybody else because it's an integral part of our life and how we practice our traditions. It took us about sixty years to battle the United States in court. In the end we got agreement with not only New Mexico senators, but all the other senators and legislative people to sign Public Law 91-550 that gives back forty-eight thousand acres to Taos Pueblo, which includes Blue Lake, the source of our water that comes through our village. Next year we're going to be celebrating fifty years.

If you look at places like Chaco Canyon and Mesa Verde, where we talk about in my culture, water is very important. Now there's no water in both places, or it is very sparse. Knowing that in our genes—I want to say genes because it's passed on verbally—why did we move from Chaco Canyon? It was a nice place, man! And we're over here now. Well, water. Mesa Verde? Yup. So, it's in our DNA. I love to say that. We have to have that relationship [with water] otherwise we'll probably be moving, maybe to Colorado. Taos Pueblo reestablished in Colorado, or Washington State.

We had a drought last year. For whatever reason, there was less precipitation, and that impacted a lot of the crops that we grow here. And so we had to, as a community, back off so that we're not expending all the water that we could. We know that other people need water as well. So we have that in mind. A lot of our philosophy here in relation to land, or to natural resources, is it's here for everyone, and we all need to be good neighbors and good stewards to the land and water so that everybody benefits. Because if everybody benefits, then the world is a better place, to put it simply. So that's what we strive for here. Tribal members that had cornfields or vegetable gardens, they were proportionate in size to the amount of water that we had.

We look at parcels of land that border our lands to lessen the development and keep it wild. The thing about all these lands is that we take a long time to consider whether they'll be developed. If you look at a lot of tribal land in the West, there is a lot that is undeveloped and is just land. Sometimes realtors will say, "This land is located right next to Indian land with fantastic views!"

So when there were discussions about the whole length and width of

Rio Grande del Norte, to us, it was like, yeah, let's do it. Because why did we need to develop everything? We don't need to have a home here or there. Just leave it wild. That way the animals could roam free.

Taos Pueblo reintroduced river otter to the Rio Grande valley. It fell within our philosophy of restoring animals that were once thriving in the area. So we did an entire evaluation of the stream where it was going to be relocated. Since our tribal land boundary—if I were to take the non-Native point of view—is in the middle of the Rio Pueblo and Rio Grande, we reintroduced the otter into the lower reaches of the Rio Pueblo as a connection to the Rio Grande. And we also reintroduced rocky mountain bighorn sheep. Now we have a thriving herd. The Rio Grande del Norte Monument, that just enhances a more wild and undeveloped area that we were told to continue by our ancestors.

The monument keeps in mind the values of the first Americans that were here in this valley, preserving it for future use, scenic enjoyment, and exploration. Not for minerals, but exploring what is there like our ancestors did. I never thought it was gonna be named a national monument, and I was happy it did. A lot of it falls within our Taos Pueblo original homelands. We don't mind sharing it. The monument follows along with our philosophy of let's enjoy it, but don't destroy it. Use it, but don't overuse it. You are on this Earth, so you take care of this land. You don't own it, but you take care of it and everything on it.

AFTER JIM GAVE INSTRUCTIONS about how to navigate Big Rock rapid—the biggest we would see all day—he paddled the raft back into the current. I watched him float away and realized I could no longer back out. I had to float the rapid and I didn't want to make a mistake.

I gave Jim some space, holding onto reeds until he was a few boat lengths away. Then I pushed off the shore and dipped my paddle gently to point the boat's nose straight. The ducky was carried along in the current and I sat motionless but ready on its rubbery surface. Ahead, Jim steered the raft river left, bypassing a large boulder on the right. It looked as though the raft was going to smash right into an even larger boulder, which must be Big Rock, but instead the raft slowed in still water. Just as Jim had instructed, he overcorrected by bringing the raft far left, then pointed it the opposite way. My smaller boat was gaining on him. I angled left around the first rock, hoping I wouldn't bump the raft. Just before we collided, the raft dropped down a slip of water between the huge boulder and the shelf along the right shore and disappeared out of sight.

My ducky rushed toward the large boulder. I pointed the nose right, and my shoulders flexed as I dug deep with the paddle. The current pushed my boat's vulnerable wide side toward the boulder. The boat bumped onto Big Rock and begins to lift as quick water bombarded the other side. I pulled hard on the paddle, tried not to think about swimming or recirculating, just paddling. The boat slipped forward and down the tongue of water, gliding swiftly past the raft waiting in an eddy below. I was jubilant, filled with adrenaline, relief, and joy.

"Great job!" Jim smiled over at me.

This river is fragmented, divided, and distributed through legislation and treaties, dams and diversions. People, countries, and groups "own" rights to the water. Yet, when in the water, I can't sense those partitions or boundaries. The enormous river feels like a living being that determines its own way in the world; it chose to follow fault lines instead of digging its own path in the earth. It has personality; it can be serene and slow, rough and raging, gurgling and gleeful. And like the river, people have wide-ranging relationships to the land and water around them, different for every person, for every place.

In Rio Grande del Norte, where the claims to the land are varied and have ancient and conflicting precedents, it is incredible that disparate groups united to agree about protecting the land with a monument. This consensus is hopeful. Maybe agreement is possible in Bears Ears and other places too. This won't be achieved without sacrifice, compromise, and a willingness to listen and understand different perspectives, but Rio Grande del Norte shows it can be done.

It appears that the question of who owns the land here has not been answered. Each stakeholder still believes it is their land. Members of Taos Pueblo rightfully claim that it is their homeland. Ester, land grant heirs, and *acequia parciantes* believe the land belongs to them and have legal documents to prove it. A rancher or mountain biker or kayaker might say the same thing because they each have a strong connection to the place through using it. And this is what I find beautiful: they don't have to agree. It can mean something different to everyone, be there for everyone. In his book *Enchantment and Exploitation*, William deBuys writes of New Mexico: "Whether as sacred space, communal inheritance, or private property, the mountains have demonstrated again and again that the life of societies and the life of the land cannot be separated."

Now the task is to care for the life of this land, like Garrett said, planning for one hundred years from now. Because in one hundred years, our descendants will call this inherited land theirs too.

10. On Reactions

HANFORD REACH NATIONAL MONUMENT, WASHINGTON

We're not the most scenic monument, but we are the weirdest and the wackiest." In mid-December 2018, I was riding in the passenger seat of a government SUV listening to Dan Haas narrate our drive through Hanford Reach National Monument in eastern Washington. Dan had close-cut, tight silver curls and wore jeans and a hooded sweatshirt. He worked for the U.S. Fish and Wildlife Service and was graciously accommodating me into his workweek. I came to Hanford Reach to volunteer, ostensibly to help out, but over the course of four days I didn't feel that I completed a single helpful task. My stint of "volunteering" ended up as a private, behind-the-scenes tour of the monument, complete with a knowledgeable and eccentric guide. Dan has worked in the area since 1992, helped draft the monument proclamation, then helped write the management plan, and he had a habit of referring to random government officials by their first names as if I knew who they all were. As we made the twenty-minute drive from Dan's office at the McNary National Wildlife Refuge to the monument, he burbled facts

HANFORD REACH

NATIONAL MONUMENT

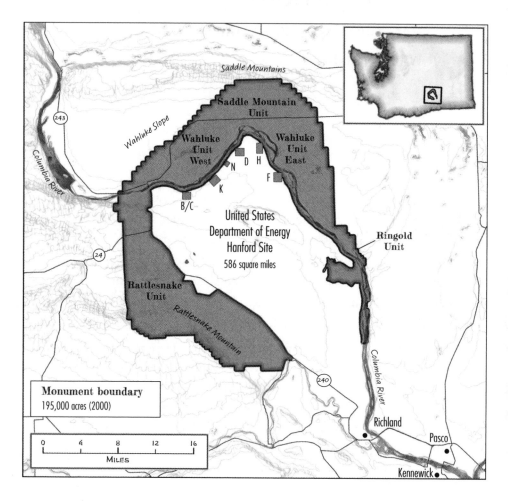

Saddle Mountains

Saddle Mountain Unit

Wahluke Slope

Wahluke Unit West

Wahluke Unit East

Columbia River

N D H

F

K

B/C

United States
Department of Energy
Hanford Site
586 square miles

Ringold Unit

Rattlesnake Unit

Rattlesnake Mountain

Columbia River

240

Monument boundary
195,000 acres (2000)

Richland

Pasco

Kennewick

0   4   8   12   16
MILES

about nuclear history, geology, office gossip, and the monument's designation.

In the 1990s, the Hanford Site was known as the most polluted place in the United States. Curving around this toxic trash heap is the Hanford Reach, a horseshoe bend in the Columbia River that is a major spawning site for Chinook salmon and the last free-flowing stretch of the Columbia. Here, devastating waste coexists with wildlife and a shining river.

The Hanford Site produced plutonium, referred to as "the most toxic substance known to man," for the first atomic bomb in the 1940s. Plutonium occurs naturally when dying stars shatter to smithereens in supernova explosions, but this means it can be hard to find on Earth. So to use this radioactive element to create a bomb, it needed to be manufactured.

Glenn Seaborg discovered plutonium at University of California, Berkeley in 1940 and covertly wrote to President Franklin D. Roosevelt to explain how it could be used in weapons. In 1942, after the Japanese had bombed Pearl Harbor on the Hawaiian Island of Oahu the previous December, Roosevelt authorized the Manhattan Project with the classified directive to build a nuclear bomb for use in World War II.

My first volunteer task was to assist Dan in a bald eagle survey opposite the Hanford Site. The Department of Energy, which still manages Hanford and the defunct nuclear reactors, was conducting monthly eagle surveys on their side of the river throughout the winter, so the Fish and Wildlife Service decided that they should conduct coordinating surveys on the monument side. Dan signed us up for the survey, thinking it would be fun for me. As a novice bird-watcher, I was eager to participate. The survey started in the eastern portion of the monument, wound along the bend of the Columbia River on closed roads, and finished on the western side. This would give me an up-close view of the part of the monument that closely bordered the Hanford Site.

After the Manhattan Project was authorized, a search began for a place to house the plutonium factory. Dan enumerated the requirements for the site: it had to be remote with a low population to reduce risks to the public, it had to be defensible since it was a classified government operation during wartime, and it required large quantities of water for cooling the reactors. This area outside Richland, Washington, embodied these characteristics, and 670 square miles within a bend of the Columbia River was identified as the perfect location for the Manhattan Project's factory. At the time, this area was perceived as empty, a wasteland. It was unproductive in an agricultural sense and was considered economically useless, so few people cared that the government took over this small corner of river and sagebrush. Instead, it was put to work for "the good of the nation." The Department of Energy seized private landholdings in the area by eminent domain, ordered residents of the small communities of White Bluffs and Hanford to evacuate in less than thirty days, and forbade Indigenous people from being in the area, which cut them off from sacred hunting, fishing, and ceremonial sites.

Construction began at the Hanford Site in 1943 with a workforce of more than fifty thousand people. Almost no one knew what was being built and speculation was forbidden. Workers whispered but were fired if their curiosity ever became too public. Everyone believed that they were contributing to the war effort in an important way, but the actual mission was a closely guarded secret. In a little over a year, Hanford's B Reactor—the first large-scale nuclear reactor ever built—was responsible for producing the plutonium used in the bombs tested at the Trinity Site in New Mexico and used in the Fat Man bomb dropped on Nagasaki, Japan. Fat Man killed seventy thousand people.

HANFORD REACH

Our first survey stop was the White Bluffs boat launch, but on the way we stopped at White Bluffs overlook. The air was cold and the sun was bright. Dan pointed out one of his favorite plants, White Bluffs bladderpod. It is a low-growing plant with feathery pistachio-colored leaves similar to sagebrush petals. In summer it blooms with bright-yellow flowers. "This is the only place in the world it grows," he said. From the high point at the overlook, I could see sage-covered ripples, round Rattlesnake Mountain in the distance, geometric reactors at the Hanford Site, and the curving blue of the Columbia in between. Though there are many dams both up- and downstream, this is the one remaining section of the Columbia that still functions as a natural river, evidenced by the salmon that continue to return here. I pondered the possibility that fish swim into radioactive water, lay eggs, hatch, and swim to sea, then are pulled out of the ocean to land on my lox bagel along with capers and cream cheese.

Plutonium was manufactured from uranium, a mineral more common than silver. After mining and milling, powdered uranium took a pale neon form called yellowcake, which was packed into aluminum rods and inserted into a thirty-six-foot-tall graphite box, the reactor. Through a chain reaction, the chemical composition of uranium was changed to plutonium by exposing it to extra neutrons. The process produced millions of tons of solid waste at Hanford. Water pumped directly from the Columbia River was used to cool the reactors during production, and that became billions of gallons of liquid waste. Focused on the emergency of the war and not on environmental responsibility, the Hanford Site dumped 440 billion gallons of radioactive and chemical waste onto the ground. The site still houses millions of gallons of high-level waste in 177 underground tanks. In total, nine reactors were built and operated at Hanford, and they continued production throughout the weapons stockpiling of the Cold War era.

Dan and I climbed back in the car and passed through a locked gate. As we drove, Dan migrated from discussing nuclear history to geologic history. During the last ice age, between thirteen thousand and fifteen thousand years ago, glaciers formed ice dams that created the ancient Glacial Lake Missoula over western Montana. Periodically the dams would break, and water would go rushing down what is now known as the Columbia River Gorge, flooding most of eastern Washington. The ice dams reformed, and the process, known as the Missoula floods, would repeat. Dan pointed out the window and explained this was how the landscape got its rippled topography. "Those floods gouged the landscape seven ways to Sunday," he said.

At the boat launch I climbed out of the vehicle with binoculars around my neck and startled a great blue heron in nearby grasses. With childlike excitement I scanned the trees across the river to find where the heron had landed in cattails, while Dan set up his spotting scope. My lenses halted on a regal white head, a flicker amid brown branches.

"Dan! I think I see an eagle. On that tall tree," I pointed to the Hanford side of the river.

He swung his scope around. "Yeah, you're right, that is an eagle."

My first confirmed eagle sighting: I was proud and in awe. Dan spotted a juvenile eagle; brown and speckled, the young birds were more difficult to find since they camouflaged with the winter branches and lacked the telltale white head. I continued my search, vibrating with thrill, but Dan was unruffled. An expert at identifying birds, he was bored by the eagles. He aimed his scope away from the trees and searched for other wildlife instead. He zeroed in on a coyote lounging on the opposite beach, and we took turns looking at it through the glass. A high-pitched yipping echoed across the water. Other voices joined in an orchestra of yips and howls.

HANFORD REACH

I scoured branches for more eagles. With an air of triumph Dan refocused the scope and motioned me over to spy a small, spiny clump high in a tree. I had not realized that porcupines hung out in trees.

In total we counted six adult bald eagles and three juveniles, all on the Hanford side of the river. It was curious to me that they seemed to prefer the nuclear waste site to the wildlife refuge.

We headed to the next survey location. "Where is your favorite part of the monument?" I asked after closing the next gate.

"Oh . . . it burned," Dan said mournfully. Hanford Reach National Monument includes the largest remaining shrub-steppe habitat in Washington. Shrub-steppe is like a miniature forest: open grassland with woody shrubs that function like a forest canopy. Rabbitbrush, bitterbrush, and sagebrush form a thermal layer that provides shade, roosts, and food for birds, small animals, and wildflowers. The shrubs are interspersed with clumps of bunchgrass and surrounded by macrobiotic soil crusts. However, like elsewhere in the West, shrub-steppe is being overtaken by cheatgrass. Native bunchgrass grows in isolated clumps, but invasive cheatgrass grows in a consistent blanket on the ground. Cheatgrass is tall and oily and burns extra hot: an ideal fuel. Bunchgrass naturally resists fire because it forces the flame to jump from bunch to bunch, but cheatgrass fills in all the blanks and turns shrub-steppe into tinder. Fires are a problem here. Since I come from California, forest fires are on my mind often, but I had never considered sagebrush fires as damaging or tragic. In fact, I had never considered sagebrush fires at all.

We turned onto the highway, and Dan decided to detour to his old favorite spot at the top of Saddle Mountain. We drove past blank brown earth and circular black patches that indicated the obliteration of bushes. "It used to be spectacular up here. It was covered with amazing old sagebrush and balsamroot flowers and was filled with sage sparrows. Then it burned about a year or so ago. It is so sad." I noticed a film of young green cheatgrass coated the hills. "Cheatgrass sprouts earlier in the year than bunchgrass, so it makes it hard for the native grasses to compete. By the time bunchgrasses start to grow, the cheatgrass has already begun to dry out."

Sagebrush plains take a long time to recover from a fire. The bushes only germinate every seven years, and each plot spreads outward only a few feet with each germination. There was a restoration zone in this burned area, but the restoration was failing because of continued fires. "It is almost not worth the effort to try and have areas like this anymore," Dan said.

On the summit of Saddle Mountain, I took in a panorama of wrinkled hillsides, stark plains, and tall, gnarled sagebrush still growing on the other side of the slope. We climbed back in the vehicle. As we pulled onto the highway, we passed a large falcon on the side of the road. I expected it to fly up as we passed, but it stayed defiantly in place. I stared out the passenger window at the peregrine guarding a meal of dead duck.

We turned onto a dirt road toward Saddle Lakes, approaching Hanford from the opposite side of the bend in the river, and found a pile of dead coyotes on the roadside. Dan climbed out of the car, disgusted, and called it in to his supervisor. I squatted and counted seven animals with blood-matted fur, thinking of the live coyote we had seen earlier and its lonely calls. Dan explained that some ranchers think of coyotes as pests and like to shoot them. Coyotes are protected by the monument, so the bodies were dumped here, likely to make a statement.

We passed through another locked gate, and as we drove, the SUV flushed birds from cattails. We spied several more eagles, all on the Hanford side. Dan's phone burst to life with the George Strait

HANFORD REACH

song "All My Exes Live in Texas." I focused my binoculars out the window and tried not to eavesdrop as he discussed shared-beagle-custody logistics with his ex-wife.

IN THE 1950S scientists contracted by the Atomic Energy Commission injected beagles with plutonium to predict the health effects of radiation on humans. This is how scientists learned that plutonium is malevolently bone loving. Dan's canine companion, whom he loves like a child, is a beagle. Beagles were chosen for these plutonium tests because of their docile temperament, hardy physique, and robust digestive system. I witnessed the beagle's resilience firsthand when Dan's dog gobbled half a bar of dark chocolate from atop my notebook. After a momentary panic that I had just killed my host's best friend, Dan shrugged and said that beagles could handle just about anything.

We drove along dirt roads through wetland near the river, with views of the N Reactor on the far bank and tall green cattails filled with birds on our bank. The N Reactor was the final and most advanced reactor built at Hanford. It produced plutonium and generated energy and was the only dual-purpose reactor in the United States. By 1971 the other reactors had been shut down, leaving N as the last operating reactor at Hanford until it, too, was shut down in 1987. A misty cloud obscured N on the other side of the rippling river. The reactor could not have functioned if it weren't for this water. And the river might have been dammed or developed like the rest of the Columbia if it weren't for the reactor. A strange symbiosis.

I kept a running tally of the wildlife we saw in the wetland region of our survey: juvenile bald eagle, 1; adult bald eagles, 2; red-tailed hawks, 3; great blue herons, 7; snowy egret, 1; tundra swans (with black bills), 8; porcupine in a tree, 1 (yes, another one); coyote running across the road, 1; and a small herd of grazing mule deer.

The B Reactor began producing plutonium in 1944, all production ceased in 1987, and two years after that, Hanford was declared a Superfund hazardous waste site. Throughout this time, the Department of Energy controlled thousands of acres surrounding the Hanford facility, which had been acquired as a protection buffer. The government didn't want farmers nearby if something exploded. By the year 2000, this region had been removed from development for over fifty years and had become, in its own way, a de facto park. Consequently, President Bill Clinton designated almost 200,000 acres as Hanford Reach National Monument, the first monument to be managed by the U.S. Fish and Wildlife Service.

"Bob did a good job of writing a lot of things in there," Dan said, referring to Bob Anderson, special counsel to Bruce Babbitt, the secretary of the interior at the time. Bob was responsible for writing the monument's proclamation. This proclamation established protection for the largest remnant of shrub-steppe habitat in the Columbia River basin, fifty-one miles of the last free-flowing, nontidal stretch of the Columbia River, and an array of flora and fauna. Since Dan had already been working in the area for a while, he fed Bob important tidbits to include. "It even mentions beavers. No one is going to manage for beavers."

Paradoxically, this protected region would not exist if it wasn't for the Hanford nuclear site. The very site responsible for manufacturing a death weapon is also responsible for preserving life for many wild plants and animals. War and eminent domain unintentionally paved the way for wild.

DAN, considerate of the fact that I hoped to learn as much about the monument as I could, arranged for me to accompany ecologist Sheri Whitfield on a native plant restoration project for my second day. I envisioned spending the day with my hands and knees in dirt, but professional planters were hired to do the actual work. Instead, I helped Sheri organize the seedlings and "supervise" the planting effort. We met at six in the morning so we could drive out to the monument before the planting crew arrived.

Sheri, a nervous brunette, drove the SUV through early darkness and lamented the looming possibility of a government shutdown. Congress and President Trump were in disagreement over funding for a wall along the U.S.–Mexico border. Sheri explained that if employees of the U.S. Fish and Wildlife Service had a vacation planned and the government shut down, something that happened during the Obama administration, too, they were not supposed to take their trip. First, they had to report to the office to collect and sign furlough slips, and then they had to be available to report back whenever the government reopened, which was unpredictable. It was almost Christmas, and Sheri did have a trip planned with her use-it-or-lose-it vacation time.

We passed through a gate into the monument, parked, and walked through chilly, gray light into a garage filled with large tractors, cardboard boxes of plants, and big bags of seed. Sheri sliced open the boxes to reveal infant plants with roots carefully encased in soil and plastic wrap. We organized them by plant type. Sheri had acquired a mix of woody shrubs and forbs, or wildflowers: blue flax, phlox, purple sage, Wyoming sage, bitterbrush, fleabane, Shasta daisy, and winterfat.

Sheri explained that after a fire, government agencies like the national monument have ten days to create a restoration plan if they are going to get money for that project. All public land agencies are dealing with similar problems, and they are all competing not just for funding but for the seeds and plants themselves. The area we were replanting was known as the Range 12 fire, which happened in 2015. Not long after the fire, they drill-seeded native grasses: bluebunch wheatgrass, bottlebrush squirreltail, Sandberg bluegrass, thickspike wheatgrass, and prairie junegrass. The grasses had already sprouted and grown, with some cheatgrass mixed in. A full three years after the fire comes the final rehabilitation phase: shrub replanting. For shrubs, hand planting is much more effective than seeding. If successful, the shrubs will live for many years, but the forbs will last only about a decade. Hopefully that will be enough time for them to germinate and spread across the prairie.

It was time to meet the planting crew at the gate, so we headed outside. The sage plains glowed pastel pink and lavender while the sky swirled an electric mix of canary and grape, raspberry and slate. Sheri walked matter-of-factly to the truck; I lingered dumbfounded in front of the sky and the thought-to-be-empty land. To my left I could just see the Hanford Site on the horizon: tiny square structures and miles of sagebrush overtaken by brilliance.

Sheri and I helped the crew transport the plants from the shed to the Range 12 plot and got the four-man team set up with a four-wheeler that could roam the plain and deliver plants to each worker. Each man loaded up a stiff fabric bag with seedlings, slung it over his shoulder, and walked into the grass carrying a tall metal tool similar to a scythe. I watched the first man swing the tool in a big, lazy stroke into the soft ground, yank it back to create a small triangular hole, and drop a seedling inside. Then he packed the seedling in with a foot stomp and walked several erratic steps to plant the next one.

As the men planted, Sheri and I waded through stiff yellow grass, tying neon-pink flagging to stakes to mark the plot perimeter. "Once the sagebrush is burnt, this becomes a grassland habitat instead of shrub-steppe habitat. Right now, this is grassland," Sheri said. "The shrubs provide shade and habitat for wildlife, but they also provide food. Sage grouse actually eat the sagebrush petals. Mule deer eat

Looking across the Columbia River toward Rattlesnake Mountain, Hanford Reach National Monument, Washington. Photograph by the author.

bitterbrush. You can see that there are no birds out here right now. I used to come out here and count the different birds: sage sparrow, Brewer's sparrow, sage thrasher, western meadowlark, and lark sparrows. Now I come out here and hardly see any birds all day."

We circled around the plot to where the planters had already been. I couldn't find any seedlings amid the bunchgrass. "Look for the footprints," Sheri instructed. In between dry clumps of grass I spied a muddy footprint, and in the center a small silver seedling.

"We no longer have fire seasons, we have fire years," Sheri said.

"People think of trees as burning down, but they don't think about sagebrush burning. Yet the sagebrush ecosystem is one of the most threatened ecosystems on the planet."

Sheri recently worked on restoration at the Saddle Lake transect, Dan's former favorite part of the monument. It was an area that she loved as well. "At Saddle Lake, the new seedlings were not even there a year when another fire ran over the same plot. If I have 1 percent survivability, I will be surprised. It really breaks my heart. It is so sad to see all the work and money we put into restoration go up in flames. But if we do nothing, it will all go to cheatgrass. It feels futile but we have to do it."

Invasive species like hot-burning cheatgrass are not a perfect parallel to human action, but much invasion has happened here. European settlers displaced Indigenous people. The government took land by force from farmers, ranchers, and landowners. Defying the natural process for plutonium production, radioactive materials were manufactured. Waste was dumped onto the ground and into the river, an invasion of the land's purity and integrity. And finally, those radioactive materials were used to invade and subdue another country, another community.

The relationship between humans and land has been defined by dominance since agriculture and cities were conceived. Here in America, mapping, mining, settling, farming, fencing, building, ranching, logging, and owning are all methods of control, all ways that the land has been "put to use." Places like Hanford Reach call to mind how our domineering attitude toward the landscapes around us sometimes mirrors our relationship to our fellow humans. First the land was seized, then it was tainted, and then we used the land's product to control and destroy other people.

Now there is a hint of renewal. The destruction, at least here, has paused. Mess is being cleaned up as best as it can, wildlife is thriving, habitat is being restored. I'm not certain that attitudes of subjugation have changed much.

We drove back to McNary, and I was filled with a dual sense of beauty and degradation, gloom and hope.

FOR MY FINAL VOLUNTEER TASK, I accompanied Dan and his co-worker Lamont Glass out to Rattlesnake Mountain to assess where parking, signage, and bathrooms should go when the road is opened to hikers and visitors. Currently, the entire Rattlesnake Unit is closed to the public. Rattlesnake Mountain, or *Laliik* in Yakama language, which means "land above water," is considered sacred by the Nez Perce, Yakama, Umatilla, Wanapum, Walla Walla, and Cayuse tribes. The monument closed it out of respect. However, the public pushed for access to the 3,531-foot peak, which is the highest in the region. In December 2014, Congress passed a law directing the secretary of the interior to provide public access to the mountain. Indigenous communities objected. Negotiations continue. For now, the monument's staff members are following the legal directive by creating a plan to open the peak to hikers and bikers for one or two weekends a year. Our task was to figure out what kind of infrastructure would be needed for those weekends, if and when they happened.

Our first stop was the shed and garage near old Nike missile site barracks, the same garage where Sheri and I had sorted seedlings the day before. During the Cold War, the War Department developed antiaircraft missiles as a defense system and installed them at key locations around the country. Several missile sites were built around Hanford since a plutonium factory was an obvious potential bomb target. We measured how many parking spaces could fit in the cement pad in front of abandoned emergency bunkers. In Dan's plan, people could park here and then either bike eighteen miles up the road that leads to the summit or hike from here using a shortcut to meet the road. If more people attend than this lot can hold, the state park across the street could serve as overflow parking.

"Are you sure there are going to be enough visitors to fill all these spaces?" I asked once we tallied fifty.

"Oh yeah, people are always asking us about coming up here. This has been a long time coming," Dan said.

Next, Dan and I walked into the field behind the shed to see if we could find any disturbed land for the hiker shortcut. A shortcut would save hikers at least two miles of walking around on the road, but we did not want to create a new footpath through sagebrush. I discovered the stump of a sawed-off telephone pole behind a patch of non-native weeds. Dan pointed to an out-of-place hunk of granite amid the shrubs, noting that it was glacial erratic, swept down during the time of the Missoula floods. We hiked farther in what seemed like faint road ruts and found a second sawed-off telephone pole. Dan was relieved that this old power-line road could serve as the hiker shortcut.

We drove slowly up the crumbling one-lane road to the summit of Rattlesnake, searching for flat spots along the edge where porta-potties would fit, and clocked the mileage to ensure they would be placed at appropriate intervals. We reached the summit, and it was bald and bare. Some small structures remained, but for the most part it was empty. Since Rattlesnake Mountain is the tallest point for miles, a research telescope and observatory were constructed at the summit in 1971 and used by scientists from NASA. To clear the summit of the sacred mountain, the observatory was relocated south of the Tri-Cities to Wallula Junction in 2012.

I popped open the car door, but the wind slammed it shut before I could exit. I forced it back open a crack and squeezed out. "This is a great spot to see elk," Dan hollered over the wind, indicating the golden, rolling hills below us. The Yakima elk herd comprises about 1,000 animals that live in the monument, but a subset of that herd, the Rattlesnake Hills elk herd, consists of 350 animals that live on the lower flanks of Rattlesnake. "I would get my spotting scope out, but it's far too windy," he yelled. My hair whipped about my face, and I spotted a few elk-brown specks on the distant hillsides. Beyond them, the silhouettes of cocooned reactors jutted up from the horizon.

To clean up the Hanford Site, the reactors were cocooned inside buildings, also known as Interim Safe Storage. The plan is these cocoons is to prevent anything from getting in or out for at least seventy-five years while radioactivity decays enough for the reactors to be dismantled. The first reactor cocooned was C in 1998.

Starting in 1989 and originally planning to take thirty years, the cleanup effort was not even half finished by 2008. In 2014 it was considered the largest environmental cleanup effort in the world. The process will cost hundreds of billions of dollars and will never leave the area completely "clean." The groundwater below the Hanford Site will never be safe to drink.

The biggest problem Hanford faces is what to do with the radioactive waste. All the equipment used in the facility is now contaminated by radiation; everything, down to the uniforms of the workers, counts as waste. Then there is the by-product from the production of plutonium that now sits in underground tanks in the form of toxic sludge. A plant is being built onsite to vitrify the sludge—transform it into solid glass rods, which will be easier to store and won't leak onto the ground or into the river.

But these rods will still be dangerous. Even in the form of glass, this waste will remain radioactive and harmful for at least 10,000 years. Plutonium itself has a half-life—the time it takes for radioactivity to decay by half—of 24,100 years. In 24,000 years, plutonium will just begin to approach a state where it is safe to handle. That is a mind-boggling length of time. Ecological philosopher Timothy Morton also classifies nuclear waste as a hyperobject. Like those of climate change, nuclear waste's effects on the planet are so large and span so much time that they can be difficult to comprehend. The waste from this plutonium factory will linger on Earth for thousands of years beyond the lives of the people responsible for creating it, and thousands of years longer than the people attempting to clean it up.

Radioactive waste can't be left long-term at Hanford, an area vulnerable to earthquakes and near a river that provides drinking water for many. The waste, including the yet-to-be-made glass rods, was supposed to go to Yucca Mountain, a proposed long-term nuclear waste storage site in Nevada, but that site was never completed. Without a dedicated storage facility, Hanford had to improvise and settled on burying the waste underground. It became the trash heap for other contaminated bits and sundry, accepting radioactive waste from the Trinity Site in New Mexico and decommissioned nuclear submarines, and even, reportedly, radioactive dog poop from the beagle project. In anticipation of a better long-term solution, the tanks containing toxic liquid were designed to last for only forty years, and now some of them have begun to leak.

Meanwhile, across the river, we were concerned with population management for a controversial tourist trip. We drove the route again, confirmed our restroom sites, and decided where signage was needed to direct people to parking, the shortcut hike, and the bike route. The bathrooms needed to be there so people didn't go trampling sagebrush to relieve themselves. Visitors required places for their cars to rest while they ventured up the mountain, and signage was essential to instruct people to stay on the pre-disturbed roads and pathways. And yet, I couldn't shake the sense that this was all so trivial in the face of the neighboring environmental disaster and its destructive history.

"It only took sixteen months from the time they broke ground to the production of plutonium," Lamont said. "In contrast, it has taken us five years to a plan a trip to the top of Rattlesnake Mountain."

On the way back to McNary we stopped at the Manhattan Project National Historical Park Visitor Center. The National Park Service offers tours of the B Reactor and tells the story of America's wartime effort through interpretive sites here and at the park's other locations, in New Mexico and Tennessee. The walls contained maps of the Hanford Site, historic photos of its construction and daily life there, images of the B Reactor, and diagrams detailing the primary chain reactions that happened within the reactor. As at any historic interpretive site, a fair bit of nostalgia was intermixed with instructive facts.

The region's attitude about this nuclear past is not what I had expected. In my mind, the thought of the nuclear bomb conjures images of mushroom clouds and black-and-white photos of panicked people, of death and devastation, of great sadness that this is what humans are capable of. Yet in the Tri-Cities, the nearby population centers of Richland, Pasco, and Kennewick, people take a lot of local pride in the area's participation in this part of history. Richland High School's sport teams are referred to as "the bombers," and their illustrated mascot is a mushroom cloud. Dan and I first met at a bar called Atomic Ale, which serves Plutonium Porter, Half-Life Hefeweizen, and Rubidium Red Wheat. Hanford directly contributed to the economic growth of the Tri-Cities area and continues to employ around nine thousand people to work on the decommission and cleanup, meaning the Hanford Site is still one of the largest employers in the region even though it no longer produces anything.

Here the mood is a celebration of American ingenuity, pride that our country's intelligence and work ethic led directly to success and the end of the war. Some take the view that because of the bomb, the war ended earlier than it would have without it, and ultimately saved lives. Others point out that because the Allies won the war, many people were saved from oppressive governments, and genocides were stopped. That might be true, but I can't help but think of the vast number of people who died because of the bomb, almost entirely Japanese civilians, people who were perceived as different and far away and therefore removed from American consciousness. Denying the horror of the effect of the atomic bomb is a way for us to live with that tragedy. If we don't think too long on the destruction, we can instead be proud of accomplishment. The bomb should be remembered for what it truly was, and that means recognizing both triumph and depravity.

At Hanford, they created in order to destroy, and that in turn formed this accidental park. The ecological processes on display in the shrub-steppe reveal another form of growth and combustion and regrowth. It all exists here concurrently: life, destruction, restoration, re-creation, reverence, ambition, success, catastrophe. Places like this are important because they embody the great complexity that is the human-earth interface. Hanford Reach gifts us with a recognition of that entanglement.

If people could clearly see this coexistence of creation and devastation, perhaps decisions would be made differently. When we understand that humans are capable of both greatness and horror, that progress can lead to tragedy, that success is not one-sided, it might allow us to rethink how we care for what is around us: human, animal, or place.

We build an observatory on a sacred peak, then take it down. We close that sacred peak out of respect, and then we open it back up. We

HANFORD REACH

create a refuge for coyotes, and then we shoot them and discard their carcasses on the roadside. We manufacture a harmful element and use it to bomb others at a time of great emergency. Its by-product threatens us for thousands of years. Meanwhile, bald eagles perch on branches overlooking cocooned reactors and radioactive earth.

11. On Walls

ORGAN MOUNTAINS–DESERT PEAKS NATIONAL
MONUMENT, NEW MEXICO

I will build a great wall—and nobody builds walls better than me,
believe me—and I'll build them very inexpensively. I will build a
great, great wall on our southern border, and I will make Mexico
pay for that wall. Mark my words.

—DONALD J. TRUMP, June 16, 2015, shortly after announcing his
presidential campaign

Mexico does not believe in walls.

—MEXICAN PRESIDENT ENRIQUE PEÑA NIETO

W hat kind of trees do you think these are?" my mom wondered as we drove through geometric rows of an orchard
outside Las Cruces, New Mexico. The trees were tall and
bare, anchored in red sand. A quick phone search told us that they
were pecan trees, known as "thirsty" trees because of their great need
for water.

I looked at the dry landscape and wondered aloud, "Why would
you grow thirsty trees in the desert? Wait—is that the Rio Grande?"

ORGAN MOUNTAINS-DESERT PEAKS
NATIONAL MONUMENT

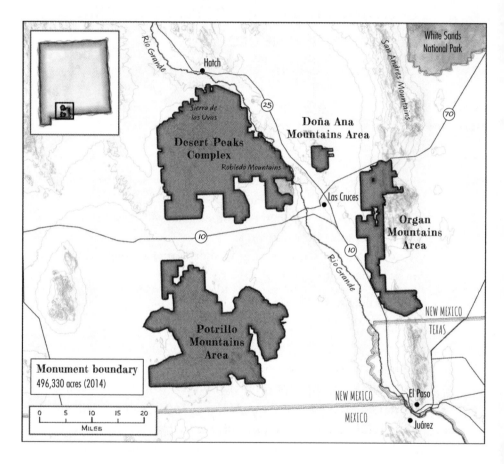

Rio Grande

Hatch

White Sands
National Park

San Andres Mountains

25

Sierra de
las Uvas

Doña Ana
Mountains Area

70

Desert Peaks
Complex

Robledo Mountains

Las Cruces

Organ
Mountains
Area

10

10

Rio Grande

NEW MEXICO
TEXAS

Potrillo
Mountains
Area

Monument boundary
496,330 acres (2014)

NEW MEXICO
MEXICO

El Paso

Juárez

0   5   10   15   20
MILES

I almost swerved off the road as I crossed a culvert, craning my neck to see the river underneath. The map said we were crossing the wide, famed river of New Mexico and Texas, but what lay below us was an empty expanse of sand, a lone set of tire tracks weaving down the center. In Rio Grande del Norte I learned that dams and diversion left parts of *Río Bravo* dry for some of the year. Now I could see that in February, near the U.S.–Mexico border, the river was nonexistent.

My mom and I had come to New Mexico to visit Organ Mountains–Desert Peaks National Monument, which is composed of five noncontiguous mountain ranges. Nearby, just outside Las Cruces, lies the White Sands Missile Range and the Trinity Site, where the Manhattan Project detonated the first nuclear device. Like the sage-steppe surrounding Hanford, this desert had been perceived as empty and expendable. As William deBuys puts it, New Mexico is the land of "Enchantment and Exploitation." I was keeping an eye out for both.

We drove past the orchard off pavement and onto dirt. We crossed railroad tracks. We turned from a wide, well-graded dirt road onto a single-lane road with three-foot-tall sandbanks on either side. It felt committing. In our two-wheel-drive rental, we had no way to turn around. Eventually we approached rounded hills rising from pale sand and creosote bush: the Potrillo Mountains. Just beyond that lay *la frontera*, the border. In his 2017 monument review, Ryan Zinke flagged the Potrillo Mountain district as problematic. He requested stricter border regulations to prevent drug trafficking through these mountains. President Trump's campaign-promised border wall was a perceived solution and would stand very near this monument.

My mom and I arrived at Kilbourne Hole, a mile-wide, three-hundred-feet-deep volcanic crater. We climbed out of the car, passed two men shooting at clay pigeons in the bottom of the crater, and began traversing the rim. Kilbourne Hole is a maar crater, which forms when magma superheats groundwater below the surface. The pressure builds and builds until eventually steam explodes out of the earth. Essentially this crater is like a volcano without a mountainous rim but the inverse: a depression in the ground. We picked up our pace, following intermittent sandy trails. Our aim was to hike six miles as we circumnavigated the hole.

Something shiny caught my eye. "Hey, look at this," I said as I stooped and picked up a rock. One side was warm, rough gray basalt, and the other was a sparkling cluster of pale-green crystals. "I bet that's peridot," my mom said. "You know, the green gem. I think it might be Veronica's birthstone." She stopped, picked up another shining stone, and looked closer. "Yeah, I'm pretty sure this is peridot."

I looked around. The dry desert bristling with sharp spiny plants unveiled a treasure trove. Glittering celadon gemstones littered the sand. Like diamonds, peridot forms deep in the earth's mantle under intense pressure and heat. The green tint is the result of iron present when the gems form. Volcanic activity brings these emerald-colored crystals to the surface. In this case, when steam released from underground in an explosion, it shot out gemstones at the same time.

We ambled along, eyes glued to the ground as we overturned pebbles in search of the perfect peridot specimen. Our hike, now transformed to a treasure hunt, led us slowly around the crater's edge until it began to sprinkle rain. We pulled on raincoats and assessed our options. We were walking much too slowly to make it all the way around the crater, so we would have to turn around. "Or we could climb down into the crater and back out the other side so we don't repeat the hike we already did," I suggested. Afraid of heights, my mom looked at me with wide eyes.

"But where would we get down?" she asked, not immediately refusing. Along the edge of the crater, the basalt walls were tall and sheer, but a section of broken columns formed a low-angle ramp downward. I clambered down the rocks to make sure it was suitable for her and found myself on a small walkway of stone. Summoning bravery, Mom scooted down the rocks as I spotted her from below. Soon we were walking through tall bunchgrass and fourwing saltbush on the flat, sandy bottom of the crater, surrounded by basalt walls on all sides. Apollo astronauts performed training exercises in here in the late 1960s and early 1970s. I wondered how similar this landscape was to the moon's.

On the other side of the crater I scouted another low-angle passage that led back up. We topped out, and it began to rain harder. We pulled our hoods up and hurried the last couple hundred feet back to the car. Our legs dampened as we rushed through the rain. We both reached for the door handles at the same time. I took a breath as I prepared to step into the dry interior but then paused. "Wait, do you smell that?" Mom paused too. We stood, breathing as raindrops speckled our cheeks. The air smelled smoky, sooty, with a tinge of green. Creosote bush. I had read that creosote emits fragrance during rain but had never experienced it. Creosote grew in every direction, and its almost industrial yet lively fragrance engulfed us. We looked at each other through the rain and grinned.

THE MOUNTAINS IN THIS DESERT HOLD STORIES. As philosopher Edward Casey says, "Places not only *are*, they *happen*." More than natural splendor or impressive geology, the cliffs here speak of people.

There is a legend about the famed Apache warrior Geronimo that takes place here. Some tellings place this story in the Superstition Mountains in Arizona, but most versions claim it happened in the Robledo Mountains, in Organ Mountains–Desert Peaks National Monument.

Geronimo was not particularly well liked. He was known for his surly attitude and roaring temper when drunk. Even among his followers, he had a reputation for fighting for personal glory rather than for the welfare of all, and his battles often left too many civilians and young warriors dead. But Geronimo was also said to possess supernatural powers. He was called on to start rain or to control the sun. It was also rumored that rifles jammed and misfired if aimed directly at him.

Geronimo hated Mexicans; Mexican soldiers had invaded his village and killed his family. Later he hated Anglo-Americans, who took over his land and tried to force his roaming people onto reservations. Geronimo did not want to be contained. He wanted freedom. Freedom to travel through the desert and feel life prickling on his skin. Fighting, always for freedom, Geronimo became famous for killing Mexican and American soldiers in raids as well as for his surprising escapes. He was elusive and hard to capture. He surrendered at least three times, then promptly ran away, before his final surrender.

As this legend goes, Geronimo was being pursued by soldiers, most likely American troops. To evade the soldiers, Geronimo fled into a cave in the Robledo Mountains. The soldiers, smug in their belief that they had trapped the warrior, set up camp beside the cave entrance, content to wait until the Apache, humbled and hungry, crawled back out.

But he never came.

Geronimo escaped unseen out an exit that no one has been able to find. He wiggled through stone passageways, using his intimate knowledge of the earth and, perhaps, even his powers to control natural forces, to squeeze his way to freedom. In defiance of containment, impervious to walls, his silent footsteps receded into the creosote-filled night.

ORGAN MOUNTAINS–DESERT PEAKS

AT THE TIME of Donald Trump's presidential campaign, 705 miles of fence already existed along the 1,969-mile-long border between the United States and Mexico. The Rio Grande naturally divides the two countries for 1,252 miles. This was not enough for Trump: as one of his first acts in office, President Trump issued an executive order that called for tougher border security measures, including the construction of a physical wall. The stated goal of the barrier was to "achieve complete operational control of the southern border."

In September 2019, David Bernhardt, the secretary of the interior who succeeded Ryan Zinke, transferred 560 acres of public land in California, Arizona, and New Mexico from the Department of the Interior to the Department of Defense. This land was now for the wall. Two hundred thirteen acres were near Organ Mountains–Desert Peaks. Just like that, the land went from public and open to all to militarized and part of an exclusionary plan.

OUTSIDE LAS CRUCES, my mom and I went on another hike, this time in the Organ Mountains, so named because the pointed granite needles resemble the gleaming metal pipes of an organ. We walked toward this jagged skyline under ethereal light: one half of the sky darkened by heavy clouds, the other half glowing golden. The winter air carried a hint of rain as we crunched over the trail, passing dry yellow grasses, deep-green juniper, and the sharp spears of narrowleaf yucca, known as Spanish bayonet. Born and raised in Ohio, my mom has a special fondness for New Mexico. When I invited her to join me here, my dad said to her, "You love that desert. You have to go."

We came to some crumpled wooden structures that were the livery and mercantile buildings of Confederate colonel Eugene Van Patten's Mountain Camp, referred to as Dripping Springs Resort. In the late 1800s, visitors would ride a stagecoach seventeen miles from Las Cruces to vacation here. The hotel had two stories, fourteen rooms, a dining hall, and a gazebo for a bandstand. A barn housed chickens and cows, a vegetable garden provided fresh produce for meals, and a brick reservoir collected water that dribbled through stone.

After Van Patten's Confederate career, he was a U.S. Marshal for Western Texas, when Billy the Kid reportedly surrendered his rifle to him. Then he became a captain in the New Mexico Territorial Militia during the Apache Wars, when he may have crossed paths with Geronimo. Later in life he married Benita Madrid Vargas, a half-Piro and half-Spanish woman, and he settled down to run this resort in the mountains.

"You know, we have a relative who fought in the Civil War and then moved to New Mexico," my mom said as we walked down the trail. We debated if it could have been Van Patten but decided it wasn't. "I love seeing the bare bones of the mountains," she said, thinking about how she shared that with our relative. "You can see great distances, but it isn't just flat." We passed below tawny cliffs streaked with black watermarks and neon lichen, and I understood why Van Patten and my ancestor had moved here. Something about this place called to us. It called to them too.

Farther down trail we passed the still stately remains of the hotel and came to the spring, where a shock of green moss sprouted from damp cracks in the brick reservoir. Above the spring was another abandoned building.

Eventually Van Patten, bankrupted by land ownership disputes, sold his precious resort to Dr. Nathan Boyd for one dollar. Boyd's wife had come down with the white plague, or tuberculosis. He watched in anguish as she suffered, but even with the medical expertise of a doctor, he was unable to cure her. At the time it was commonly believed that dry desert air could cure the damp coughs of tuberculosis; this idea had brought Billy the Kid's ill mother to New Mexico years earlier. In a desperate last-ditch effort to help his wife,

ORGAN MOUNTAINS–DESERT PEAKS

Boyd built a mountain respite for her near Dripping Springs, where she lived until her death.

I looked up at the tall sepia walls and wondered if Mrs. Boyd had also found them lovely, or if she had found them imprisoning. Colonel Van Patten and his guests sought out this place as a refreshing retreat, an escape from the dusty toil of daily life. But perhaps for her, suffering from an incurable illness in this remote canyon felt like being fenced off from the world she loved.

BILLY THE KID earned his legendary reputation with bewildering escapes. His first crime, committed at age fourteen the day after his mother died of tuberculosis, was stealing clothes from a Chinese laundry. He was found, arrested, and jailed for the night as an admonition. But when the guards returned the next morning and unlocked the heavy wooden door, his cell was empty. The wiry youth had squirmed up the chimney, emerging into the world of an outlaw.

In the Robledo Mountains, about fifteen miles north of Las Cruces, there is a hideout that was supposedly used in 1880 by Billy the Kid and three of his gang members. Sheltered from wind and with a high view of the approaching wagon road, it was the perfect place to camp while being pursued. Very faintly, you can see "O.F.," "Bowdre," "DR," and "Bonney" carved into the stone, indicating that Tom O'Folliard, Charles Bowdre, Dave Rudabaugh, and William Bonney, aka Billy the Kid, had been there.

Known for his protruding front teeth and cheerful personality, Billy made friends almost as easily as he made enemies. Fluent in Spanish and with blue eyes that blazed like gunfire, he was rumored to be popular with Hispanic ladies. He fell in with a group of cowboys and ruffians who stole cattle and eventually became entangled in a deadly local dispute between ranchers known as the Lincoln County War.

223

In spring 1881, Billy the Kid was imprisoned in Mesilla, New Mexico, under the serrated silhouette of the Organ Mountains. He was found guilty of killing Lincoln County sheriff William Brady and was sentenced to death by hanging. First he had to be transferred to the custody of Pat Garrett, the new Lincoln Country sheriff, so that the hanging could take place in the same county as the crime. Billy was shackled in handcuffs and leg irons and transported by wagon, accompanied by six guards. It took the party five days to travel over 150 miles across the sharp Chihuahuan desert.

According to Sheriff Garrett, Lincoln didn't have a prison "that would hold a cripple," so he arranged for Billy to be housed in the second-story room next to his office, still in handcuffs and leg irons and with two full-time guards. Garrett warned the guards that if Billy saw an opportunity to run, he would take it.

One of the guards, Bob Olinger, hated Billy the Kid. He believed Billy was responsible for the death of his friend, so he spent his days tormenting the prisoner. The other guard, Deputy James Bell, got along with Billy, charmed by his easy humor.

On the morning of April 28, Olinger sat in front of Billy and slowly, menacingly loaded his shotgun with eighteen grains of buck-shot per barrel. "The man that gets one of these loads," Olinger said with a hard stare, "will feel it."

Billy leaned back in his chair, his ankles straining against the irons. "I expect he will. But be careful, Bob, or you might shoot your-self."

Later in the day, as the sun stretched long over cactus and creo-sote, Olinger took a group of prisoners across the street to a hotel for supper. Billy asked Bell if he could use the privy. On the way back in-side, Billy walked with a quicker step than Bell and made it to the top of the stairs before his guard. He ducked behind a wall and slipped a handcuff over his hand, which was thinner than his thick wrist. As

Bell reached the top of stairs, Billy swung the loose metal cuff into Bell's face. Metal crunched skin, and Bell toppled over. Billy grabbed the guard's revolver as he fell. Knowing the danger he was in, Bell scrambled to his feet and ran for the door, but Billy shot him in the back. Bell tumbled down the stairs, dead.

Billy then went back into his holding room and picked up Olinger's shotgun, the one loaded with buckshot, and hovered at the window. Having heard the gunshots and curious as to the cause, people congregated in the streets. Olinger emerged from the hotel as a neighbor called to him, "Bob, the Kid has killed Bell!"

At nearly the same moment Billy threw open the upstairs window and shouted, "Hello old boy!" Olinger saw Billy framed by the window and answered, "And he has killed me too . . ." As he turned his face upward, Billy blasted him with the buckshot that he had loaded into his own gun that morning.

After killing his guards, Billy stole several guns from the sheriff's office and convinced a townsperson to saddle up a pony and lend him an ax. Billy hacked apart the chain between his legs with the ax, pulled the broken ends up and tucked them into the waistband of his pants, and mounted the pony. The residents of Lincoln lined the streets and watched him ride away, chains slapping against his thighs.

I DROVE SOUTH ON I-25 from Santa Fe to Las Cruces to visit Organ Mountains–Desert Peaks a second time, this time to speak with Ángel Peña, who worked for the Conservation Lands Foundation, and with other advocates for the monument. The highway runs parallel to the White Sands Missile Range. It also follows the path of the El Camino Real de Tierra Adentro.

Today this north–south route is a highway, with points along it designated as a National Historic Trail. Previously, it was the earliest

Spanish trade route in the United States, spanning sixteen hundred miles linking Mexico City to Ohkay Owingeh (San Juan) Pueblo, north of Santa Fe.

Long before it was a Spanish trade route, it was an Indigenous trade route. Footpaths connected Mexico's ancient cultures with the ancients of the American Southwest. Based on out-of-place evidence like bright red and blue feathers from a scarlet macaw, a bird native to South America, it is believed that these trails reached much farther south than Mexico City. This enduring pathway travels through Organ Mountains–Desert Peaks and has been connecting cultures and continents for thousands of years. Now the trade route is interrupted by a wall.

"I HAVE HIKED THIS CANYON probably hundreds of times," Ángel Peña said as he turned his Jeep off the highway onto a dirt road.

"And you aren't sick of it?" I asked.

"No. Not even close." With dark eyes, dark hair, and dark tattoos covering his left arm, Ángel is young, handsome, and filled with infectious enthusiasm for the desert. His eleven-year-old daughter Gabriella rode in the backseat. Ángel made it clear it was important she came with us because Gabi gave him his love for the outdoors.

Valles Canyon is in the Sierra de las Uvas, part of the Desert Peaks district of the monument. They consist of brown hills that don't look particularly distinctive. I would struggle to point out which brown mounds are the Sierra de las Uvas without first consulting a map. On the other side of Las Cruces, the Organ Mountains rise from the lowlands in a jagged, recognizable skyline. It is no surprise that here the Organ Mountains get all the attention: they are dramatic and beautiful. But to Ángel, the Sierra de las Uvas hold more appeal.

When advocacy efforts had successfully convinced the Las Cruces community and New Mexico's politicians that there was a need for a monument, Senator Martin Heinrich said that he would work to protect only the Organ Mountains. At that point, Ángel switched his efforts from convincing people that there should be a monument to convincing people that the Sierra de las Uvas, the Robledo Mountains, the Potrillo Mountains, and the Doña Ana Mountains should be included in the monument too. Ángel planned numerous hikes into Valles Canyon with politicians and business leaders to show them its value. I was being treated to a similar tour.

The Jeep rambled down the dirt road. We sat in silence for a few moments, then Ángel asked, "So, where is *your* place?" He was not asking me "Where are you from?" or even "Where were you born?" He was asking me something less tangible but more important: Where are you happiest? What place has changed you?

I told him about Indian Creek and how the red buttes and towers vibrated my soul.

I recognized that Ángel was bringing me to *his* place. "I'm a first-generation Mexican American," he said. "My mom and grandfather moved to El Paso from Mexico."

"And I'm first-generation from here!" Gabi chimed from the back.

"Yes, first-generation *New* Mexican," Ángel smiled at her in the rearview mirror. "I did not grow up doing anything outdoors," he continued. "My wife took me on my first-ever camping trip when we were in college. When we had Gabi, I was nineteen. I was raised, as a Hispanic, to believe that the man needs to provide for his family, to be in charge. I felt like I needed to have all the answers, but I didn't. Being outside was the cheapest way that I could spend time with my daughter, so I would take her with me and go out hiking. When we would get out there, all those pressures would fall away, and I would feel free to just be myself and enjoy where we were. We could both be kids together."

Ethereal desert light in the Organ Mountains, Organ Mountains–Desert Peaks National Monument, New Mexico. Photograph by the author.

Ángel parked near the mouth of a canyon. He pulled a shotgun out of the back of the Jeep and handed it to Gabi. She scampered ahead, and Ángel whispered to me that "enticing her with dove hunting was the only way I could get her to come, since today is her day off school." Now that she is older, hunting is their preferred way to spend time outside together.

The three of us headed down a dry pebbled wash that fed into a narrow canyon with chocolate-and-ivory-colored walls. We rounded a bend to face a wall covered in petroglyphs. These petroglyphs were unusual. Among the more common spirals and depictions of bighorn

ORGAN MOUNTAINS–DESERT PEAKS

sheep there were drawings of things that seemed out of place: a fish, a macaw, a big amorphous creature that looked like it had a small bird inside it. Ángel, an archaeologist by training, pointed out the most interesting drawings.

"See this?" he pointed at a carving of a deerlike animal with horns, its rear legs drawn in a ninety-degree bend. "An antelope with a bend in its legs means the animal was harvested; straight legs means that it lived for another day." The macaw, he explained, indicated trade that happened up and down the continent. Perhaps this canyon was part of that ancient route to South America. He described more petroglyphs farther up canyon that look as though they depict aliens. I got the sense that he loved this place partly because of its mysteriousness and partly in amazement that people had been traveling through here for so long.

As we walked, Ángel and Gabi told me about a recent time they came here to hunt deer. They had been walking along a hillside and saw the ears of a doe mule deer peeking up over sagebrush. It was buck hunting season, so they couldn't shoot, but sat there and watched her as she watched them back. After searching for bucks all day with no luck, the two of them climbed onto their ATV to head back to the truck. Suddenly a group of deer burst from the bushes and bounded in front of the ATV: several does and a huge buck that strutted boldly across their path. "But we couldn't shoot because we were riding!" Gabi exclaimed.

"All day we were being quiet, and we didn't see a buck until we were on a noisy ATV," Ángel added. As they laughed fondly over the memory, I realized then that this was not only Ángel's place—it was Gabi's too. More specifically, it was their place together. Ángel had brought me here, with Gabi, to demonstrate that this particular place had a profound effect on their lives. It had shaped who he had become.

We drove back toward Las Cruces past open desert filled with shrubs, windows down and air tickling our faces. "This area used to be mostly grassland. Overgrazing has changed the landscape," Ángel said, echoing what Garrett had told me about northern New Mexico. "Creosote has taken over where there used to be more diversity." Ángel swung the jeep toward the edge of the dirt road. "Reach out and grab some of that there," he said, motioning out the window. I pulled off a sprig of leaves and handed it to him. "This bush smells like water," he said, pressing the leaves to his nose and offering it back to me to do the same. "When I am hot or tired from hiking, I pick some of this and smell it, and I feel refreshed."

I inhaled. It smelled exactly like warm, wet pavement after a rain. I had thought that was the scent of asphalt, but perhaps Ángel is right, and it is actually the scent of water. Ángel took another whiff of creosote and his eyes sparkled. "When it rains, the entire city smells like this."

JUAN DE OÑATE, credited as the founder of New Mexico, was born in New Spain (present-day Mexico) to Spanish-Basque silver miners. In the late 1500s, Oñate was selected by the viceroy of Spain to explore unknown lands to the north, so he eagerly set out with a contingent of colonists to spread Catholicism to Native inhabitants in the province of Nuevo Mexico.

When the party crossed the rushing Rio Grande near present-day El Paso, Oñate looked around at the creosote- and yucca-filled desert and claimed all the territory across the river for the Spanish Empire, even though large populations and intricate cities already existed in this land. Shortly thereafter, the oldest member of his expedition became the first casualty of it. Pedro Robledo, a native of Toledo, Spain, had joined Oñate's party along with his wife and five children but died on May 21, 1598. He was buried near the folded, fossil-filled mountains that later came to bear his name: the Robledo Mountains, one of the five ranges included in Organ Mountains–Desert Peaks. Later that same winter, Robledo's twenty-year-old son and namesake would also perish. The young Robledo traveled with Oñate's nephew, Juan de Zaldívar, to collect supplies before reuniting with Oñate, who was on a scouting mission. Zaldívar's group possibly traded with the Acoma people and then camped below the Acoma Pueblo.

The Acoma Pueblo, also known as Sky City, resides in central New Mexico on top of a red sandstone mesa that rises 365 feet above the desert. It was accessed by steep trails and in some places by small depressions for fingers and toes carved in the soft stone. It was likely built around 1144, approximately 450 years before the Spanish came to convert people to their religion. Today, Acoma Pueblo is known as one of the longest continuously inhabited communities in North America.

But in December 1598, Zaldívar's group was rounded up in the pueblo and slaughtered. These killings may have been retaliation for an attack on a group of Acoma women by Spanish men. Or possibly the Acoma were upset by reports of the Spanish enslaving Natives, and feeling safe in their city in the sky, they planned to send a message that they would not be overtaken. Whatever the reason, twelve men were killed, and young Pedro Robledo was pushed—or perhaps in an attempt to escape, jumped—over the edge of the tall cliff. His body smashed against the rock wall and tumbled to the ground below, leaving bright-red stains on the ruddy walls.

After hearing reports of this violence toward his men, Oñate retaliated with overblown brutality. An army of seventy men sieged Sky City, climbing crimson cliffs toward the sad, cloudless blue overhead, and massacred most of the inhabitants of the pueblo. Oñate punished the rest with forced servitude and ordered one foot cut off every man over age twenty-five.

Some tribal authorities believe that the name *Acoma* derives from a word in a Native language that means "place of preparedness." Sky City is thought to be this place, where high on a bluff with wide-reaching views, surrounded by sheer walls, people believed they were immune to invasion.

Walls have long been thought to be a form of protection. But walls can be breached.

A THIRTY-FEET-HIGH SOLID WALL along the U.S.–Mexican border would be the only physical wall in the world to split a continent. If a continuous wall is constructed, it will bisect six different ecoregions and interrupt the ranges of more than fifteen hundred plant and animal species, sixty-two of which are listed as critically endangered or vulnerable. This barrier through the Chihuahuan and Sonoran Deserts would impede the movement of black bears, mountain lions, and javelinas. The jaguar is essentially extinct in the United States, but wild populations exist in the mountains of Mexico. Several male jaguars have recently migrated into Arizona, indicating that the species could make a recovery in the United States if a female would travel north too, but a wall makes this impossible. The wall would block the migration of ocelots, jaguarundi, and the declining population of monarch butterflies. Also, Peninsular bighorn sheep, Mexican gray wolves, Sonoran pronghorn, Quino checkerspot butterflies, and ferruginous pygmy owls.

It would interrupt the movements of people too.

In fall 1993, to address rising tensions over immigration in towns along *la frontera*, the U.S. border patrol implemented Operation Blockade. On a Sunday morning in September, four hundred border patrol agents stationed themselves a few yards apart along a twenty mile stretch of the border outside El Paso. Boots planted firmly in sand, they could see and communicate with the agents on either side of them. This human wall prevented anyone from getting into the United States without official permission and interrupted the daily back-and-forth between Juárez and El Paso. Suddenly working, shopping, and visiting family and friends became much more difficult for the entwined populations of these sister cities.

This area has a history of people mingling regardless of borders, physical or cultural. José González from Latino Outdoors has said that modern New Mexicans are "both the conquered and the conquerors." Their ancestry is a blend of Indigenous populations and Spanish conquistadors, white American settlers and Mexicans. Despite this mingling, borders have recently become more pronounced.

Operation Blockade was supplanted by Operation Hold the Line, which continued to impede illegal border crossings, beginning an era of fighting and fleeing over this imaginary line. Today, it is estimated that more than ten thousand migrants have died since 1994 while attempting to cross the hot, waterless desert. Tougher immigration enforcement in border cities pushed people crossing the border without visas into neighboring open land where there are fewer resources and backup options. These deaths are partially the result of walls and tighter travel restrictions.

"IN MY OPINION, Organ Mountains is one of the most culturally rich and diverse national monuments because it spans so much time," said Lucas Herndon, previously the executive director of the nonprofit Friends of Organ Mountains–Desert Peaks. "One of my favorite things is at Rattlesnake Peak. There's a megafauna scratching post. It's a rock that's like twelve feet tall."

"Yeah, it's huge. It's bigger than me," Ángel added.

"And the top of it is rubbed smooth, which makes no sense. Well, it's because mammoths would go scratch their shoulders there."

"How can they tell?" I asked, amazed.

"The oils. The oils break down the rock in a specific wear pattern," Ángel explained. Ángel had arranged an evening at a local bar with several people who were influential in the designation of the national monument. They included Lucas, local bike shop owner Pablo Lopez, local rider Matt Mason, and others. Pablo and Matt created a 333-mile mountain bike loop that connects all four units of the monument and provides a unique way to experience the desert. Their route has become popular with bike-packers and has brought numerous people to Organ Mountains–Desert Peaks. The group of us sat on a roadside patio on a warm evening with beers in hand and discussed challenges to getting the monument designated, the public outreach involved, and the celebration held after the monument's creation in 2014.

"My job at that time was to make sure everyone got a picture with Martin," said Gabe Vasquez, a former staff member at Senator Martin Heinrich's office, and who, like Ángel, is a Mexican American whose family lives across the border. "I'm doing crowd control, and I'm like, okay, your turn, your turn. And there was this lady standing in the very back with a big folder that was overflowing, and she was sitting there patiently. She was wearing a long skirt, and she was definitely the odd person out because everybody else knew each other. I thought she was trying to get a picture, but every time somebody else cut in front of her—and, to be honest, it was a white guy or a white lady, and this was an Indigenous woman. So I was paying attention, and I was thinking I gotta get her in. Martin said, 'Oh, I gotta go.' And I'm like, 'No, no, no. She's been waiting.' So she opens her folder and pulls out all these maps, and she says, 'Senator, thank you so much for protecting this beautiful mountain range, but I just want you to know that before they were the Organ Mountains, this was the Sierra de los Mansos. And I wish that there was a way to honor them. I wish that there was a way we could somehow honor that this was stolen land. This was Indigenous land, and my people are part of the community."' Gabe paused for a moment. I took a sip of my beer.

"I still remember that very clearly. There's a very real social justice, environmental justice component to what we should be doing, starting with connecting our own people in our community to these lands. So that's my approach to the work that we do now, is to try to tell their stories and make sure that everybody has a voice and make sure everyone's included."

These lands *were* stolen. So were the lands in every monument in this country. In the time since these lands were forcibly taken from Indigenous people, generations have passed, people have blended, ideas about equity have slowly begun to evolve. We can't ignore our nation's violent past. And we need to consider the needs of the increasingly diverse people who access these lands. Gabe stressed the importance of elevating suppressed voices and bringing people to land who are least likely to have access to it.

"If we create a monument and only white folks get to enjoy it, and we create all these new tours and opportunities for people to come and mountain bike and bird, but our own kids don't get any opportunities, then who's really winning? Who is really winning?"

Everyone around the table nodded in agreement.

"This is the poorest state in the nation," Gabe continued.

"It's a three-way battle between Mississippi, Louisiana, and New Mexico every year," Pablo interjected.

"Here we have a state with tons of public land, the poorest kids in the country, and some of the worst education. I was always like, How the fuck is a national monument going to feed kids? How is a national monument going to fix broken homes? Are protected public lands going to do anything to actually improve the lives of people in New Mexico? It's great for people who get to go out on them, right? But that's like 1 percent of the entire state population."

In response to his own questions, Gabe has devoted much of his career to getting kids outdoors. He helped found the Nuestra Tierra Conservation Project, which works to provide communities of color near the border access to public land. Gabe and Nuestra Tierra were then instrumental in the creation of the New Mexico Outdoor Equity Fund, which develops programs and opportunities on public land for New Mexican youth.

Because of people like Gabe and Ángel, who now serves as president of Nuestra Tierra Conservation Project, Organ Mountains–Desert Peaks provides access to land for people who would not have had it before. They know that experience with land is more than merely an adventure: it shapes how people perceive themselves. It can alter someone's life. Ángel showed me a place that profoundly affected him, a place that gave meaning and dimension to his life. Gabe's mission is to share this type of connection and experience with the children of New Mexico, to give people, as Ángel would say, their own place.

IN TOTAL, the Trump administration built 453 miles of wall along the border and spent roughly $15 billion dollars. That is about $33 million per mile. Only forty miles are new barriers. Construction came to a halt after President Joe Biden was inaugurated on January 20, 2021, and hours later signed an executive order that terminated construction and spending on the project. In anticipation of this order, construction crews scrambled in a final push to build as much wall as possible, blasting through desert even after Biden had been sworn in.

Mountains have been cleaved apart, leaving isolated quarter-mile lengths of wall standing where rugged peaks used to be. Service roads switchback up hillsides to islands of wall, providing an easy path for foot travel around the walls' unconnected ends. Once pristine desert is now spiderwebbed with roads, staging areas, disjointed walls that serve no purpose, and dynamited mountains susceptible to erosion. These massive, unfinished structures were built to prevent anything from crossing over them. Meanwhile, the sun rises on one horizon and sets on the other, clouds traverse between countries, breezes blow back and forth, and the scent of creosote wafts between walls.

BEFORE WE LEFT NEW MEXICO, my mom and I hiked into Soledad Canyon on a rainy winter morning, me in a dark-blue raincoat, Mom in a baby-blue poncho. The rain enhanced the color of the desert: brick-red sand, coppery rocks, flaming-yellow grasses, verdant cactus. Tall spears of dry desert spoon, or *Dasylirion wheeleri*, populated the hillsides like sentinels. We didn't mind the weather and hiked through misty, low clouds while discussing details we had learned about Billy the Kid. The trail dead-ended at a tall brown wall smeared with the first glisten of a waterfall.

We looped back to the car on a different path, marveled at the fresh scents that emanated from blooming cactus and the water fragrance of creosote. To us, the desert felt mystical, vibrant, enlivening.

The trail wound past the crumbing foundation of an old building. Only one wall remained standing, with stacked rocks cradling a wooden window frame. I peered through, curious about the people who had chosen to build here in this desert. I wondered what had happened in and around these old walls. I'm sure there is a story. Stories are resilient, walls are temporary.

We poked at the stones that lay in scattered disarray around the foundation, then turned and walked toward the emerging sunshine.

237

12. On Patterns

BASIN AND RANGE NATIONAL MONUMENT, NEVADA

A fter viewing one of the largest sculptures in the world, Nevada senator Harry Reid felt compelled to ensure that others could see it too. In the early 2000s, he introduced bills to Congress to protect Garden Valley, where the sculpture was located. When those bills went nowhere, he personally appealed to President Obama, citing the unusual earthwork as one reason to create a national monument in the Great Basin. The *Washington Post* reported their conversation:

"Explain it to me," Obama said, referring to the artwork.

"I can't." Reid replied.

IN THE DESERT OF SOUTHEASTERN NEVADA, surrounded by a sea of sagebrush, there is a life-size work of art that mimics a city. Concrete curbs swoop in graceful curves toward negative space pits balanced by positive space structures. All clean lines and geometric shapes, triangular constructions rise from the ground like buildings. They could be temples; they could be apartments.

BASIN AND RANGE
NATIONAL MONUMENT

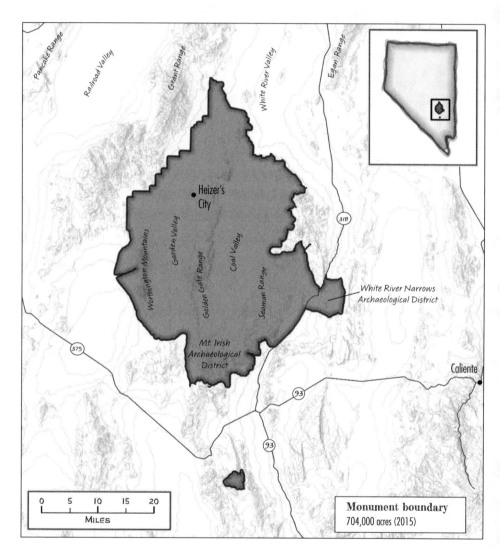

Pancake Range

Railroad Valley

Grant Range

White River Valley

Egan Range

Heizer's City

Worthington Mountains

Garden Valley

Golden Gate Range

Coal Valley

Seaman Range

318

White River Narrows
Archaeological District

375

Mt. Irish
Archaeological
District

93

93

Caliente

| 0 | 5 | 10 | 15 | 20 |
MILES

Monument boundary
704,000 acres (2015)

In 1972, the artist Michael Heizer bought a ranch in isolated Garden Valley and used bulldozers to begin construction on a large-scale sculpture he calls *City*. Heizer is known for his earth art, such as *Double Negative*, a fifteen-hundred-foot trench dug into sandstone in Moapa Valley, Nevada. For *City*, he used rock and dirt from the desert to construct a 1.25-mile-long compound that can be viewed up close as well as from afar, an environment that fuses ancient and modern, natural and man-made forms. You can immerse yourself in this artwork: walk through it, crunching sand and pebbles beneath your feet while unfiltered sun causes sweat to bead on your forehead and distant mountains form a craggy frame against a blue-sky backdrop.

In a profile in *ARTnews* in 1977, Heizer is quoted as saying about his work: "You don't have to relate to it. It's not a requirement. All you have to do is just be there. . . . You've got to understand that a lot of my thinking is based on preliterate societies. . . . So, when you talk about relating to my work . . . well, how do you relate to Maya or Egyptian pyramids?"

ROUGHLY THIRTY MILES FROM *CITY*, Veronica and I arrive in Basin and Range National Monument at night. We set up camp in the dark to the melodic hoots of an owl. A medley of birdsong wakes us when the early morning light is warm and new and casts a golden glow on the valley.

Basin and Range National Monument is named after the rhythmic topography of the region stretching between the Sierra Nevada and the Rocky Mountains. Parallel mountain ranges are separated by valleys ten to fifteen miles wide. Basin. Range. Basin. Range. Basin. Range. When I attended art school, one of my first assignments was a line interval project. Using only black-and-white cut paper, I explored alternating line widths. What happened if I paired wide lines with wispy ones? Sharp, emotional contrast. What cadence is created if the lines are the same width? Steady constancy. What emotion is evoked if the lines get fatter in one direction and finer in the other? Dynamic, uplifting movement. The Basin and Range Province stretches across the West in a natural interval study, rising and falling in an elemental pattern.

John McPhee describes the formation of Great Basin topography in his book *Basin and Range*: "Most mountain ranges around the world are the result of compression, of segments of the earth's crust being brought together, bent, mashed, thrust and folded, squeezed up into the sky. . . . The ranges of the Basin and Range came up another way. The crust . . . is spreading out, being stretched, being thinned, being literally pulled to pieces."

On this stretched and folded landscape, cattle forage amid sagebrush, nuclear bombs were dropped, ATVs share trails with hikers, and endangered sage grouse live alongside wild horses. "Perhaps more than any other region within the United States, and because it has often been seen as an empty wasteland, the Great Basin is a perceptive hole in the nation's mental map," writes public lands historian Leisl Carr Childers. This perceived wasteland status and the multiple-use land management philosophy that grew in the absence of agriculture or development have resulted in the Great Basin being "a landscape filled with activities that are not always compatible." According to Carr Childers, "multiple-use broadly permitted grazing, nuclear testing, wildlife and wild horses, and a host of outdoor recreational activities."

As land users of a recreational type, Veronica and I drive through a narrow sandstone canyon formed by the White River during the last ice age. The sun crests the canyon walls, and the road ends in a grassy meadow surrounded by an amphitheater of penny-colored cliffs. Pale lines are etched into dark varnish: human figures, animal figures, squiggles, and circles. The carvings overlap and intertwine, some faded with varnish beginning to regrow over them, some fresh and sharp. Very little of the wall's surface is untouched.

We climb out of the car to get a better view, and Veronica pulls out her camera. Her shutter clicks. "This is a weird thing I am doing," she says, "making art out of someone else's work." She shifts her angle to get better light on the rough rock.

Some drawings on the rock are nothing more than long, horizontal rows of tidy vertical stripes. Archaeologists speculate that these hatch marks could depict a hunting strategy. Or they could be a calendar, an old way of marking time that somehow still feels familiar.

In his book *The Rocks Begin to Speak*, LaVan Martineau examines petroglyphs, what he calls rock writing, with a cryptographer's eye. He has developed the start of a system to interpret rock writing and has deciphered many pictorial symbols. Martineau cites examples where petroglyphs point to water sources or give directions to hidden locations. He is adamant that rock writing was intended to communicate and was not merely decorative. According to Martineau, "The existence of such a writing system among Indians offers a solution to the mystery, so long ignored, of why tribes had their own words for *reading* and *writing*. Such words were not borrowed from English or Spanish. . . . They are retained from a recent time when the Indians practiced their own form of picture writing."

The White River Narrows was a travel corridor for people as far back as four thousand years ago. Hunter-gatherers moved seasonally across the landscape in small family groups and left marks on the stone to communicate with one another. Most of the rock writing here is in the appropriately named Basin and Range style from that time period, which is characterized by abstract shapes that combine to form complex images, depictions of stick-figure humans, and a pecked process, rather than scraped or carved. Also found along these walls is rock writing in the Fremont style, distinguished by stylized human figures. These were drawn on the same stone by farming communities that lived here two thousand years after the wandering hunter-gatherers.

Then there is a smattering of graffiti carved over the weathered drawings. RICKY '76 and STEVE 1977, bold and white, obscure a human form with wide shoulders and skinny, dangling arms. Long after the Fremont people lived here, this canyon served as unpaved State Route 38, now Nevada 318, directing Euro-Americans through the same travel corridor as the ancients. Just as conflicting uses occur in the same landscape, drawings intermingle on the same stone, and travel overlaps at the same location on different planes of time.

MICHAEL HEIZER is part of a land art movement that began in the 1960s. Growing from a postminimalist atmosphere at the same time as the environmental movement, land art became a way for artists to explore the human relationship to landscape, and they did it on a large scale. Along with Heizer's *Double Negative*, some of the most famous land artworks were *Spiral Jetty* by Robert Smithson, a huge basalt spiral that extends into the Great Salt Lake, and *Sun Tunnels* by Nancy Holt, a grouping of cement tunnels arranged in the Utah desert to align with the sun on the solstices.

One of the key elements of land art is framing. Seeing the world through Holt's tunnels, viewers focus more intently on the silhouette of the surrounding mountains, notice how the sun and the stars move, and recognize how this setting influences humans. Heizer's *City* attempts to do something similar: as your eyes move from built shape to natural ground, from the surrounding hills to fabricated form, the artwork forces you to notice the landscape, and the landscape points you back to the sculpture. It makes the viewer see what is there.

People have been making land art since they have been on Earth. There are several ancient, large-scale earthworks, like Serpent Mound near my hometown of Cincinnati, Ohio. Built by either the Adena culture around 320 BCE or the Fort Ancient culture around 1070 CE (it is debated which one), this effigy mound is three feet high and more than thirteen hundred feet long. It spirals in the shape of a snake with a mouth opening around an egg, but this shape is visible only from the sky. The mound does not include any burials or artifacts, so is believed to have been built for aesthetic reasons rather than to house something. I have memories of rolling around on nearby soft grassy hills as a child, enjoying the earthen folds, oblivious to the larger image.

Now, in Nevada's pebbled, rippled desert, I am seeing land art as a way of expressing an intense, personal relationship to land. And just like human relationships, this bond takes many different forms.

In 2017, artists Kade Twist, Raven Chacon, and Cristóbal Martinez created a land artwork along the U.S.–Mexican border called *Repellent Fence*. Unlike Heizer's signature style of transforming a landscape, their work was ephemeral, part of a new wave of land art that seeks to complement the land rather than permanently alter it. Their piece consisted of a series of massive balloons installed in a line that bisected the border to "symbolically demonstrate the interconnectedness of the Western Hemisphere by recognizing the land, Indigenous peoples, history, relationships, movement, and communication." Partly because their work was temporary, they filmed a documentary, *Through the Repellent Fence*. In the film, Chacon says, "Humans of the past, when they made land art works, it was to celebrate the land they lived on or that they were from. Or they tried to harmonize themselves with that land. I think what those guys in the sixties, Robert Smithson and Michael Heizer, tried to do was destroy the land. . . . They just continued the destruction of the earth and continued to go and colonize different places they felt were theirs."

Chacon is wise in his criticism. To make *Double Negative*, sandstone that took millions of years of heat and pressure to form was dredged and crumbled and crushed to form a fake canyon. Heizer bulldozed and blasted his way into the rock to make a statement. This doesn't seem any different than the sculpted pink walls of the pit mine in Castle Mountains. Chacon is also correct that this previous generation of land artists viewed these places as theirs: Heizer purchased the land on which he is building *City*. And since he is notoriously secretive, very few people have been allowed to view his work. It is something he believes he owns.

IN THE 1970S, when Heizer began work on *City*, it was becoming apparent that the country needed a place to store radioactive waste. The Hanford Site in Washington had tons of radioactive waste left over from plutonium production and nuclear power plants across the nation were storing waste at their individual facilities. The threat of leaks and contamination was worrying. In the nuclear industry, it is generally agreed that radioactive waste should be entombed underground until radioactivity naturally declines over time. After a sharp drop in radioactivity over the first fifty years, it can then take tens of thousands of years to become completely safe.

The U.S. Department of Energy began studying several sites across the country as possible storage facilities to collect and contain all of the country's nuclear refuse. Yucca Mountain in southwestern Nevada, surrounded by miles of sandy desert punctuated with spiny yucca and cactus, was proposed as a repository. Yucca Mountain lies just outside the small town of Beatty, in the transition zone between the Mojave Desert and the Great Basin Desert. It is also situated adjacent to the Nevada Test Site, where nuclear weapons were tested from the 1950s through the 1990s, meaning this landscape had been labeled as empty for years. "Landscapes once seen as isolated wastelands became optimum sites for scientific inquiry into the greatest of new weapons technologies," wrote Ryan Edgington in *Range Wars*. "They include the Nevada Test Site and the Yucca Mountain Nuclear Waste site in Nevada, the Hanford plutonium production site in Washington, and the Trinity Site and the Waste Isolation Pilot Plant in New Mexico."

Yucca Mountain is about 160 miles south of Basin and Range National Monument and only a three-hour drive to the urban center of Las Vegas. After decades of studying the site for suitability, Congress voted to approve the Yucca Mountain Nuclear Waste Repository in 2002.

One of the perplexing problems of a nuclear waste storage facility is how to communicate the danger of what is stored there to people of the future. Language decays, changes, and evolves. In ten thousand years, the version of English that we speak today may be as unintelligible as old English is to us now, and may not even be the language of this future society. The oldest petroglyphs in the Basin and Range area are thought to be from 8,000 to 10,000 years ago, with most of them dated around 4,000 years old. A few were drawn as recently as 850 years ago. Even the meaning of these newer illustrations has been mostly lost.

LaVan Martineau has dedicated his life's work to understanding and interpreting rock writing, and he is only partway there. "It will take lifetimes and the dedication of more than just one man to exhume the body of evidence and recall the spirit of a great vanished people as manifested in their writings," he wrote. For the most part,

Petroglyphs at Mt. Irish Archaeological District, Basin and Range National Monument, Nevada. Photograph by Veronica Palmer.

we can only speculate what the artists and authors were trying to express as they chiseled images into varnished stone. If we have already lost the context for forms of communication that have been in existence far longer than other written forms, how can we expect a warning about the dangers of radioactivity to be read and correctly interpreted ten thousand years from now?

In the 1990s, an "Expert Judgment Panel" composed of linguists, anthropologists, archaeologists, material scientists, cognitive psychologists, and futurists was formed to address the construction of a communication marker for the country's proposed nuclear waste storage facilities. The panel divided into teams, wrote a standard statement, debated where and in what material this message should

BASIN AND RANGE

be constructed, and brainstormed ways of communicating a basic warning message. One suggestion was to exhibit a chart of the stars when the repository was closed and a second chart showing what the stars would look like ten thousand years in the future, when it would be safe to open.

In 2002, after Congress voted its approval of the repository site, Joshua Abbey of Desert Space Foundation launched a design competition to conceive of a warning marker for Yucca Mountain that considered these long-range communication problems. The entries included mostly land art solutions, such as a plan for creating intensified heat and disturbing low-frequency sound waves to keep people away through physical discomfort; *The Great Lie*, an image of the mountain dated November 25, 22001, smoking and smoldering from internal nuclear combustion; and the Best in Show entry, *Blue Yucca Ridge*, which depicts the surrounding yucca plants with their bladed leaves radiating an eerie, nuclear blue.

VERONICA AND I SCRAMBLE among cinnamon-colored volcanic tuff boulders and twisted juniper trees at Shaman Knob and discover drawings hidden in piles of rock. Turning a bend, we face a large, round figure that dominates a rock panel at eye level. The pale, pecked form has skinny arms that end in three claws. Pahranagat man: a style found only in the Pahranagat Valley, which depicts humans with solid oval or rectangular bodies, often with big blanks for eyes. We walk farther through the sand, and the boulders open in a gallery around a tall copper rock accented with lime-green lichens. Dancing across the panel is a herd of bighorn sheep.

I imagine how it happened. Someone picked up a tool, swinging one precise stroke at a time, painstakingly hammering out these drawings, forming figures from their mind's eye. Were they trying to convey an important message, or were they trying to capture a

249

feeling? Was it a duty they had to perform, or was it a way to pass time? Did they know that humans thousands of years in the future would see their etchings and wonder about them?

Land art and the nuclear waste storage problem raise interesting questions about time. As the submissions in the Desert Space Foundation's contest suggested, land art is perhaps the most effective method for communicating far into the future. If petroglyphs and effigy mounds have survived for thousands of years, it is possible that today's land art will be around equally as long. We can only wonder what *Double Negative* and *City* will mean to humans who view them in ten thousand years, and what these works will say about the people of today.

The fact that we have produced something as dangerous as nuclear waste to begin with raises a slightly different time consideration: what is our responsibility to future humans? In the early 1990s, environmental activist and writer Joanna Macy spearheaded a Nuclear Guardianship movement. After events like the Chernobyl nuclear reactor meltdown in Ukraine, the increasingly apparent negative health effects from nuclear weapons testing, and faulty storage of radioactive materials in the United States, we were only beginning to grapple with nuclear problems. Macy's idea was to establish human guardians of waste sites who would perpetuate the knowledge of what was stored there into the future. In her vision, this task took on a spiritual significance, like monks with a mission for humanity. Part of this work was reimagining society's relationship to time.

"We in western industrialized culture have a very unusual, unprecedented, and idiosyncratic experience of time," Macy said in an interview in 1991 with Alan AtKisson from the Context Institute. "We are increasingly cut off from the past and the future in a shrinking box—in which we race like a squirrel in a cage, at increasingly frenetic speeds. . . . We've done this as a nation because we ran out of frontier—we canceled the future so that we could keep on using up the Earth as though it were limitless."

I am struck by how Macy's depiction of relationship to time is entwined with relationship to land. On the surface, these two concepts seem separate, but the more one thinks about time and place, the more they are united. You can't be in a place without being in a moment of time, and vice versa. Our perceptions of the future and time must be related to our perceptions of place. The Nuclear Guardianship project included a bill of rights for citizens of the future. Article I of this bill reads: "Future generations have a right to an uncontaminated and undamaged Earth and to its enjoyment as the ground of human history, of culture, and of social bonds that make each generation and individual a member of one human family."

If future generations have a right to an uncontaminated and undamaged Earth, then in addition to properly dealing with nuclear waste, we need to place much more emphasis on protecting land, combatting climate change, and caring for the one human family to ensure that this is so. Macy's understanding of the impact nuclear waste has on the physical world and on humans now and far into the future is not unlike Timothy Morton's classification of nuclear waste as a hyperobject. Now that we recognize the scale of the problem and the way that place and time are linked, something must be done. Monuments like Basin and Range, where place, time, and people converge in sharp relief, are the beginning of a solution.

A MORE IMMEDIATE PROBLEM with the Yucca Mountain repository site than erecting a communication marker was establishing how to transport nuclear waste to the facility. If waste was going to be brought there from places like the Hanford Site, dangerous radioactive material would need to be shipped across the country.

251

Semitrucks full of the stuff would traverse highways and sit in traffic jams in populated cities. The agreed-on transportation route collected the waste in the remote Nevada town of Caliente, and from there a railroad would wind through Garden Valley to cart it to Yucca Mountain.

The proposed railroad would shuttle trains of nuclear waste directly past *City*. Heizer had already been working on his earthwork for nearly thirty years when the transportation plan was developed, but it was obvious to him that the natural resonance of his work would be voided when loads of hazardous materials rattled past. He told his neighbors that he would use bulldozers to bury his masterpiece if the railroad was built.

That was when Harry Reid got involved. In early 2015, five art museums, including the Museum of Modern Art and the Nevada Museum of Art, joined Reid's campaign to protect *City* from a contaminated fate. Although approved by Congress years before, Yucca Mountain was still being evaluated, and construction of the storage facility had not yet started. Not long after the museums began petitioning to protect the artwork, and likely in part due to Reid's urging, President Obama established Basin and Range National Monument in July 2015. The boundaries surround Heizer's private ranch and *City*. Now protected land blocks the path of the nuclear waste railroad. Robert Halstead, the director of the state Agency for Nuclear Projects, called the monument "the final nail in the coffin" for the Yucca Mountain plan.

Contrary to the original and false national park concept of untrammeled wilderness unaffected by humans, this protected place is notable *because* of human effects on the land. Now the marks of both Heizer and those of ancient inhabitants reverberate throughout time with new meanings and significance.

Yucca Mountain, that poor volcanic rock now riddled with test tunnels, is still being examined for suitability for radioactive waste storage more than twenty-five years later. Politicians around the country agree on the project on mostly bipartisan lines, with the exception of Nevada politicians, who vehemently oppose it. The Obama administration ignored the project, though technically the 2002 law that approves the repository is still in place. Some people viewed Basin and Range National Monument as Obama's way of killing the idea. Several officials within the Trump administration hoped to reinvigorate the project, but President Trump never supported establishing the repository. It languishes in uncertainty. Nuclear waste still sits aboveground around the country in more than a dozen locations.

Forty-plus years and approximately $17 million later, *City* is still under construction. It is unknown if or when it will ever be open to the public. Heizer purposely used nonvaluable materials to prevent looting and to root the structure into the landscape. It is art that will last, perhaps like petroglyphs. It is made from sand and stone, without pigments that will fade or a surface that can wrinkle and crack, at once a product of and a part of the ancient desert.

As humans, it is impossible for us not to shape and transform and interpret the world around us. Every act is a demonstration of our relationship to land. We build cities composed of roads and buildings, sidewalks and gardens, murals and trash heaps. We dig mines, we farm grassland, we build bombs, we pollute rivers, we reserve parks to be free from development. Each of these places defines our culture. Heizer mimicked this human compulsion, leaving behind his own modification of the world around him, an expression perhaps more about dominance than harmony. Ancient societies chiseled drawings into rock possibly to convey messages, to create familiarity, to illustrate their view of the world, or perhaps to claim the place as theirs in a small way. Now we have a national monument, which marks the land with an invisible boundary, designates it as something unique, and influences what will happen at this place next, hopefully in a way that invokes celebration despite a past of displacement.

Article 2 of the Nuclear Guardianship Bill of Rights reads: "Each generation, sharing in the estate and heritage of the Earth, has a duty as trustee for future generations to prevent irreversible and irreparable harm to life on Earth and to human freedom and dignity." Protecting a place with a political stamp does in many ways consider our collective responsibility to humans of the future. Reserving part of this planet instead of using up every last resource is an act of guardianship.

Indigenous and aboriginal cultures often have very different understandings of land and time than industrialized Western cultures. Joanna Macy hinted at limited Western views, where land is a resource to be consumed and time is linear, both subject to the forward march of progress. Non-Western cultures often see land as sacred and time as cyclical, where all events and beings are related to one another and many truths exist at once. Cameron Martinez from Taos Pueblo insinuated that in the *Tiwa* language, names for things change at different times of the year. The way things change in time is built into his culture's understanding. Like the pecked and carved lines that overlap on a single stone, people, relationships, stories, and truths overlay and exist in tandem. There is no separation from the humans of the past, the places of the future, and the humans of today. All truths are relevant. Therefore, the responsibility to each is the same.

VERONICA AND I DRINK steaming mugs of tea and coffee as the sun paints the monochrome desert in fresh color. Across the valley I see three mountain ranges separated by more valleys. Pahranagat Valley, Hiko Range, Sixmile Flat, South Pahroc Range, Dry Lake Valley,

Burnt Springs Range. Though the movement of the earth is slowly pulling them apart, to my eye the ranges flatten onto one another, looking like three shades of cut-paper silhouettes pasted onto a pastel sky. The sun washes the rosy mountain skylines whiter.

An Arab proverb says, "Man fears time, but time fears the pyramids." Though humans cannot live for eternity, there are things, like mountains, but also man-made things, that survive long beyond our lifetimes. Almost as if time does not matter. As if all things separate and collide in time.

13. On Possession

GOLD BUTTE NATIONAL MONUMENT, NEVADA

If you take I-15 east from Las Vegas and leave blinking lights and clinking casinos behind, the scenery dissolves into the middle of nowhere fast. This is how you get to Gold Butte National Monument. Exit the highway, turn onto a dirt road, and you will pass the Bundy ranch. This ranch belongs to the same Bundy family who had an armed standoff with the federal government over twenty years of unpaid grazing fees in 2014 and who occupied the Malheur National Wildlife Refuge in Oregon for forty-one days just two years later. I have heard that Cliven Bundy grows delicious melons.

I drove slowly past and rubbernecked at irrigation-green grass, fences, and a squat house. After the ranch, a twenty-mile gravel road leads to Gold Butte, marked by a sign that warns HIGH-CLEARANCE, 4-WHEEL-DRIVE VEHICLES REQUIRED. Alone, I braked and considered my low-clearance, two-wheel-drive hatchback. At least I had a full six-gallon jug of water in the back seat. That should last me a few days no matter what happened. I kept driving.

For more than an hour, I crept down the deserted dirt road,

GOLD BUTTE
NATIONAL MONUMENT

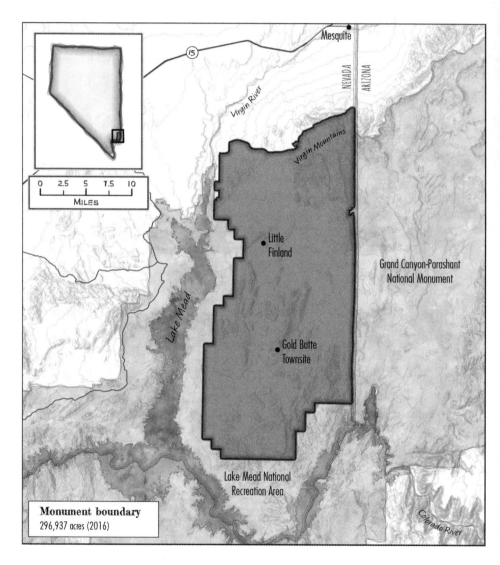

15

Mesquite

NEVADA

ARIZONA

Virgin River

Virgin Mountains

0   2.5   5   7.5   10
MILES

Little
Finland

Gold Butte
Townsite

Lake Mead

Grand Canyon-Parashant
National Monument

Lake Mead National
Recreation Area

Colorado River

Monument boundary
296,937 acres (2016)

grateful that no boulders or deep holes blocked my way. There was no cell phone service. Creosote grew for as far as I could see. Ridgelines scalloped the skyline. The landscape was a creamy beige and tan with flecks of gold, distinct from the electric red of Utah, the deep pine green of Oregon, the silvery sage of eastern Washington, and the rainbow of Hawaii.

The Gold Butte region of Nevada, a rectangle sandwiched between the Lake Mead reservoir and the Arizona border, was proposed as a national conservation area in 2008 and 2015 but was never signed into law. Obama stepped in and declared it a 296,937-acre national monument during the waning days of his presidency. The proclamation cites "vital plant and wildlife habitat, significant geological formations, rare fossils, important sites from the history of Native Americans, and remnants of our Western mining and ranching heritage" as the resources to be protected. Of course, this designation had critics. Cliven Bundy said that a national monument reduced his family's ability to make a living off the land, land that he considers his and not the federal government's. He claimed that since he is descended from Mormon settlers, his family has an ancestral right to this ground.

But others have ancestral rights that extend much further back. The land of Gold Butte is known as *Mah'ha gah doo*, or "land of many bushes," and is the homeland of the Paiute, or *Nuwu* people. Before the Nuwu, the nomadic Tudinu roamed this desert.

"Songs were one of the primary means through which ownership of land and resources were recognized," said Shanandoah Anderson, a Southern Paiute and daughter of author LaVan Martineau. "The men who owned the song owned the territory to which it was associated. When one approached a stranger in their land they would ask, 'What song do you come from?' The stranger would then have to sing the song from which his bloodline came to show which land

259

he belonged to. [Songs] were oral maps of the territory. If you knew the songs, you knew which area it was talking about."

I navigated with maps and GPS and followed a dirt road built by others. I imagined navigating by songs that told of Joshua trees, golden boulders, and hidden washes.

In the 2017 national monument review, Interior Secretary Ryan Zinke suggested that Gold Butte's proclamation be amended to protect grazing and historic water rights, but nothing was changed. The Bundy family used to legally graze cattle on land that became the national monument. When Bundy's permit was revoked due to unpaid grazing fees, he never applied for a new one but continued grazing his cattle in the desert anyway. Existing leases and rights are usually left in place when new national monuments are established. In this case, no grazing leases were active at the time of Gold Butte's proclamation, so no grazing is allowed within the monument. Even if Bundy wanted to reapply for a permit, he cannot.

After the standoff at his ranch and the Malheur occupation, Cliven Bundy sued the federal government to declare that all federal land in Nevada, in particular Gold Butte National Monument, belongs to the state. "Bundy Insists U.S. Government Can't Own Land—No Matter Who's President," read a 2018 *Salt Lake Tribune* headline. Bundy backed up this claim with Article 1, Section 8, Clause 17, of the Constitution, known as the Enclave Clause. This clause authorizes Congress

To exercise exclusive Legislation in all Cases whatsoever, over such District (not exceeding ten Miles square) as may, by Cession of particular states and the Acceptance of Congress, become the Seat of the Government of the United States, and to exercise like Authority over all Places purchased by the Consent of the Legislature of the State in which the

Same shall be, for the Erection of Forts, Magazines, Arsenals, dock-Yards, and other needful Buildings.

Bundy zeroed in on the "not exceeding ten Miles square" phrase, but this clause refers to the nation's formation of a physical capital, not its ability to own land overall. Bundy's interpretation ignores numerous other laws, Supreme Court cases, and decisions by Congress that absolutely ensure the federal government can own land. "Cliven Bundy's Public Lands Claim Is 'Simply Delusional,' Judge Rules," read *The Oregonian* after his case was dismissed.

In the United States, federal land that is considered accessible to the public is administered by the Bureau of Land Management, the U.S. Forest Service, the U.S. Fish and Wildlife Service, the National Oceanic and Atmospheric Administration, and the National Park Service. All citizens can access and use this land. But to many in a society that exalts private property rights and personal liberties, the concept of a shared space runs contrary to the American culture of individualism. Bundy feels that it is his distinct right to do what he wishes on land near his home; he does not want to share. He certainly must love this amber desert that he has lived in his entire life, even if he is unwilling to acknowledge others' rights to it.

I TURNED ON A SIDE ROAD and found a comfortable dirt patch behind a boulder to set up my tent. The dropping sun electrified the stone. Boulders blazed fluorescent pink and neon orange and then, as if a switch was flipped, paled as the sun eased below the horizon. As darkness settled in, the glow of distant Las Vegas rose.

The next morning I woke after a deep, silent sleep and hiked down Mud Wash Road to an area with unique rock formations called Little Finland. I passed a dilapidated wooden corral and bright-crimson hills that erupted from yellow sand. I navigated over a red rock ramp to climb onto the sandstone band with whimsical rock sculptures and wandered through them like a kid in a playhouse. Wind and weather had shaped rosy rock into swooping modern art. Flat plates of stone balanced improbably on curving, crumbling towers. Rippled rock stretched outward like flames frozen in time. Hallways opened through mazes of waving solid sand.

I was at once alone in the wild and reminded of people and civilization. The overhead roar of planes going to and from Las Vegas was constant. Across a deep gully a parked truck waited near a yapping dog and a buzzing four-wheeler.

I climbed into an alcove, wriggled through a small tunnel onto a second-story platform, and wondered what living in America would be like without public land. This land gave me a great sense of personal freedom: I can explore out here completely by myself and feel safe in my solitude. Only a couple hours from crowded Vegas, I am free to wander in the desert without a building for miles. Just knowing that I could be here in this strange and wonderful place gave me a sense of possibility and adventure. Without this, cities would feel like cages.

IN 2019, Secretary of the Interior David Bernhardt appointed a man as acting director of the Bureau of Land Management who, like the Bundy family, does not believe the federal government can or should own land. It was like electing an atheist as the pope.

"The Founding Fathers intended all lands owned by the federal government to be sold. . . . as James Madison put it, the new government would 'promote the sale of the public lands,'" wrote William Perry Pendley in the *National Review* in January 2016, three years prior to his federal appointment. It is difficult to fathom how

Pendley, with these views, could manage the 244 million acres of federally owned BLM land in United States.

In the same article, Pendley disparaged the environmental movement and its effect on public land in the West:

> Beginning with the National Environmental Policy Act (1969) and continuing through a plethora of other federal laws, Congress dramatically enhanced the power of the "public" to intervene in land-use decision making. For decades the only people interested in such parochial issues as grazing on barren expanses of western land were affected westerners. Now scores of environmental groups that are not affected by federal decisions but are interested anyway have stepped forward as the hyperengaged public. (There is a difference. As we say out west, a chicken is interested in what you have for breakfast, but a pig is affected.)

According to Pendley, it seems that only people who graze livestock are affected by public land—no one else should care. This sentiment ignores people indigenous to western lands, who are more affected than ranchers. It also ignores people who want to visit western places and recreate on land that they do not consider "barren expanses," and ignores the plants and animals who depend on that land for survival. Pendley, like Bundy, clings to a vision of public land that is notably exclusionary.

The federal government first came to own land not long after the United States was formed. Europeans settled and colonized parts of what became the United States, and seized land from Indigenous groups through conquest and treaties. In 1781 the colony of New York agreed to surrender its claim to "unsettled" lands west of the Mississippi, giving them to the federal government. Other colonies followed suit until all land between the Appalachian Mountains and the Mississippi River was considered public domain by the young government. Throughout the nineteenth century, land temporarily controlled by Spain, France, England, Russia, Mexico, Hawaii, and Canada was claimed through war, treaty, and purchase for the new nation of the United States. To encourage settlement, the government gave away much of this territory to citizens for homesteads, ranches, farms, mines, railroads, cities, and schools. Land was also granted to individual states when they joined the union. This process of giving or selling land to individuals and states was referred to as "disposal."

As the seemingly endless, abundant West was divided and fenced, there became a clear need for some publicly shared space. Largely due to the work of early environmentalists like John Muir, national parks, monuments, and forests were "reserved" instead of "disposed." This again resulted in Indigenous groups removal. When Yellowstone became the first national park, twenty-six tribes that lived in, traveled through, or considered that land sacred were forced out of the region so the new park could embody an illusion of an uninhabited wilderness. Though celebrated today, public land in America began as stolen and exclusionary.

ON ANOTHER TRIP states away in Idaho, I visited a friend in a small town called Island Park. Island Park is a gateway community to Yellowstone National Park and sits near the borders between Idaho, Wyoming, and Montana. Island Park's national forest land has unsuccessfully been proposed for national monument status several times. The same tensions and debates about land use exist here as in Gold Butte or Bears Ears before their monument proclamations went into effect.

As I wound my way through a rural, conservative part of Idaho on highways lined with lodgepole pine and spruce, I passed over a

GOLD BUTTE

bridge where three old men tossed bread to gulls hovering over a river. A wooden sign in a small parking area read "Warm River." I U-turned and parked.

I hadn't even closed my car door when one of the men called over, "Hey, do you want some bread?" He grinned and held out half a loaf. I don't think that feeding white bread to wildlife is particularly healthy for animals, but the man was filled with such joy and welcoming cheer that I couldn't refuse. I accepted the bread and joined them, leaning on the bridge's splintery railing. They tossed chunks into the center of the shallow river where gulls swooped. A family of fluffy baby ducks floated just downstream of me, so I dropped tiny crumbs below my feet and let the current carry the bread to them.

"So where are you from?" the man who handed me the bread asked. I looked up and noticed that two of my three companions were sporting faded, well-worn "Make America Great Again" hats.

"Mammoth Lakes, California," I said, expecting a cringe. The MAGA guys both smiled and mentioned they had family in California. We went back to tossing bread.

"Do you see them out there?" The man next to me pointed to the center of the river where they had been aiming their throws. Under the sun-speckled water hovered several rainbow trout, about two feet long. They floated motionless in the current, as if water were not rushing around them. I thought the men had been feeding gulls, but they were feeding fish. I changed the trajectory of my tosses and watched the fish swallow the breadcrumbs in big, hungry gulps. We stood there in companionable silence, admiring the sun on the water and the waiting fish.

I was offered another loaf, and I tossed more white bread into brown ripples, feeling warm about how eager these men were to share the fish with me. Then I thought, if my skin were any other shade, if I wore a hijab, if I spoke with an accent, or if I had an

265

androgynous look, would I have been as welcome? It is possible that these men would have invited anyone to join them, but many people would not feel safe because of the political statement made by their hats. Public land, though intended for everyone, has mostly bene-fited and been accessed by the dominant white culture, leaving oth-ers to feel excluded, even unsafe. If protecting and conserving land are justice for Earth itself, ensuring that all people feel welcome to access these places is justice for Earth's inhabitants.

GOLD BUTTE AND ISLAND PARK inhabit opposite quadrants on the landscape color wheel; they are complementary. Each night in Gold Butte, the cream-colored stone blended into zinging magenta as the sun slid below the horizon. Brown and tan peaks radiated rose gold in alpenglow. Though the landscape is dry and sandy, the stone and earth resonated with warm fuchsia tones. Island Park, on the other hand, is dark evergreen needles and sun spots bouncing in rivers, shaggy brown moose, and bright greenery growing on the edges of springs.

Morning light pinged off the Island Park Reservoir as I walked into the nearly empty Lakeside Lodge to meet a man named Ken Watts for breakfast. Ken runs the Island Park Preservation Coali-tion, an organization against the proposed Caldera National Mon-ument. The group was so successful at preventing a monument designation here that they advised anti–Bears Ears groups. With a tanned and lined face and snow-white hair, Ken was already seated and drinking coffee when I arrived. A manila folder with my name Sharpied on the front rested on the checkered tablecloth near his elbow. "You look just like your picture," Ken said with a sly smile, as he lifted the cover of the folder to reveal a printed photograph of me pulled from the internet.

I decided not to interpret this as intimidation and ordered eggs and toast and asked him where the monument idea started. He went back to 2012. It began with money from a sustainability grant from the Department of Housing and Urban Development. Part of that project involved evaluating water quality in the Island Park region, which is the Henry's Fork watershed. When the project was over, there was money left, and it was decided that it should be used to assess whether the region should be considered for a national monument designation. At this point, Ken described a convoluted series of secret meetings, lies, and environmental organizations from outside the area trying to make changes here, in his town.

Ken responded by forming the avidly anti-monument Island Park Preservation Coalition, which champions keeping the area as it is. "Our first meeting was in a barn," he told me. "It stunk in there. I thought it was a conservationist, but they told me it was just a skunk."

His coalition arranged to have a measure put on the county ballot that read "Do you favor or oppose a national monument in any part of Fremont County?" Ninety-three percent of the county voted no, in part because of the Preservation Coalition's outreach efforts. From his folder he plucked a leftover promotional postcard. Black-and-white type screamed:

ISLAND PARK NATIONAL MONUMENT GOVERNMENT JURISDICTION:

NO ACCESS	NO HUNTING
NO FISHING	NO RECREATION
NO GRAZING	NO SNOWMOBILING
NO WATER	NO OFF-ROAD VEHICLES

Protect your rights! Vote to oppose a national monument
on the Fremont County ballot in November.

No water? This is not an accurate depiction of what a national monument would change about an area. It is true that new monu-

Sunset near the Falling Man Petroglyph Site, Gold Butte National Monument, Nevada. Photograph by the author.

ments can come with restrictions such as a ban on building new roads and limits to off-road vehicle access; however, most monuments preserve existing rights, meaning if grazing is allowed in an area, it will continue. The same goes for off-road vehicles and recreation. Typically, monuments continue to allow use and access but attempt to manage uses in a responsible way that also takes the health of the land into consideration. To me, this flyer seemed like hyperbole.

But hyperbole is not restricted to one side. I messaged the Caldera National Monument Idaho Advocacy group on Facebook to

GOLD BUTTE

ask if the monument idea was dead or just on hold. Like Ken's flyer, the answers I got were long on passion and short on facts. "Many are interested and the idea is far from dead. The problem has been Fremont County locals, many of which are anti-wildlife and anti-government Bundy supporters. . . . Many are very ignorant and believe government conspiracies are at play. The monument may be designated in spite of them, however." I couldn't help but think that they were referring to Ken Watts, who did have some ideas that bordered on government conspiracy, though I would not describe him as ignorant or anti-wildlife.

I asked why the advocacy group wanted a monument in Island Park, and the response was almost indignant: "The area is being destroyed by development, by ATVs, and by ignorance. To anyone who's been around for the past several decades, it's obvious. The wildlife is disappearing."

In Ken's view, the Caldera advocacy group wanted to establish this monument as a trophy, a way to say, *Look, Idaho did this great thing.* And they wanted it in time for the National Park Service's centennial anniversary, which did not happen. "They are always going to try to expand Yellowstone this way. We are always going to be a target," he said. "When Trump got elected, that gave us a reprieve. A four-year window when we don't have to worry about this monument idea moving forward. I sure hope he gets reelected. If only that man would keep his tweets to himself."

Vocal monument opponents often repeat canned lines about monuments being federal overreach, which to me reveals a lack of deeper thought and understanding of the issues. Ken doesn't do this. Though he is quick to paint environmentalists as enemies, he is against a monument primarily because its designation would change all the rules. "I oppose a national monument because the process stinks," Ken said. "You don't know if a monument will be good or bad until after the management plan is created, which can take ten years. Why trust the government to create a plan that is in your best interest? Let me write the management plan and I'd love a monument."

Ken wants to keep Island Park the way it is. His coalition supports multiple use and believes that logging, grazing, and all forms of recreation, including motorized recreation, can be conducted in harmony. "The area is pristine and nice, what do we need to protect it from?" He noted that more and more people are coming to Island Park, and there are more transient rentals. He doesn't like the feel of that change. In his view, a monument would bring more tourists, more infrastructure to support them, and more regulation.

Keeping the area the same is also the motivation for monument advocates. They want to preserve the wilderness character, habitat for bears, moose, and elk, and clean water in Henry's Fork with protections that are stronger than the current Forest Service regulations.

In Gold Butte, opponents to the monument there expressed similar sentiments to Ken's. Nevada local Dustin Nelson has familial ties to the Gold Butte area that go back generations. He started the website savegoldbutte.com to advocate against monument status. In a post dated January 2017, Nelson wrote:

> By designating Gold Butte as a monument, it is intentionally prioritizing cultures and history by what today's values dictate while minimizing others. . . . The history of many of these cultures will slowly be erased and forgotten by the federal land managers as they focus their resources on making a monument based on a single narrative. . . . I agree that it is critical that we protect the Native American sites found within Gold Butte, but I also know it is critical to protect, with the same significance, the Pioneer Sites, the Mining Sites, the corrals, the water tanks, the springs, the access to the roads and the camping spots.

GOLD BUTTE

This view is reversed in its fear that white settler history will be erased in favor of Indigenous narratives, when historically white settler culture has led to the erasure of Indigenous people and their history, as well as that of other minorities.

Like Ken, Dustin doesn't want anything to change in this place that he loves. He was afraid that a monument would come with restrictions and reduced access. "I want to see public lands preserved for my children and grandchildren. A national monument designation is not the best path to ensure Gold Butte is preserved for my grandchildren," Nelson wrote.

I agree with Ken that the process of creating a monument management plan can be unfair, no matter which side you fall on. When the management plans for the reduced Bears Ears and Grand Staircase–Escalante National Monuments were written, the public did not have an effect on the outcome, though there was the pretense that they did. Thousands of public comments were submitted in support of those monuments, against the reduced borders, and against increased resource extraction on monument land, but final management plans were approved to confirm smaller borders and to invite mining and expanded grazing anyway.

The process does need to be reconsidered. Perhaps on larger yes-and-no issues, the number of comments for or against a monument or a change to one should be counted individually and tallied like a vote instead of all lumped into one comment. Maybe comments that illustrate a personal connection to place should be considered alongside the in-depth scientific arguments instead of being tossed aside.

Of course, it might not always be in the public's best interest to fully dictate policies. The knowledge base of the people working in government can often result in a better understanding of the best course of action for certain areas or issues. Managing agencies, when run correctly, are more likely to evaluate issues from the widely varied perspectives of different stakeholders, whereas members of the public are more likely to see things only through the lens of their personal interest. Without some oversight, recreation could destroy the very places that people love for their natural beauty. These agencies are often forced to compromise when opinions conflict. But since land and access to it are a personal issue as well as a governmental one, people who care about places should have more of a say than they do. Frustration about monuments and opposition to their designations often stem from people feeling powerless and hating the sense that they have no say in a place's future. If it were easier for the public to affect a monument's management plan, I wonder what Ken would advocate for then.

However, even with things as they are now, I don't agree that avoiding a monument designation is necessarily the way to keep Island Park or Gold Butte the same. Island Park is already changing. When I drove into town, a huge Marriott Hotel was under construction along the highway. Tourism here has been increasing for years as visitors to Yellowstone search for less crowded places to stay. In Gold Butte before the monument designation, vandalism had been on the rise. Pottery and arrowheads were being stolen, petroglyphs were being chipped away with bullet holes, and even mining history was being destroyed: the grave of miner Arthur Coleman was dug up and his remains stolen.

Arthur Coleman and William Garrett were two men enticed to Nevada's bright desert in the early 1900s by the promise of gold. They became close friends and lived together in the desert for forty years, prospecting, distilling whiskey, and welcoming travelers to their home. They were buried next to each other in Gold Butte. Dustin

Nelson gave the eulogy at the rededication of Coleman's grave site, though his remains were never found.

A monument could enhance protection for exactly the things that Ken and Dustin claim they want to preserve: wild open land and access for recreation. Their fear of change reminded me of how I began this journey: speaking with George Rice and Josh Ewing about Bears Ears. George opposed Bears Ears National Monument because he did not want to see changes to a place that he loved. Josh was pro-monument for the very same reason.

I would not lump Ken Watts into the same category as Cliven and Ammon Bundy, but his opposition to Caldera National Monument has a "locals only" mentality similar to their opposition to Gold Butte. Ken feels very strongly that environmental groups from outside Island Park should have no say in what happens in his town. I understand that local feeling of ownership. I even understand feeling annoyed when tourists flood your town, and yearning for the quiet and emptiness that comes when visitors leave. But the idea that no one else gets to share in a place doesn't feel right.

The fact that American public land is designed to be for everyone is stated in numerous laws. The National Park Service Organic Act states that the purpose of public land managed by the NPS is "to provide for the enjoyment of the same in such manner and by such means as will leave them unimpaired for the enjoyment of future generations." The Federal Land Policy and Management Act of 1976 states that "public lands be managed in a manner that will . . . provide for outdoor recreation and human occupancy and use."

The language of these laws includes all people. Enjoyment and use by people are primary purposes for reserving public land from settlement or sale. The laws do not limit who gets to enjoy and use the land or where they come from.

ON MY RETURN HIKE from Little Finland, I passed a detailed panel of petroglyphs carved midway up a wall. The author would have had to scramble onto a ledge and perch twenty-five feet above the ground to carve spirals, human figures, bighorn sheep, and many other symbols into the scene on this rock. LaVan Martineau reveals that bighorn sheep are often representative of the people who carved the illustrations. A complex panel such as the one I was looking at mostly likely told an intricate story of an event that took place in this desert.

"The Southern Paiutes, the *Nuwuvi*, span across Southern Utah, Southern Nevada, Northern Arizona, and Southern California. And we're all connected by the Salt Song Trail," said Fawn Douglas, a member of the Las Vegas Band of Paiutes and former board member for the nonprofit Friends of Gold Butte. "The Salt Song Trail goes around those four states. We're connected by these songs that describe the mountainsides, the plants, the animals, everything that is within that trail. And so, when we have ceremonies, those songs are sung to remind the spirits of where they come from and the attachments that we have to these lands."

In the late 1800s, government boarding schools were created with the goal of assimilating Indigenous people into white culture. Many Southern Paiute were forcibly taken from their families and sent to boarding schools for years at a time. There they were not permitted to participate in sacred rituals and were forbidden from speaking their native languages and singing their traditional songs. Largely because of this, many customs, much of the language, and even most of these Salt Songs have been lost.

"The story behind the salt trail needs to be told to understand the balance between land and people and song and language," says Vivienne Jake in the short documentary *The Salt Song Trail*. Jake is Kaibab Paiute and the codirector of a project to revive salt songs.

"All of those are interrelated, and you can't have one without the other."

Land that was owned only so much as someone could sing about it in detail—about peaks and cactus and potholes holding precious water—is now recognized as "owned" through fences and deeds and managing agencies. As property ownership took hold in the United States, the idea of the world as a place where people share and partake in nature around them was suppressed in favor of advancement, wealth, dominance, and individualism. The rise of land ownership and industrialization coincided with the loss of connection, the silence of song.

"It was important to get the monument designated," Douglas told me, referring to Gold Butte. "There were many different tribal groups that pushed for that designation. Under national monument status there are stronger protections and rights for that land. I was an activist involved in the fight for protection of that area. I found it really important, especially in the Las Vegas area, working with different groups and getting people to speak up with stories about these places. And it's those specific stories—some of them, we didn't tell all of them—[that help] people understand why it's so important to the Paiute people. Because we identify with the lands we come from. It's pretty much drilled into who we are as a people: this is our identity and we're connected to it. We have this covenant to protect those places. They're in our songs, they're everything."

Douglas speaks a truth that must be honored and understood: public land in America is the sacred land of Indigenous people; it is vital that they participate in or lead management and decision making for land that is integral to their past, their present, and their future. Public land in this country was predicated on Indigenous people's removal; this should not be forgotten. But it need not continue to be public land's legacy. We can create a new legacy, one of collaboration. Indigenous history should be celebrated and respected. People of all ethnicities and backgrounds should feel welcome. What has brought all people to this place in time—the actions of our ancestors, the wrongdoings of the past—are shared histories that are lived in land.

In *The Salt Song Trail*, Jake says, "We need to explore a little bit deeper into what we have had for a long time, and yet be able to share it with a lot more people so that they can get an understanding of themselves and their attachment to Mother Earth." Protecting land is not just about the land. It is about us. We need to preserve ecosystems: habitat for plants and animals, biodiversity, waterways, trees and plant life and coral reefs that provide us with clean air. But we should also consider what the land does for people.

When Ángel Peña asked me, *Where is your place?* embedded in his question was the understanding that a person needed a place to shape their understanding of themselves. Clearly places like Gold Butte and Bears Ears are places that shape many people. Even many who oppose monuments are united by their deep care for those same places, places that inform their lives, their identities. We need these places so that we can be ourselves.

I USED THE REMAINING JOLTS of sunlight to visit the Falling Man Petroglyph site. I scrambled up and over boulders, traversed sandy slabs, and wound through washes. I didn't find the drawing of the falling man, but I did find a boulder covered in overlapping etchings of people, bighorn sheep, spirals, and a tortoise. I also found pale spatters of bullet holes in chocolaty desert patina. Elsewhere in the monument are abandoned mining sites, the graves of Arthur Coleman and William Garrett, perhaps even some of Cliven Bundy's feral cows.

"We treat the land and everything within it as our relative because it is alive and deserves the utmost respect. This value is the

GOLD BUTTE

foundation for how we treat each other and the land," wrote the Nuwuvi Working Group in "Nuwu Kanee, Nuwu Tooveenup (Our Home, Our Story)," a document created in collaboration with the U.S. Forest Service about Nuwuvi culture, sacred sites, and stories. "The Creator placed us on the Earth to help to keep the land in balance. This is very different than non-native thinking that sees nature as something that does not need human interference. We believe that the land needs us to be healthy."

This struck me. Through all of my visits to national monuments, it was achingly obvious that people need land. But perhaps the land also needs us. Just as people are incomplete without the places that make them whole, maybe the land is incomplete without people. Western culture often views land and nature as separate from people. Language reveals this with phrases like "natural world" and "the outdoors," which signify something wholly apart from our daily experience. If society could adopt the Nuwuvi view and understand humans and land as two parts of a working whole, perhaps both humans and Earth could be treated with more care. We have more responsibility to a place when we realize that it needs us as much as we need it.

National monuments revealed to me in a tangible way that the well-being of the world and the well-being of humans are intertwined. Monuments exemplify how we can't separate ourselves from what we love, what we need, what we use, and who we are.

When I spoke with Lucas St. Clair about Katahdin Woods and Waters, we discussed how land needs advocates for protection to happen. "Land needs people to love it," St. Clair said. "Then a person needs to make their voice heard and to find ways to increase the volume of their voice. This is best achieved with more voices. Turn your single voice into a chorus."

A chorus. A ringing of voices about love for land. Perhaps even a song.

Looking Forward

First a pandemic, and now this.

I drove north to Washington to escape smoke. It was September 2020, and California was on fire. All of it, really. On the Cal Fire incident website the state was so dotted with red, it looked infected with chicken pox. I thought 2017 was bad, when the Camp Fire burned near Santa Rosa and the sky over Berryessa Snow filmed over. Now the Creek Fire burned less than fifteen miles from my house. The granite crest of the Sierra lay between it and me, but people in my town were divided over whether it was possible for the fire to breach that crest and rage through our neighborhoods. Meanwhile, smoke coated the town in sepia. Ash collected in grainy tufts on my car's windshield. I walked outside, and the smoke scratched the corners of my eyes like a finger with a hangnail. I sealed myself in my not-well-sealed cabin, stuffing towels underneath the doorjambs and window frames.

Because of extreme risk of more fires igniting while the firefighting system was already overloaded, California closed all of its

279

national forests. I discussed with friends how every climbing area was closed, but the air quality was so bad that being outside was unbearable anyway. Then the wind changed and we had a miraculously clear day. Enticed by blue sky, I pedaled my mountain bike toward my favorite trail, thrilled to escape the confines of walls. I rode right up to a metal gate blocking the road to the trailhead. I had completely forgotten that the forest was closed. I admonished myself. I *knew* it was closed; how could I have been so forgetful? As I coasted home, I understood how the patterns of my life are so entwined with being outside and on land I could barely envision my days without it. I returned to my house and felt more imprisoned than ever.

Orange smoke returned the next day, thicker and more pungent than before.

After a few more days breathing fire inside my house, I fled north. It would have been wiser to head east, where Nevada and Utah were a little hazy but mostly nice, but a writing residency awaited me in a cabin surrounded by damp green woods on the Olympic Peninsula.

I passed through a region that had recently burned: orange rubber traffic cones and roadblock signs were piled on the embankment, turquoise government fire trucks lined roadside ditches, and grubby firefighters worked in a row. The ground oozed smoke like a rising fog, which obscured the sun and darkened everything. Charred tree trunks stood forlorn without underbrush.

I drove on, unsettled. Climate change was no longer the far-off, possibly avoidable future I had learned about as a child. The climate has already changed. Longer, drier, warmer summers and winters with less snowfall than in years past are creating more hazardous fire seasons in the West. The fires that disrupted California when I visited Berryessa Snow were not an anomaly but a new normal. We can no longer avert climate disaster: we are living this disaster.

EPILOGUE

EARLIER THAT SUMMER, George Floyd's murder by a police officer in Minneapolis prompted a reexamination of public monuments. During the demonstrations that followed Floyd's death, protesters toppled hundred-year-old monuments to confederate soldiers and politicians, as well as other statues of controversial figures. In Albuquerque, protesters defaced a statue of Juan de Oñate, the one-time governor of New Mexico who slaughtered and tortured the Acoma people. With these acts, some Americans chose to reexamine what deserves recognition and what they want our country to memorialize and celebrate.

This shift in perspective led me to consider the legacy of the park-like national monuments in our country. Like other forms of public land, national monuments unite the environmental and the social. By changing the way we think about land, national monuments could serve as an opportunity for a deeper relationship with the people and places around us, a way to heal the broken. To achieve this, we need to complicate our perception. Monuments and the land they encompass can't be viewed simplistically, as good or bad or shaded in a black-and-white opinion. The first step is embracing the complexity, welcoming the duality of both tragedy and beauty present in these places. Making room for story.

I began this journey by looking for the in-between, using middle gray to calibrate my view. I started by appreciating colors: the gradation of blues in the sky, the numerous reds and pinks of desert sandstone, the variations of yellow sun glinting off rivers. I came away looking not at the colors but at what forms the colors. How those same blues and yellows combine into pine-needle green and spring-shoot green and silver sage green. How blue and red mingle to become Kayenta Formation purple, lavender morning glory, and sunset indigo.

A monument is more than just a land designation; it is the story of everything that happened in that place before, everything that continues to happen there, and the story that comes next. Monuments encapsulate long stretches of history, numerous plants, animals, rocks, and waterways, and uncountable ways that each of these things relate to one another. Land contained within monuments faces challenges posed by climate change, nuclear waste storage, a border wall, and conflicting human needs and desires. The impacts of reserving and remembering these places cross cultural and political lines and linger for longer than one human lifetime.

The lands that we have termed national monuments can and often do represent the worst of America's story. They tell of genocides perpetrated so that sacred land could be stolen, the torture and dehumanization of slavery, the continued injustice of racial inequality, the ways in which land and animals and people are harmed through development, pollution, and the climate disaster. But alongside the horrible exists the incredible. Opposing groups united for a common cause, one person changing hundreds of minds, lives improved through bonds formed with land. Sagebrush reflecting the sunrise's persimmon and lavender, soft petals on a cactus flower unfurling next to its spines, the song of whales trumpeting through the ocean.

WHEN PRESIDENT BIDEN TOOK OFFICE in January 2021, he announced a plan to protect 30 percent of American land and ocean before 2030. This goal is an attempt to mitigate the effects of climate change and prevent mass extinction of species. As of the time of this announcement, the United States had conserved roughly 26 percent of its oceans and 12 percent of its land. For this goal to be met, another 440 million acres will need to be conserved in the next ten years. This will require the purchase of private land, consultation

EPILOGUE

with tribal governments, and new conservation regulations on federal land that does not prioritize protection. One of the ways the Biden administration plans to achieve the 30 percent goal is by making access to land more equitable: establishing more parks and green spaces in underserved communities that lack access to the outdoors. Some of this work will be made possible through the Great American Outdoors Act, federal legislation passed in 2020 that provides needed funding for parks and recreation.

National monuments could also be key to achieving Biden's goal. The language of the Antiquities Act is broad enough that preserving biodiversity and hindering climate change can be reasons for the creation of new monuments. Plus, monuments can be created quickly and avoid an argumentative stall in a divided Congress. Monuments could become the instruments of radical change in our society, a new direction for our nation that prioritizes land, equality, and diversity, both human and nonhuman.

Upon taking office, President Biden did something else truly historic. He nominated the first-ever Indigenous person to serve in a presidential cabinet by tapping Congresswoman Debra Haaland, a citizen of the Laguna Pueblo, to be the secretary of the interior. This position oversees the National Park Service, the Bureau of Land Management, and the Bureau of Indian Affairs. This is also the position with the most influence over an administration's decisions about national monuments.

As an elected representative from New Mexico, Haaland authored a bill called the Thirty by Thirty Resolution to Save Nature, which laid out the land protection plan that President Biden endorsed in his early executive order. The bill claims that "the United States faces a conservation and climate crisis, with nature in a steep decline," and it asserts that "conserving and restoring nature is one of the most efficient and cost-effective strategies for fighting climate change." As secretary of the interior, Haaland may advocate for more monuments to further this goal.

Secretary Haaland's leadership will be key to a new public lands narrative, in which stories might begin to shift in ways that represent a broader, more inclusive view of the land around us. "Our national parks and our public lands should tell the story of our country and of all Americans," Haaland told *Outside Magazine* in 2021. "There are a lot of ways that the National Park Service hasn't fully been able to highlight those particular areas, but certainly, Asian Americans, African Americans, Native Americans, and Hispanic Americans are all part of our country's history." During her confirmation hearing, when asked why she was interested in taking on a job as contentious and difficult as the secretary of the interior, Haaland responded by saying, "the Navajo Code talkers, the first word they decided to use when working on the code was *Nihimá,* and that means 'our mother.' That was the code they used for the United States of America. . . . This is all of our country. This is our mother. It is difficult to not feel obligated to protect this land."

Monuments are a form of guardianship. In the words of the Nuclear Guardianship Bill of Rights, it is our duty to "prevent irreversible and irreparable harm to life on Earth and to human freedom and dignity." As Haaland put it in the Thirty by Thirty Resolution to Save Nature, "access to public land, nature, and a healthy environment should be a right of all people."

If I have learned anything through this journey, it is that humans change the land around them. But the land also changes us. In profound, tangible, and intangible ways, land shapes us all. Who would Ángel Peña be without Valles Canyon? Who would Roxanne Quimby and Lucas St. Clair be without the Maine woods? Who would Cameron Martinez and the *Tiwa* be without the Rio Grande? I certainly would not be the same person without Indian Creek and each of the monuments I visited. I lament to think about who we would become without these places.

SMOKE FOLLOWED ME. I had hoped I would drive out of it, but as I passed through Reno, Nevada, and then Susanville, California, the bile-colored haze still clung to everything. I knew there were mountains to the west of me, but they were completely invisible. Night fell as I neared the California–Oregon border, and I needed to find a place to sleep. The national forest was closed. I turned onto a dirt road toward Lava Beds National Monument. Maybe the monument was still open, and I could camp on its outskirts. Questionable. I rationalized the choice by promising I would not use a stove or anything that could cause a spark.

In the dark, I found a pullout along the main road. I began to set up my tent in loose, pale pumice. As my poles snicked together, I looked up and saw stars. Glittering, shining, resilient stars. Somehow the smoke had lifted, or I had found the one place between fires in California and fires in Oregon that wasn't stifled under grunge. I remembered the stars in Katahdin Woods and Waters, and how they revealed an infinite universe. I recalled the wonder of seeing a Hawaiian green sea turtle floating up close, the marvel of squeezing my body through mazelike slot canyons, the improbability and ecstasy of climbing a featureless sandstone crack, how creosote smells like life itself. I sensed the shift inside me that had occurred as I came to know these places and felt their meaning. Despite the numerous challenges we face in this country, I am filled with love and hope for this contested land.

Acknowledgments

WRITING THIS BOOK HAS BEEN A JOURNEY—a physical journey to new places but also a journey in learning and in creating. My greatest joy in this process came from people and conversations. I was astounded by the passion, openness, and generosity of people who shared stories, expertise, and opinions about something as intimate as connection to land. Without them and their perspectives, this book would lack meaning and depth: Shanandoah Anderson, Russell Beesley, Cassandra Begay, Andrew Bossie, Brian Bowen, Matthew Brown, Fawn Douglas, Josh Ewing, Ester Garcia, Lamont Glass, Dan Haas, Lori Hargrove, Lucas Herndon, Pablo Lopez, Cameron Martinez, Matt Mason, Len Necefer, Ángel Peña, Gabriella Peña, Matt Redd, George Rice, Lucas St. Clair, Bob Schneider, Mililani Trask, Phil Unitt, Gabe Vasquez, Garrett VeneKlasen, Ken Watts, and Sheri Whitfield. I also want to thank those who helped facilitate connections and fact-finding: Caroline Britton, John Casey, Roger Fragua, Jeff Keay, Doug Robinson, and Roberta Salazar.

In addition to stories, this project has gifted me with relationships with other writers. These women provided enthusiastic support, clever insight, and a literary community: Laura Jenkins, Joan Meiners, Emi Nietfeld, Andrea Sauder, Amy Sugeno, Heather Von

Bargen, and Tori Weston. A special thanks goes to Jeff Keay, who offered much needed perspective and encouragement, hosted me at his home in Island Park, and has become a friend. Sarah Browning and Todd Gilens shared residency space and creative time with me. Gilens introduced me to new sources and helped develop my thinking on perception of time. Two peer reviewers, Kim Todd and Leisl Carr Childers, provided careful feedback that enhanced my work. Carr Childers was especially generous, and conversation with her helped clarify some of the central points of this work. Thank you to others who provided education, inspiration, or suggestions: Wendy Call, Waverly Fitzgerald, Katie Ives, Jennifer Sahn, Kim Stravers, and Paula Wright.

In the messy middle of this project I was accepted to the Writer to Writer mentorship program hosted by the Association of Writers and Writing Programs and was wonderfully matched with author Kathryn Aalto. She offered wisdom and writing advice, pushed me to go deeper than I otherwise would have, and encouraged me to pursue more interviews and gather more perspectives. I am extremely grateful for this opportunity and for her time and close attention.

Two different residencies supported me during my writing of this book: Hypatia-in-the-Woods in Shelton, Washington, which hosted me twice, and Mesa Refuge in Point Reyes, California. I am very grateful to the people behind these nonprofits and their nurturance of me and other artists, especially Peter Barnes, Carolyn Maddux, Shelley Spaulding, Susan Tillett, Kamala Tully, and Norma Yardeners.

A very warm thank you to artist and scientist Ann Piersall Logan, who visited Grand Staircase–Escalante with me, read my entire book in draft form, and provided valuable feedback. She also created the beautiful bases to the maps in each chapter. Most important, she is a dear friend who enriches my life.

ACKNOWLEDGMENTS

I am overwhelmed with gratitude for my editor, Kristian Tvedten at the University of Minnesota Press. It has been a joy to work with someone who shares the same vision for my work and who pushed me to find its best possible form without altering my message or goals. He allowed this book to become real.

Thank you to the team at University of Minnesota Press for all the effort that went into producing and promoting this book: Shelby Connelly, Emily Hamilton, Daniel Ochsner, Heather Skinner, and Anne Wrenn.

Thanks most of all to my marvelous family. My mother, Linda Long, traveled with me and served as a sounding board as I wrestled with ideas. My father, John Long, unflinchingly supports and loves me. My sister Dr. Alexandra Long is six years younger but mentors and inspires me in many ways. Veronica Palmer accompanied me on my very first monument research trip, took many of the gorgeous photographs you see in these pages, and has been a cheerleader and friend my entire life. My husband, Jack Cramer, visited several monuments with me and offered his expert interpretation of economic reports and fishery studies. His painstaking word tinkering improved my manuscript. He fills my life with love, curiosity, creativity, and adventure.

Heartfelt appreciation goes to all the individuals and organizations that advocate for and support monuments and other public land. Without their effort and care there would be less wildness to experience and fewer stories to learn. With deep respect, I am grateful to all the Indigenous peoples who call this land home and who cared for it first and still.

American Antiquities Act of 1906

16 USC 431–433

Be it enacted by the Senate and House of Representatives of the United States of America in Congress assembled, That any person who shall appropriate, excavate, injure, or destroy any historic or prehistoric ruin or monument, or any object of antiquity, situated on lands owned or controlled by the Government of the United States, without the permission of the Secretary of the Department of the Government having jurisdiction over the lands on which said antiquities are situated, shall, upon conviction, be fined in a sum of not more than five hundred dollars or be imprisoned for a period of not more than ninety days, or shall suffer both fine and imprisonment, in the discretion of the court.

Sec. 2. That the President of the United States is hereby authorized, in his discretion, to declare by public proclamation historic landmarks, historic and prehistoric structures, and other objects of historic or scientific interest that are situated upon the lands owned or controlled by the Government of the United States to be national monuments, and may reserve as a part thereof parcels of land, the limits of which in all cases shall be confined to the smallest area compatible with proper care and management of the objects to be protected: Provided, That when such objects are situated upon a tract covered by a bona fide unperfected claim or held in private ownership, the tract, or so much thereof as may be necessary for the proper care and management of the object, may be relinquished to the Government, and the Secretary of the Interior is hereby authorized to accept the relinquishment of such tracts in behalf of the Government of the United States.

Sec. 3. That permits for the examination of ruins, the excavation of archaeological sites, and the gathering of objects of antiquity upon the lands under their respective jurisdictions may be granted by the Secretaries of the Interior, Agriculture, and War to institutions which they may deem properly qualified to conduct such examination, excavation, or gathering, subject to such rules and regulation as they may prescribe: Provided, That the examinations, excavations, and gatherings are undertaken for the benefit of reputable museums, universities, colleges, or other recognized scientific or educational institutions, with a view to increasing the knowledge of such objects, and that the gatherings shall be made for permanent preservation in public museums.

Sec. 4. That the Secretaries of the Departments aforesaid shall make and publish from time to time uniform rules and regulations for the purpose of carrying out the provisions of this Act.

Approved, June 8, 1906

Presidential Monument Proclamations

THE FOLLOWING LIST includes all national monuments created under the Antiquities Act. Entries are organized by administration and include the date and acreage at the time of establishment or other action. The final line of each entry states the land's current status, managing agency, and federal acreage. This total does not include private or state land holdings that exist within the boundaries of some parks and monuments.

This information is based in large part on a table compiled by Harmon, McManamon, and Pitcaithley (2006). The current acreages were taken from the National Park Service Acreage Report published December 31, 2021, and similar reports released by the U.S. Forest Service and Bureau of Land Management in October 2021.

ADMINISTRATION OF THEODORE ROOSEVELT
(18 MONUMENTS)

Devils Tower, Wyoming
Established September 14, 1906
(1,194 acres)
Current: Devils Tower National
Monument (NPS), 1,347 acres

El Morro, New Mexico
Established December 8, 1906
(160 acres)
Current: El Morro National Monument
(NPS), 1,040 acres

Montezuma Castle, Arizona
Established December 8, 1906 (161 acres)
Current: Montezuma Castle National Monument (NPS), 999 acres

Petrified Forest, Arizona
Established December 8, 1906 (60,776 acres)
Current: Petrified Forest National Park (NPS), 147,144 acres

Chaco Canyon, New Mexico
Established March 11, 1907 (10,643 acres)
Current: Chaco Culture National Historical Park (NPS), 32,840 acres

Cinder Cone, California
Established May 6, 1907 (5,120 acres)
Incorporated into Lassen Volcanic National Park, 1916 (NPS), 106,505 acres

Lassen Peak, California
Established May 6, 1907 (1,280 acres)
Incorporated into Lassen Volcanic National Park, 1916 (NPS), 106,505 acres

Gila Cliff Dwellings, New Mexico
Established November 16, 1907 (160 acres)
Current: Gila Cliff Dwellings National Monument (NPS, USFS), 533 acres

Tonto, Arizona
Established December 16, 1907 (640 acres)
Current: Tonto National Monument (NPS), 1,120 acres

Muir Woods, California
Established January 9, 1908 (295 acres)
Current: Muir Woods National Monument (NPS), 523 acres

Grand Canyon, Arizona
Established January 11, 1908 (808,120 acres)
Most of monument incorporated into Grand Canyon National Park, 1919 (NPS), 1,180,651 acres

Pinnacles, California
Established January 16, 1908 (1,320 acres)
Current: Pinnacles National Park (NPS), 26,675 acres

Jewel Cave, South Dakota
Established February 7, 1908 (1,275 acres)
Current: Jewel Cave National Monument (NPS), 1,274 acres

Natural Bridges, Utah
Established April 16, 1908 (120 acres)
Current: Natural Bridges National Monument (NPS), 7,636 acres

Lewis and Clark Cavern, Montana
Established May 11, 1908 (160 acres)
Abolished 1937; incorporated into Lewis and Clark Caverns State Park (Montana FWP)

Tumacácori, Arizona
Established September 15, 1908 (10 acres)
Current: Tumacácori National Historical Park (NPS), 358 acres

Wheeler, Colorado
Established December 7, 1908 (300 acres)
Abolished 1950; incorporated into Rio Grande National Forest (USFS)

Mount Olympus, Washington
Established March 2, 1909 (639,200 acres)
Current: Olympic National Park (NPS), 913,574 acres

ADMINISTRATION OF WILLIAM HOWARD TAFT

(10 MONUMENTS)

Navajo, Arizona
Established March 20, 1909 (unspecified acreage)
Current: Navajo National Monument (NPS), 360 acres

Oregon Caves, Oregon
Established July 12, 1909 (466 acres)
Current: Oregon Caves National Monument and Preserve (NPS), 4,554 acres

Mukuntuweap, Utah
Established July 31, 1909 (16,000 acres)
Incorporated into Zion National Park, 1919 (NPS), 143,793 acres

Shoshone Cavern, Wyoming
Established September 21, 1909 (210 acres)
Abolished 1954; lands under BLM jurisdiction

Gran Quivira, New Mexico
Established November 1, 1909 (160 acres)
Current: Salinas Pueblo Missions National Monument (NPS), 985 acres

Sitka, Alaska
Established March 23, 1910 (57 acres)
Current: Sitka National Historical Park (NPS), 58 acres

Rainbow Bridge, Utah
Established May 30, 1910 (160 acres)
Current: Rainbow Bridge National Monument (NPS), 160 acres

Big Hole Battlefield, Montana
Established June 23, 1910 (5 acres)
Current: Big Hole National Battlefield (NPS), 656 acres

Colorado, Colorado
Established May 24, 1911 (13,466 acres)
Current: Colorado National Monument (NPS), 20,536 acres

Devils Postpile, California
Established July 6, 1911 (798 acres)
Current: Devils Postpile National Monument (NPS), 800 acres

ADMINISTRATION OF WOODROW WILSON
(13 MONUMENTS)

Cabrillo, California
Established November 14, 1913 (less than 1 acre)
Current: Cabrillo National Monument (NPS), 160 acres

Papago Saguaro, Arizona
Established January 31, 1914 (2,050 acres)
Abolished 1930; lands transferred to State of Arizona and local agencies

Dinosaur, Colorado and Utah
Established October 4, 1915 (80 acres)
Current: Dinosaur National Monument (NPS), 205,766 acres

Walnut Canyon, Arizona
Established November 30, 1915 (960 acres)
Current: Walnut Canyon National Monument (NPS), 2,923 acres

Bandelier, New Mexico
Established February 11, 1916 (23,352 acres)
Current: Bandelier National Monument (NPS), 32,654 acres

Sieur de Monts, Maine
Established July 8, 1916 (5,000 acres)
Current: Acadia National Park (NPS), 48,207 acres

Capulin Mountain, New Mexico
Established August 9, 1916 (640 acres)
Current: Capulin Volcano National Monument (NPS), 793 acres

Old Kasaan, Alaska
Established October 25, 1916 (43 acres)
Abolished 1955; incorporated into Tongass National Forest (USFS)

Verendrye, North Dakota
Established June 29, 1917 (253 acres)
Abolished 1956; lands transferred to State of North Dakota

Casa Grande, Arizona
Established August 3, 1918 (480 acres)
Current: Casa Grande Ruins National Monument (NPS), 473 acres

Katmai, Alaska
Established September 24, 1918 (1,088,000 acres)
Current: Katmai National Park and Preserve (NPS), 3,944,965 acres

Scotts Bluff, Nebraska
Established December 12, 1919 (2,054 acres)
Current: Scotts Bluff National Monument (NPS), 2,954 acres

Yucca House, Colorado
Established December 19, 1919 (10 acres)
Current: Yucca House National Monument (NPS), 34 acres

PRESIDENTIAL MONUMENT PROCLAMATIONS

ADMINISTRATION OF WARREN G. HARDING

(8 MONUMENTS)

Lehman Caves, Nevada
Established January 24, 1922 (593 acres)
Current: Great Basin National Park (NPS), 77,180 acres

Timpanogos Cave, Utah
Established October 14, 1922 (250 acres)
Current: Timpanogos Cave National Monument (NPS), 250 acres

Fossil Cycad, South Dakota
Established October 21, 1922 (320 acres)
Abolished 1957; incorporated into South Dakota Resource Area (BLM)

Aztec Ruins, New Mexico
Established January 24, 1923 (5 acres)
Current: Aztec Ruins National Monument (NPS), 267 acres

Mound City Group, Ohio
Established March 2, 1923 (57 acres)
Current: Hopewell Culture National Historical Park (NPS), 1,146 acres

Hovenweep, Utah
Established March 2, 1923 (286 acres)
Current: Hovenweep National Monument (NPS), 785 acres

Pipe Spring, Arizona
Established May 31, 1923 (40 acres)
Current: Pipe Spring National Monument (NPS), 40 acres

Bryce Canyon, Utah
Established June 8, 1923 (7,440 acres)
Current: Bryce Canyon National Park (NPS), 35,833 acres

ADMINISTRATION OF CALVIN COOLIDGE

(13 MONUMENTS)

Carlsbad Cave, New Mexico
Established October 25, 1923 (719 acres)
Current: Carlsbad Caverns National Park (NPS), 46,427 acres

Chiricahua, Arizona
Established April 18, 1924 (3,655 acres)
Current: Chiricahua National Monument (NPS), 12,022 acres

Craters of the Moon, Idaho
Established May 2, 1924 (22,652 acres)
Current: Craters of the Moon National Monument and Preserve (NPS, BLM), 738,420 acres

Castle Pinckney, South Carolina
Established October 15, 1924 (4 acres)
Abolished 1956; owned by South Carolina State Ports Authority. Listed on National Register of Historic Places, 1970.

Fort Marion, Florida
Established October 15, 1924 (19 acres)
Current: Castillo de San Marcos
National Monument (NPS), 19 acres

Fort Matanzas, Florida
Established October 15, 1924 (1 acre)
Current: Fort Matanzas National
Monument (NPS), 299 acres

Fort Pulaski, Georgia
Established October 15, 1924 (20 acres)
Current: Fort Pulaski National
Monument (NPS), 5,365 acres

Fort Wood (Statue of Liberty), New York
Established October 15, 1924 (10 acres)
Current: Statue of Liberty National
Monument (NPS), 58 acres

Wupatki, Arizona
Established December 9, 1924 (2,234 acres)
Current: Wupatki National Monument
(NPS), 35,402 acres

Meriwether Lewis, Tennessee
Established February 6, 1925 (50 acres)
Incorporated into Natchez Trace
Parkway, 1961 (NPS), 52,207 acres

Glacier Bay, Alaska
Established February 26, 1925
(1,379,316 acres)
Current: Glacier Bay National Park and
Preserve (NPS), 3,280,841 acres

Father Millet Cross, New York
Established September 5, 1925 (less than 1 acre)
Abolished 1949; incorporated into Old
Fort Niagara State Historic Site

Lava Beds, California
Established November 21, 1925 (45,590 acres)
Current: Lava Beds National Monument
(NPS), 46,692 acres

ADMINISTRATION OF HERBERT HOOVER

(9 MONUMENTS)

Arches, Utah
Established April 12, 1929 (4,520 acres)
Current: Arches National Park (NPS),
76,546 acres

Holy Cross, Colorado
Established May 11, 1929 (1,392 acres)
Abolished 1950; incorporated into
White River National Forest (USFS)

Sunset Crater, Arizona
Established May 26, 1930 (3,040 acres)
Current: Sunset Crater Volcano
National Monument (NPS), 3,040
acres

Great Sand Dunes, Colorado
Established March 17, 1932 (35,528 acres)
Current: Great Sand Dunes National Park and Preserve (NPS), 136,374 acres

Grand Canyon II, Arizona
Established December 22, 1932 (273,145 acres)
Incorporated into Grand Canyon National Park, 1975 (NPS), 1,180,651 acres

White Sands, New Mexico
Established January 18, 1933 (131,487 acres)
Current: White Sands National Park (NPS), 146,344 acres

Death Valley, California and Nevada
Established February 11, 1933 (848,581 acres)
Current: Death Valley National Park (NPS), 3,355,172 acres

Saguaro, Arizona
Established March 1, 1933 (53,510 acres)
Current: Saguaro National Park (NPS), 88,031 acres

Black Canyon of the Gunnison, Colorado
Established March 2, 1933 (10,288 acres)
Current: Black Canyon of the Gunnison National Park (NPS), 30,730 acres

ADMINISTRATION OF FRANKLIN D. ROOSEVELT

(11 MONUMENTS)

Cedar Breaks, Utah
Established August 22, 1933 (5,701 acres)
Current: Cedar Breaks National Monument (NPS), 6,155 acres

Fort Jefferson, Florida
Established January 4, 1935 (47,125 acres)
Current: Dry Tortugas National Park (NPS), 61,481 acres

Joshua Tree, California
Established August 10, 1936 (825,340 acres)
Current: Joshua Tree National Park (NPS), 781,909 acres

Zion II (Kolob Section), Utah
Established January 22, 1937 (49,150 acres)
Incorporated into Zion National Park, 1956 (NPS), 143,793 acres

Organ Pipe Cactus, Arizona
Established April 13, 1937 (330,690 acres)
Current: Organ Pipe Cactus National Monument (NPS), 329,365 acres

Capitol Reef, Utah
Established August 2, 1937 (37,060 acres)
Current: Capitol Reef National Park (NPS), 241,223 acres

Channel Islands, California
Established April 26, 1938 (1,120 acres)
Current: Channel Islands National Park
(NPS), 79,019 acres

Fort Laramie, Wyoming
Established July 16, 1938 (214 acres)
Current: Fort Laramie National Historic
Site (NPS), 872 acres

Santa Rosa Island, Florida
Established May 17, 1939 (9,500 acres)
Incorporated into Gulf Islands National
Seashore, 1946 (NPS), 99,779 acres

Tuzigoot, Arizona
Established July 25, 1939 (43 acres)
Current: Tuzigoot National Monument
(NPS), 382 acres

Jackson Hole, Wyoming
Established March 15, 1943 (210,950
acres)
Incorporated into Grand Teton National
Park, 1950 (NPS), 308,664 acres

ADMINISTRATION OF HARRY S. TRUMAN
(1 MONUMENT)

Effigy Mounds, Iowa
Established October 25, 1949 (1,000
acres)
Current: Effigy Mounds National
Monument (NPS), 2,489 acres

ADMINISTRATION OF DWIGHT D. EISENHOWER
(2 MONUMENTS)

Edison Laboratory, New Jersey
Established July 14, 1956 (2 acres)
Current: Thomas Edison National
Historical Park (NPS), 21 acres

**Chesapeake and Ohio Canal,
Maryland, Washington, D.C., and
West Virginia**
Established January 18, 1961 (5,264
acres)
Incorporated into Chesapeake and Ohio
Canal National Historical Park, 1971
(NPS), 14,449 acres

ADMINISTRATION OF JOHN F. KENNEDY

(2 MONUMENTS)

Russell Cave, Alabama
Established May 11, 1961 (310 acres)
Current: Russell Cave National
Monument (NPS), 310 acres

Buck Island Reef, Virgin Islands
Established December 28, 1961 (850
acres)
Current: Buck Island Reef National
Monument (19,015 acres)

ADMINISTRATION OF LYNDON B. JOHNSON

(1 MONUMENT)

Marble Canyon, Arizona
Established January 20, 1969 (32,547
acres)
Incorporated into Grand Canyon
National Park, 1975 (NPS), 1,180,651
acres

ADMINISTRATION OF JIMMY CARTER

(15 MONUMENTS)

Admiralty Island, Alaska
Established December 1, 1978
(1,100,000 acres)
Current: Admiralty Island National
Monument (USFS), 1,008,069 acres

Aniakchak, Alaska
Established December 1, 1978 (350,000
acres)
Current: Aniakchak National
Monument and Preserve (NPS),
595,985 acres

Becharof, Alaska
Established December 1, 1978
(1,200,000 acres)
Current: Becharof National Wildlife
Refuge (USFWS), 1,157,000 acres

Bering Land Bridge, Alaska
Established December 1, 1978
(2,590,000 acres)
Current: Bering Land Bridge National
Preserve (NPS), 2,651,328 acres

Cape Krusenstern, Alaska
Established December 1, 1978 (560,000
acres)
Current: Cape Krusenstern National
Monument (NPS), 627,709 acres

Denali, Alaska
Established December 1, 1978
(3,890,000 acres)
Current: Denali National Park and
Preserve (NPS), 6,036,910 acres

Gates of the Arctic, Alaska
Established December 1, 1978
(8,220,000 acres)
Current: Gates of the Arctic National
Park and Preserve (NPS), 8,308,013
acres

Kenai Fjords, Alaska
Established December 1, 1978 (570,000
acres)
Current: Kenai Fjords National Park
(NPS), 603,130 acres

Kobuk Valley, Alaska
Established December 1, 1978
(1,710,000 acres)
Current: Kobuk Valley National Park
(NPS), 1,714,418 acres

Lake Clark, Alaska
Established December 1, 1978
(2,500,000 acres)
Current: Lake Clark National Park and
Preserve (NPS), 3,740,755 acres

Misty Fjords, Alaska
Established December 1, 1978
(2,285,000 acres)
Current: Misty Fjords National
Monument (USFS), 2,293,162 acres

Noatak, Alaska
Established December 1, 1978
(5,880,000 acres)
Current: Noatak National Preserve
(NPS), 6,549,220 acres

Wrangell–St. Elias, Alaska
Established December 1, 1978
(10,950,000 acres)
Current: Wrangell–St. Elias National
Park and Preserve (NPS), 12,280,599
acres

Yukon–Charley Rivers, Alaska
Established December 1, 1978
(1,720,000 acres)
Current: Yukon–Charley Rivers National
Preserve (NPS), 2,195,547 acres

Yukon Flats, Alaska
Established December 1, 1978
(10,600,000 acres)
Redesignated 1980; Yukon Flats
National Wildlife Refuge (USFWS),
8,630,000 acres

ADMINISTRATION OF BILL CLINTON
(19 MONUMENTS, 1 EXPANSION)

Grand Staircase–Escalante, Utah
Established September 18, 1996
(1,885,800 acres)
Current: Grand Staircase–Escalante
National Monument (BLM), 1,870,000
acres

Agua Fria, Arizona
Established January 11, 2000 (71,100
acres)
Current: Agua Fria National Monument
(BLM), 70,980 acres

California Coastal, California
Established January 11, 2000 (883 acres)
Current: California Coastal National Monument (BLM), 8,858 acres

Grand Canyon–Parashant, Arizona
Established January 11, 2000 (1,054,264 acres)
Current: Grand Canyon–Parashant National Monument (BLM, NPS), 1,021,030 acres

Giant Sequoia, California
Established April 15, 2000 (327,769 acres)
Current: Giant Sequoia National Monument (USFS), 328,408 acres

Canyons of the Ancients, Colorado
Established June 9, 2000 (182,422 acres)
Current: Canyons of the Ancients National Monument (BLM), 176,370 acres

Cascade-Siskiyou, Oregon
Established June 9, 2000 (65,000 acres)
Current: Cascade-Siskiyou National Monument (BLM), 112,928 acres

Hanford Reach, Washington
Established June 9, 2000 (195,000 acres)
Current: Hanford Reach National Monument (USFWS), 195,000 acres

Ironwood Forest, Arizona
Established June 9, 2000 (189,731 acres)
Current: Ironwood Forest National Monument (BLM), 129,055 acres

President Lincoln and Soldiers' Home, Washington, D.C.
Established July 7, 2000 (2 acres)
Current: President Lincoln's Cottage at the Soldiers' Home National Monument (Armed Forces Retirement Home, NPS), 2 acres

Craters of the Moon, Idaho
Expanded November 9, 2000 (661,000 additional acres)
Current: Craters of the Moon National Monument and Preserve (NPS, BLM), 738,420 acres

Vermilion Cliffs, Arizona
Established November 9, 2000 (294,160 acres)
Current: Vermilion Cliffs National Monument (BLM), 279,566 acres

Carrizo Plain, California
Established January 17, 2001 (246,048 acres)
Current: Carrizo Plain National Monument (BLM), 211,045 acres

Kasha-Katuwe Tent Rocks, New Mexico
Established January 17, 2001 (5,394 acres)
Current: Kasha-Katuwe Tent Rocks National Monument (BLM), 4,647 acres

Minidoka Internment, Idaho
Established January 17, 2001 (73 acres)
Current: Minidoka National Historic Site (NPS), 388 acres

Pompeys Pillar, Montana
Established January 17, 2001 (51 acres)
Current: Pompeys Pillar National
Monument (BLM), 51 acres

Sonoran Desert, Arizona
Established January 17, 2001 (496,337 acres)
Current: Sonoran Desert National
Monument (BLM), 486,400 acres

Upper Missouri River Breaks, Montana
Established January 17, 2001 (494,451 acres)
Current: Upper Missouri River Breaks
National Monument (BLM), 377,346 acres

Virgin Islands Coral Reef, Virgin Islands
Established January 17, 2001 (12,708 acres)
Current: Virgin Islands Coral Reef
National Monument (NPS), 11,608 acres

Governors Island, New York
Established January 19, 2001 (22 acres)
Current: Governors Island National
Monument (NPS), 22 acres

ADMINISTRATION OF GEORGE W. BUSH

(6 MONUMENTS)

African Burial Ground, New York
Established February 27, 2006 (0.35 acres)
Current: African Burial Ground
National Monument (NPS), 0.35 acres

Papahānaumokuākea, Hawaii
Established June 15, 2006 (89,600,000 acres; 140,000 square miles)
Current: Papahānaumokuākea Marine
National Monument (USFWS, NOAA,
Hawaii Department of Land and
Natural Resources, Office of Hawaiian
Affairs), 373,120,000 acres (583,000 square miles)

World War II Valor in the Pacific, Hawaii, Alaska, and California
Established December 5, 2006 (6,309 acres; 9.859 square miles)
Abolished 2019; incorporated into Pearl
Harbor National Memorial, Aleutian
Islands World War II National
Monument, and Tule Lake National
Monument

Marianas Trench, Guam
Established January 6, 2009
(60,938,240 acres; 95,216 square miles)
Current: Marianas Trench Marine
National Monument (USFWS, NOAA),
60,938,240 acres (95,216 square miles)

Pacific Remote Islands, Hawaii
Established January 6, 2009
(55,608,320 acres; 86,888 square
miles)
Current: Pacific Remote Islands Marine
National Monument (USFWS, NOAA),
316,920,960 acres (495,189 square
miles)

Rose Atoll, American Samoa
Established January 6, 2009 (8,608,640
acres; 13,451 square miles)
Current: Rose Atoll Marine National
Monument (USFWS, NOAA),
8,599,040 acres (13,436 square miles)

ADMINISTRATION OF BARACK OBAMA
(29 MONUMENTS, 5 EXPANSIONS)

Fort Monroe, Virginia
Established November 1, 2011 (325
acres)
Current: Fort Monroe National
Monument (NPS), 327 acres

Fort Ord, California
Established April 20, 2012 (14,651
acres)
Current: Fort Ord National Monument
(BLM), 14,658 acres

Chimney Rock, Colorado
Established September 12, 2012 (4,726
acres)
Current: Chimney Rock National
Monument (USFS), 4,724 acres

César E. Chávez, California
Established October 8, 2012 (10.5 acres)
Current: César E. Chávez National
Monument (NPS), 10.5 acres

First State, Delaware and Pennsylvania
Established March 25, 2013 (1,108
acres)
Current: First State National Historical
Park (NPS), 1,365 acres

Charles Young Buffalo Soldiers, Ohio
Established March 25, 2013 (60 acres)
Current: Charles Young Buffalo
Soldiers National Monument (NPS),
60 acres

Rio Grande del Norte, New Mexico
Established March 25, 2013 (242,555
acres)
Current: Rio Grande del Norte National
Monument (BLM), 242,710 acres

San Juan Islands, Washington
Established March 25, 2013 (970 acres)
Current: San Juan Islands National
Monument (BLM), 970 acres

Harriet Tubman–Underground Railroad, Maryland
Established March 25, 2013 (11,750
acres)
Current: Harriet Tubman Underground
Railroad National Historical Park
(480 acres, NPS) and Harriet
Tubman–Underground Railroad
National Monument (USFWS), 25,000
acres

California Coastal, California
Expanded March 11, 2014 (1,665 additional onshore acres)
Current: California Coastal National Monument (BLM), 8,858 acres

Organ Mountains–Desert Peaks, New Mexico
Established May 21, 2014 (496,330 acres)
Current: Organ Mountains–Desert Peaks National Monument (BLM), 496,529 acres

Pacific Remote Islands, Hawaii
Expanded September 25, 2014 (261,300,000 additional acres)
Current: Pacific Remote Islands Marine National Monument (USFWS, NOAA), 316,920,960 acres (495,189 square miles)

San Gabriel Mountains, California
Established October 10, 2014 (346,177 acres)
Current: San Gabriel Mountains National Monument (USFS), 336,876 acres

Browns Canyon, Colorado
Established February 19, 2015 (21,586 acres)
Current: Browns Canyon National Monument (USFS), 11,822 acres

Pullman, Illinois
Established February 19, 2015 (0.24 acres)
Current: Pullman National Monument (NPS), 0.4 acres

Honouliuli, Hawaii
Established February 24, 2015 (123 acres)
Current: Honouliuli National Historic Site (NPS), 123 acres

Basin and Range, Nevada
Established July 10, 2015 (704,000 acres)
Current: Basin and Range National Monument (BLM), 703,585 acres

Berryessa Snow Mountain, California
Established July 10, 2015 (330,780 acres)
Current: Berryessa Snow Mountain National Monument (BLM, USFS), 330,780 acres

Waco Mammoth, Texas
Established July 10, 2015 (7.11 acres)
Current: Waco Mammoth National Monument (NPS), 7.11 acres

Mojave Trails, California
Established February 12, 2016 (1,600,000 acres)
Current: Mojave Trails National Monument (BLM), 1,600,000 acres

Sand to Snow, California
Established February 12, 2016 (154,000 acres)
Current: Sand to Snow National Monument (BLM, USFS) 154,000 acres

Castle Mountains, California
Established February 12, 2016 (20,920 acres)
Current: Castle Mountains National Monument (NPS), 20,902 acres

Belmont-Paul Women's Equality, Washington, D.C.
Established April 12, 2016 (0.34 acres)
Current: Belmont-Paul Women's Equality National Monument, a unit of National Mall and Memorial Parks (NPS), 0.34 acres

Stonewall, New York
Established June 24, 2016 (0.12 acres)
Current: Stonewall National Monument (NPS), 0.12 acres

Katahdin Woods and Waters, Maine
Established August 24, 2016 (87,563 acres)
Current: Katahdin Woods and Waters National Monument (NPS), 87,564 acres

Papahānaumokuākea, Hawaii
Expanded August 26, 2016 (283,400,000 additional acres)
Current: Papahānaumokuākea Marine National Monument (USFWS, NOAA, Hawaii Department of Land and Natural Resources, Office of Hawaiian Affairs), 373,120,000 acres (583,000 square miles)

Northeast Canyons and Seamounts, Rhode Island and Atlantic Ocean
Established September 15, 2016 (3,144,320 acres; 4,913 square miles)
Current: Northeast Canyons and Seamounts Marine National Monument (NOAA, USFWS), 3,144,320 acres (4,913 square miles)

Bears Ears, Utah
Established December 28, 2016 (1,351,849 acres)
Current: Bears Ears National Monument (BLM, USFS), 1,363,948 acres

Gold Butte, Nevada
Established December 28, 2016 (296,937 acres)
Current: Gold Butte National Monument (BLM), 296,937 acres

Cascade-Siskiyou, Oregon and California
Expanded January 12, 2017 (47,624 additional acres: 42,349 in Oregon, 5,275 in California)
Current: Cascade-Siskiyou National Monument (BLM), 112,928 acres

Birmingham Civil Rights, Alabama
Established January 12, 2017 (0.88 acre)
Current: Birmingham Civil Rights National Monument (NPS), 0.88 acre

Freedom Riders, Alabama
Established January 12, 2017 (5.96 acres)
Current: Freedom Riders National Monument (NPS), 5.96 acres

Reconstruction Era, South Carolina
Established January 12, 2017 (15.56 acres)
Current: Reconstruction Era National Historical Park (NPS), 15.53 acres

California Coastal, California
Expanded January 12, 2017 (6,230
  additional acres in six areas)
Current: California Coastal National
  Monument (BLM), 8,858 acres

ADMINISTRATION OF DONALD TRUMP
(1 MONUMENT, 2 REDUCTIONS, 1 REGULATION MODIFICATION)

Bears Ears, Utah
Reduced and modified, December 4,
  2017 (reduced from 1.35 million acres
  to 201,876 acres, which includes an
  addition of 11,200 acres of previously
  unprotected federal land; managed
  in two smaller units, Shash Jáa and
  Indian Creek)
Current: Bears Ears National
  Monument (BLM, USFS), 1,363,948
  acres

Grand Staircase–Escalante, Utah
Reduced and modified, December 4,
  2017 (reduced from 1.8 million acres
  to 1,003,863 acres; managed in three
  smaller units: Escalante Canyons,
  Grand Staircase, and Kaiparowits)
Current: Grand Staircase–Escalante
  National Monument (BLM), 1,870,000
  acres

Camp Nelson, Kentucky
Established October 26, 2018 (380
  acres)
Current: Camp Nelson Heritage
  National Monument (NPS), 465 acres

Northeast Canyons and Seamounts, Rhode Island and Atlantic Ocean
Management plan modified,
  restrictions on commercial fishing
  removed, June 5, 2020
Current: Northeast Canyons and
  Seamounts Marine National
  Monument (NOAA, USFWS), 3,144,320
  acres (4,913 square miles)

ADMINISTRATION OF JOE BIDEN

(AS OF AUGUST 2023: 5 MONUMENTS, 2 EXPANSIONS, 1 REGULATION MODIFICATION)

Bears Ears, Utah

Expanded and restored, October 8, 2021 (expansion includes the original 2016 boundary of 1.35 million acres plus the 11,200 acres added by the Trump administration)

Current: Bears Ears National Monument (BLM, USFS), 1,363,948 acres

Grand Staircase–Escalante, Utah

Expanded and restored, October 8, 2021 (expanded to 1,870,000 acres, near its original 1996 boundary)

Current: Grand Staircase–Escalante National Monument (BLM), 1,870,000 acres

Northeast Canyons and Seamounts, Rhode Island and Atlantic Ocean

Management plan modified, restrictions on commercial fishing reinstated, October 8, 2021

Current: Northeast Canyons and Seamounts Marine National Monument (NOAA, USFWS), 3,144,320 acres (4,913 square miles)

Camp Hale–Continental Divide, Colorado

Established October 12, 2022 (53,804 acres)

Current: Camp Hale–Continental Divide National Monument (USFS), 53,804 acres

Avi Kwa Ame (Spirit Mountain), Nevada

Established March 21, 2023 (506,814 acres)

Current: Avi Kwa Ame National Monument (BLM, NPS), 506,814 acres

Castner Range, Texas

Established March 21, 2023 (6,672 acres)

Current: Castner Range National Monument (DOD [Army]), 6,672 acres

Emmett Till and Mamie Till-Mobley, Illinois and Mississippi

Established July 25, 2023 (5.7 acres)

Current: Emmett Till and Mamie Till-Mobley National Monument (NPS), 5.7 acres

Baaj Nwaavjo I'tah Kukveni–Ancestral Footprints of the Grand Canyon, Arizona

Established August 8, 2023 (917,618 acres)

Current: Baaj Nwaavjo I'tah Kukveni–Ancestral Footprints of the Grand Canyon National Monument (BLM, USFS), 917,618 acres

Selected Resources

THESE SOURCES INFORMED THE WRITING of each chapter and developed my thinking about national monuments and public lands. These works also provide further reading for those who would like to engage with the subject more deeply. Visitor information, maps, and basic history can be found about each national monument on the corresponding government websites. I also included the websites of nonprofit organizations that support individual monuments and advocate for their care and protection.

AMERICA'S NATIONAL MONUMENTS AND PUBLIC LANDS

Antiquities Act of 1906. Public Law 59-209, U.S. Statutes at Large 225 (1906).

Blackburn, Fred M., and Ray A. Williamson. *Cowboys and Cave Dwellers: Basketmaker Archaeology in Utah's Grand Gulch.* Santa Fe: School of American Research Press, 1997.

Davis, Steven. *In Defense of Public Lands: The Case against Privatization and Transfer.* Philadelphia: Temple University Press, 2018.

Federal Land Management and Policy Act of 1976. Public Law 94-579, U.S. Statutes at Large 2743 (1976).

Hale, Edward. "Can the President Modify a Monument?" *The Regulatory Review*, September 4, 2019. https://www.theregreview.org/2019/09/04/hale-can-president-modify-monument/.

Harmon, David, Francis P. McManamon, and Dwight T. Pitcaithley, eds. *The Antiquities Act: A Century of American Archaeology, Historic Preservation, and Nature Conservation.* Tucson: University of Arizona Press, 2006.

Leshy, John D. *Debunking Creation Myths about America's Public Lands.* Salt Lake City: University of Utah Press, 2018.

"National Monuments and the Antiquities Act." Congressional Research Service, November 30, 2018. https://crsreports.congress.gov/product/pdf/R/R41330.

National Park Service Organic Act of 1916, U.S. Code 54 (1916), § 100101.

Ladino, Jennifer K. *Memorials Matter: Emotion, Environment, and Public Memory at American Historical Sites.* Reno: University of Nevada Press, 2019.

Meringolo, Denise D. *Museums, Monuments, and National Parks: Toward a New Genealogy of Public History.* Amherst and Boston: University of Massachusetts Press, 2012.

Miller, Char. *Public Lands, Public Debates: A Century of Controversy.* Corvallis: Oregon State University Press, 2012.

"Petrified Forest Is Reduced Half by Taft." *San Francisco Call* 110, no. 65 (August 4, 1911).

Rothman, Hal. *America's National Monuments: The Politics of Preservation.* Urbana: Board of Trustees of the University of Illinois, 1989.

Squillace, Mark. "The Monumental Legacy of the Antiquities Act of 1906." *Georgia Law Review* 37 (2002): 473.

SELECTED RESOURCES

U.S. Department of the Interior. "Interior Department Releases List of Monuments under Review, Announces First-Ever Formal Public Comment Period for Antiquities Act Monuments." Press release, May 5, 2017. https://www.doi.gov/pressreleases/interior-department-releases-list-monuments-under-review-announces-first-ever-formal.

Zinke, Ryan. "Memorandum to the President." As reported by *Washington Post*, August 24, 2017. https://www.documentcloud.org/documents/4052225-Interior-Secretary-Ryan-Zinke-s-Report-to-the.html.

BEARS EARS NATIONAL MONUMENT

PROCLAMATIONS

Obama, Barack. Proclamation 9558 of December 28, 2016. Establishment of the Bears Ears National Monument. *Federal Register* 82 (January 5, 2017): 1139–47.

Trump, Donald. Proclamation 9681 of December 4, 2017. Modifying the Bears Ears National Monument. *Federal Register* 82 (December 8, 2017): 58081–87.

Biden, Joe. Proclamation 10285 of October 8, 2021. Bears Ears National Monument. *Federal Register* 86 (October 15, 2021): 57321–34.

SOURCES

Bears Ears Inter-Tribal Coalition. "Bears Ears: A Native Perspective on America's Most Significant Unprotected Cultural Landscape." https://bearsearscoalition.org/wp-content/uploads/2016/03/Bears-Ears-bro.sm_.pdf.

Bears Ears Inter-Tribal Coalition. "Timeline of Tribal Engagement in Protection." http://www.bearsearscoalition.org/wp-content/uploads/2015/10/Timeline-of-Tribal-Engagement-in-Protection.pdf.

Begay, Cassandra. "Sir, there are many tribal leaders here." Video, Facebook, May 2017. https://www.facebook.com/cassalsa.b/videos/10156243046698228/.

Benally, Ryan. "Rescind Bears Ears National Monument Designation." *Indian Country Media Network*, May 26, 2017. https://www.indianz.com/News/2017/05/26/ryan-benally-bears-ears-was-a-false-prom.asp.

Lavender, David Sievert, and David Lavender. *One Man's West*. Lincoln: University of Nebraska Press, 2007.

"Navajo Nation President on Bears Ears: 'Our People Fought for Bears Ears.'" *Native News Online*, August 31, 2017. http://nativenewsonline.net/currents/navajo-nation-president-bears-ears-people-fought-bears-ears/.

Necefer, Len. Instagram post, April 7, 2018.

Necefer, Len. Email correspondence with author, June 2020.

Parry, Darren. "Great American Lie That All Tribes Are for Bears Ears NM." *San Juan Record*, May 2, 2017. https://www.sjrnews.com/public-lands/"great-american-lie-all-tribes-are-bears-ears-nm".

Robinson, Rebecca. *Voices from Bears Ears: Seeking Common Ground on Sacred Land*. Tucson: University of Arizona Press, 2018.

U.S. Department of the Interior. Bureau of Land Management. *Bears Ears National Monument: Record of Decision and Approved Monument Management Plans Indian Creek and Shash Jáa Units*. Utah, February 2020. https://eplanning.blm.gov/public_projects/lup/94460/20012455/250017011/BLM_ROD_and_Approved_MMPs_for_the_Indian_Creek_and_Shash_Jaa_Units_of_BENM_February2020.pdf.

SELECTED RESOURCES

U.S. Department of the Interior. Bureau of Land Management. *Record of Decision and Approved Plan Amendment for the Land and Resource Management Plan: Manti-La Sal National Forest, Bears Ears National Monument, Shash Jáa Unit.* Utah, February 2020. https://eplanning.blm.gov/public_ projects/lup/94460/20012456/250017012/USFS_ROD_and_Approved _Manti-La_Sal_National_Forest_LRMP_Amendment_for_the_BENM_ Shash_Jaa_Unit_February2020.pdf.

BEARS EARS NATIONAL MONUMENT
https://www.fs.fed.us/visit/bears-ears-national-monument

BEARS EARS INTER-TRIBAL COALITION
https://bearsearscoalition.org

UTAH DINÉ BIKÉYAH
https://utahdinebikeyah.org

FRIENDS OF CEDAR MESA
https://www.friendsofcedarmesa.org

GRAND CANYON TRUST
https://www.grandcanyontrust.org

KATAHDIN WOODS AND WATERS NATIONAL MONUMENT
PROCLAMATION

Obama, Barack. Proclamation 9476 of August 24, 2016. Establishment of the Katahdin Woods and Waters National Monument. *Federal Register* 81 (August 29, 2016): 59121–28.

SOURCES

"Carriage Roads and Gatehouses." Acadia National Park, National Park Service. https://www.nps.gov/acad/learn/historyculture/historiccarriage roads.htm.

"Charles W. Eliot, George Dorr, and a Son's Legacy." The Maine Thing Quarterly. https://visitmaine.com/quarterly/acadia/legacy.

Eliot, Charles William. *Charles Eliot: Landscape Architect, a Lover of Nature and of His Kind, Who Trained Himself for a New Profession, Practised It Happily and Through It Wrought Much Good.* Boston: Houghton, Mifflin, 1902.

"Protecting the Night." Night Skies, National Park Service. https://www.nps.gov/subjects/nightskies/index.htm.

Quimby, Roxanne. "Burt's Bees: Roxanne Quimby." Interview by Guy Raz. *How I Built This with Guy Raz*, NPR, February 18, 2019. https://www.npr.org/2019/02/15/695247911/burts-bees-roxanne-quimby.

Tobias, Michael Charles. "Maine vs. Thoreau: The Roxanne Quimby Question." *Forbes*, October 3, 2011. https://www.forbes.com/sites/michaeltobias/2011/10/03/maine-vs-thoreau-the-roxanne-quimby-question/#50004cae4a59.

"The Wabanaki: People of the Dawnland." Acadia National Park, National Park Service. https://www.nps.gov/acad/learn/historyculture/wabanaki.htm.

Whitcomb, Howard R. *Governor Baxter's Magnificent Obsession: A Documentary History of Baxter State Park, 1931–2006.* Friends of Baxter State Park, 2008.

Wilson, Woodrow. "Sieur de Monts National Monument Established: Proclamation (No. 1339) of July 8, 1916." https://www.nps.gov/subjects/legal/upload/2_National_Parks.pdf.

KATAHDIN WOODS AND WATERS NATIONAL MONUMENT
https://www.nps.gov/kaww/index.htm

FRIENDS OF KATAHDIN WOODS AND WATERS
https://www.friendsofkww.org

SELECTED RESOURCES

BERRYESSA SNOW MOUNTAIN NATIONAL MONUMENT

PROCLAMATION

Obama, Barack. Proclamation 9298 of July 10, 2015. Establishment of the Berryessa Snow Mountain National Monument. *Federal Register* 80 (July 15, 2015): 41975–81.

SOURCES

Olson, Steve, and Proctor Reid, eds. *Protecting National Park Soundscapes.* Washington, D.C.: National Academies Press, 2013.

Cagle, Susan. "Fire Is Medicine: Tribes Burning California Forests to Save Them." *The Guardian,* November 21, 2019. https://www.theguardian.com /us-news/2019/nov/21/wildfire-prescribed-burns-california-native-americans.

"National Conservation Lands." National Wilderness Stewardship Alliance, April 27, 2016. https://www.wildernessalliance.org/national_conservation_lands.

Raskin-Zrihen, Rachel. "Study Finds Good Reason to Keep Berryessa Snow Mountain a National Monument." *Daily Democrat,* June 7, 2017. https://www.dailydemocrat.com/2017/06/27/study-finds-good-reason-to-keep-berryessa-snow-mountain-a-national-monument/.

"The Connection between Global Warming and Wildfires." Union of Concerned Scientists, September 9, 2011. https://www.ucsusa.org/resources /climate-change-and-wildfires.

BERRYESSA SNOW MOUNTAIN NATIONAL MONUMENT (U.S. FOREST SERVICE)
https://www.fs.fed.us/visit/berryessa-snow-mountain-national-monument

BERRYESSA SNOW MOUNTAIN NATIONAL MONUMENT (BLM)
https://www.blm.gov/programs/national-conservation-lands/california/ berryessa-snow-mountain-national-monument

TULEYOME
http://tuleyome.org/projects/berryessa-snow-mountain-national-monument/

CASCADE-SISKIYOU NATIONAL MONUMENT

PROCLAMATIONS

Clinton, Bill. Proclamation 7318 of June 9, 2000. Establishment of the Cascade-Siskiyou National Monument. *Federal Register* 65 (June 13, 2000): 37249–52.

Obama, Barack. Proclamation 9564 of January 12, 2017. Boundary Enlargement of the Cascade-Siskiyou National Monument. *Federal Register* 82 (January 18, 2017): 6145–50.

SOURCES

Aldous, Vickie. "Lumber Companies File Lawsuit over Monument Expansion." *Mail Tribune,* February 17, 2017. https://mailtribune.com/news/happening-now/lumber-companies-file-lawsuit-over-monument-expansion.

American Forest Resource Council. Letter to Ryan Zinke re: "Executive Order on the Review of Designations under the Antiquities Act." May 2, 2017. https://amforest.org/wp-content/uploads/2017/05/Letter-to-Zinke-CSNM-Executive-Order-review-5-2-17.pdf.

Beckham, Stephen Dow. *O&C Sustained Yield Act: The Land, the Law, the Legacy, 1937–1987.* U.S. Department of the Interior, Bureau of Land Management, 1987. https://www.blm.gov/or/files/OC_History.pdf.

Headwaters Economics. "Cascade-Siskiyou National Monument: A Summary of Economic Performance in the Surrounding Communities." Spring 2017. https://headwaterseconomics.org/wp-content/uploads/CascadeSiskiyou.pdf.

SELECTED RESOURCES

Headwaters Economics. "The Economic Importance of National Monuments to Communities." August 2017. https://headwaterseconomics. org/public-lands/protected-lands/national-monuments/.

King, Pamela. "Greens, Trump Admin Appeal Cascade-Siskiyou Limits." *E&E News*, January 27, 2020. https://www.eenews.net/greenwire/stories /1062193373.

Letter to President Obama re: "Recommended Expansion of the Cascade-Siskiyou National Monument." May 28, 2015. https://groups.google. com/a/conbio.org/forum/#!topic/nalist/otzJSe1YBS4.

Lewis, David G. "The Land Is Our Heart: Protect the Cascade-Siskiyou National Monument." *NDN History Research*, July 16, 2017. https:// ndnhistoryresearch.com/2017/07/16/the-land-is-our-heart-protect-the-cascade-siskiyou-national-monument/.

Perkowski, Mateusz. "Legality of Cascade-Siskiyou Expansion Challenged." *Capital Press*, February 16, 2017. https://www.capitalpress.com /state/oregon/legality-of-cascade-siskiyou-expansion-challenged/article _5e912912-8237-576e-9bbb-34060c7b11ca.html.

Yachnin, Jeniffer. "Court Split Sets Up Showdown over Cascade-Siskiyou's Future." *E&E News*, November 26, 2019. https://www.eenews. net/greenwire/stories/1061653639/search?keyword=Cascade-Siskiyou.

Yachnin, Jeniffer. "Win for Obama-Era Protection of Ore. Timberland." *E&E News*, September 6, 2019. https://www.eenews.net/greenwire/ stories/1061111315.

CASCADE-SISKIYOU NATIONAL MONUMENT
https://www.blm.gov/programs/national-conservation-lands/national-monuments/oregon-washington/cascade-siskiyou

FRIENDS OF CASCADE-SISKIYOU
https://www.cascadesiskiyou.org

CASTLE MOUNTAINS NATIONAL MONUMENT

PROCLAMATION

Obama, Barack. Proclamation 9394 of February 12, 2016. Establishment of the Castle Mountains National Monument. *Federal Register* 81 (February 18, 2016): 8363–69.

SOURCES

Equinox Gold Corp. "Castle Mountain Gold Mine." https://www.equinoxgold.com/projects/castle-mountain/.

Mining Law of 1872. U.S. Statutes at Large 91-96 (1872).

Scott, Timothy D., Todd Wakefield, Don Tschabrun, and Terre Lane. "NI 43-101 Technical Report on the Preliminary Feasibility Study for the Castle Mountain Project." Equinox Gold Corp., July 16, 2018.

Shumway, Gary L., Larry M. Vredenburgh, and Russell D. Hartill. *Desert Fever: An Overview of Mining in the California Desert Conservation Area.* Bureau of Land Management, 1980.

Stringfellow, Kim. "Desert Gold: Part II." KCET, Public Media Group of California, August 14, 2019. https://www.kcet.org/shows/artbound/desert-gold-part-ii.

CASTLE MOUNTAINS NATIONAL MONUMENT
https://www.nps.gov/camo/index.htm

MOJAVE DESERT LAND TRUST
https://www.mdlt.org

MOJAVE MONUMENTS
http://www.mojavemonuments.org/castle-mountains/

SELECTED RESOURCES

SAND TO SNOW NATIONAL MONUMENT

PROCLAMATION

Obama, Barack. Proclamation 9396 of February 12, 2016. Establishment of the Sand to Snow National Monument. *Federal Register* 81 (February 18, 2016): 8379–85.

SOURCES

Carson, Rachel. *Silent Spring.* New York: First Mariner Books, 1962.

Grinnell, Hilda Wood. "Joseph Grinnell: 1877–1939." *The Condor* 42, no. 1 (1940): 3–34.

Grinnell, Joseph, and Alden H. Miller. *The Distribution of the Birds of California.* Pacific Coast Avifauna Number 27. Cooper Ornithological Club, December 30, 1944.

Grinnell, Joseph, and Harry Schelwald Swarth. *An Account of the Birds and Mammals of the San Jacinto Area of Southern California with Remarks upon the Behavior of Geographic Races on the Margins of Their Habitats.* Vol. 10. Berkeley: University of California Press, 1913.

"The Grinnell Resurvey Project." Museum of Vertebrate Zoology, University of California Berkeley. http://mvz.berkeley.edu/Grinnell/.

Iknayan, Kelly J., and Steven R. Beissinger. "Collapse of a Desert Bird Community over the Past Century Driven by Climate Change." *Proceedings of the National Academy of Sciences* 115, no. 34 (2018): 8597–602.

Morton, Timothy. "Introducing the Idea of 'Hyperobjects.'" *High Country News,* January 19 2015. https://www.hcn.org/issues/47.1/introducing-the-idea-of-hyperobjects.

Morton, Timothy. "The Mesh." In *Environmental Criticism for the Twenty-First Century,* edited by Stephanie LeMenager, Teresa Shewry, and Ken Hiltner, 19–30. New York: Routledge, 2011.

Unitt, Philip, and Lori Hargrove. "Southward and Downslope Extensions of Breeding Ranges of Birds in Southern California." In *Trends and Traditions: Avifaunal Change in Western North America*, edited by W. David Shuford, Robert E. Gill Jr., and Colleen M. Handel, 85–115. Camarillo, Calif.: Western Field Ornithologists, 2018.

Unitt, Philip, Scott Tremor, and Lori Hargrove. "Grinnell Resurveys in the Mojave Desert: SDNHM Field Report #1." Museum of Vertebrate Zoology of the University of California, July 19, 2016.

Unitt, Philip, Scott Tremor, Lori Hargrove, and Drew Stokes. "Grinnell Resurveys in the Mojave Desert: SDNHM Field Report #3." Museum of Vertebrate Zoology of the University of California, July 22, 2017.

SAND TO SNOW NATIONAL MONUMENT (U.S. FOREST SERVICE)
https://www.fs.fed.us/visit/sand-to-snow-national-monument

SAND TO SNOW NATIONAL MONUMENT (BLM)
https://www.blm.gov/visit/sand-to-snow-national-monument

MOJAVE DESERT LAND TRUST
http://www.mdlt.org

MOJAVE MONUMENTS
http://www.mojavemonuments.org/sand-to-snow

PAPAHĀNAUMOKUĀKEA MARINE NATIONAL MONUMENT
PROCLAMATIONS

Roosevelt, Theodore. Executive Order 1019 of February 3, 1909. Establishing Hawaiian Islands Reservation as Preserve and Breeding Ground for Native Birds.

Bush, George W. Proclamation 8031 of June 15, 2006. Establishment of the Northwestern Hawaiian Islands Marine National Monument. *Federal Register* 71 (June 26, 2006): 36441–75.

SELECTED RESOURCES

Bush, George W. Proclamation 8112 of February 28, 2007. Amending Proclamation 8031 of June 15, 2006, to Read, "Establishment of the Papahānaumokuākea Marine National Monument." *Federal Register* 72 (March 6, 2007): 10029–31.

Obama, Barack. Proclamation 9478 of August 26, 2016. Papahānaumokuākea Marine National Monument Expansion. *Federal Register* 81 (August 31, 2016): 60225–34.

Obama, Barack. Proclamation 9496 of September 15, 2016. Northeast Canyons and Seamounts Marine National Monument. *Federal Register* 81 (September 21, 2016): 65159–67.

Trump, Donald. Proclamation 10049 of June 5, 2020. Proclamation on Modifying the Northeast Canyons and Seamounts Marine National Monument. *Federal Register* 85 (June 6, 2020): 35793–95.

Biden, Joe. Proclamation 10287 of October 8, 2021. Northeast Canyons and Seamounts Marine National Monument. *Federal Register* 86 (October 15, 2021): 57349–53.

SOURCES

Chan, Hing Ling. "Economic Impacts of Papahānaumokuākea Marine National Monument Expansion on the Hawaii Longline Fishery." *Marine Policy* (2020): 103869.

"Climate Change and Marine Disease." Department of Land and Natural Resources. https://dlnr.hawaii.gov/coralreefs/climate-change-and-marine-disease/.

"Coral Reef Condition: A Status Report for the Hawaiian Archipelago." NOAA Coral Reef Conservation Program, Fall 2020. https://coralreef.noaa.gov.

"Coral Reef Condition: A Status Report for U.S. Coral Reefs 2020." NOAA Coral Reef Conservation Program, Fall 2020. https://coralreef.noaa.gov.

Cousteau, Jean-Michel, dir. *Ocean Adventures: Voyage to Kure 1*. Ocean Futures Society. October 19, 2016. YouTube video, 25 minutes. https://www.youtube.com/watch?v=liT7kePNKSg.

Cousteau, Jean-Michel, dir. *Ocean Adventures: Voyage to Kure 2*. Ocean Futures Society. February 7, 2017. YouTube video, 25 minutes. https://www.youtube.com/watch?v=W9hlif_mMh4.

Daws, Gavan. *Shoal of Time: A History of the Hawaiian Islands*. Honolulu: University of Hawaii Press, 1968.

Lynham, John, Anton Nikolaev, Jennifer Raynor, Thaís Vilela, and Juan Carlos Villaseñor-Derbez. "Impact of Two of the World's Largest Protected Areas on Longline Fishery Catch Rates." *Nature Communications* 11, no. 1 (2020): 1–9.

Sala, Enric, and Sylvaine Giakoumi, "No-Take Marine Reserves Are the Most Effective Protected Areas in the Ocean," *ICES Journal of Marine Science* 75, no. 3 (May-June 2018): 1166–68. https://doi.org/10.1093/icesjms/fsx059.

Vowell, Sarah. *Unfamiliar Fishes*. New York: Riverhead Books, 2012.

PAPAHĀNAUMOKUĀKEA MARINE NATIONAL MONUMENT
https://www.papahanaumokuakea.gov

KURE ATOLL CONSERVANCY
http://kureatollconservancy.org

FRIENDS OF MIDWAY
http://www.friendsofmidway.org

HAWAII CONSERVATION ALLIANCE
http://www.hawaiiconservation.org

SELECTED RESOURCES

GRAND STAIRCASE–ESCALANTE NATIONAL MONUMENT

PROCLAMATIONS

Clinton, Bill. Proclamation 6920 of September 18, 1996. Establishment of the Grand Staircase–Escalante National Monument. *Federal Register* 61 (September 24, 1996): 50223–27.

Trump, Donald. Proclamation 9682 of December 4, 2017. Modifying the Grand Staircase–Escalante National Monument. *Federal Register* 82 (December 8, 2017): 58089–96.

Biden, Joe. Proclamation 10286 of October 8, 2021. Grand Staircase–Escalante National Monument. *Federal Register* 86 (October 15, 2021): 57335–47.

SOURCES

Bruner, Travis. "Cows in the Escalante: When a Win-Win Becomes a Lose-Lose." Grand Canyon Trust, September 11, 2019. https://www.grandcan yontrust.org/blog/cows-escalante-when-win-win-becomes-lose-lose.

Childers, Michael W. *Colorado Powder Keg: Ski Resorts and the Environmental Movement.* Lawrence: University Press of Kansas, 2012.

Featherhat, Harlan. Interview by Marsha Holland, June 2016, Cedar City, Utah. Grand Staircase–Escalante National Monument Oral History Project. http://archive.li.suu.edu/docs/ms130/OH/featherhat.pdf.

Friedman, Lisa. "Trump Plans to Shrink Two National Monuments in Utah." *New York Times,* October 27, 2017. https://www.nytimes.com/2017 /10/27/climate/bears-ears-utah.html.

"Geology of the Grand Staircase–Escalante National Monument, Utah." Zion National-Park.com. http://www.zionnational-park.com/gsgeology. htm.

Larmer, Paul. "A Bold Stroke: Clinton Takes a 1.7 Million-Acre Stand in Utah." *High Country News,* September 30, 1996. https://www.hcn.org/ issues/90/2795.

Long, McKenzie. Notes from in-person attendance of a public meeting on the management plan for Grand Staircase–Escalante National Monument and the Kanab–Escalante Planning Area, March 2018. Kanab, Utah.

Maffly, Brian. "Cattle Could Return to Escalante Tributaries under New Grand Staircase Monument Plan." *Salt Lake Tribune,* March 10, 2020. https://www.sltrib.com/news/environment/2020/03/10/cattle-could-return/.

"NEPA Success Stories: Celebrating 40 Years of Transparency and Open Government." *Environmental Law Institute,* August 2010. https://ceq.doe.gov/docs/get-involved/NEPA_Success_Stories.pdf.

Oldham, Jennifer. "Forests on Utah's Public Lands May Soon Be Torn Out. Here's Why." *National Geographic,* September 3, 2019. https://www.nationalgeographic.com/environment/2019/09/pinyon-pine-juniper-forests-utah-torn-out-why/.

"Public and Private Land Percentages by U.S. States." Summitpost.org. https://www.summitpost.org/public-and-private-land-percentages-by-us-states/186111.

Rogers, Jedediah S. *Roads in the Wilderness: Conflict in Canyon Country.* Salt Lake City: University of Utah Press, 2013.

U.S. Department of the Interior. Bureau of Land Management. *Analysis of the Management Situation: Livestock Grazing Plan Amendment Environmental Impact Statement.* Utah, July 2015. https://eplanning.blm.gov/public_projects/lup/69026/89782/107364/201507_GSENM_AMS_Final_508.pdf.

U.S. Department of the Interior, Bureau of Land Management. "BLM and Forest Service Grazing Fees Lowered in 2019." https://www.blm.gov/press-release/blm-and-forest-service-grazing-fees-lowered-2019.

U.S. Department of the Interior. Bureau of Land Management. *Grand Staircase–Escalante National Monument: Approved Management Plan Record of Decision.* Utah, February 2000.

SELECTED RESOURCES

U.S. Department of the Interior. Bureau of Land Management. *Record of Decision and Approved Resource Management Plans for the Grand Staircase–Escalante National Monument*. Utah, February 2020. https://eplanning.blm.gov/public_projects/lup/94706/20012470/250017029/GSENM_ROD_and_ARMPs_February2020.pdf.

U.S. Department of the Interior. Bureau of Land Management. Record of Decision and Approved Resource Management Plan for the Kanab-Escalante Planning Area. Utah, February 2020.

Wang, Sonia, Spencer Phillips, Oliver Beavers, and John Stoner. "Public Support for Public Lands: Analysis of Comments Regarding Review and Potential Loss of Protection for America's National Monuments." *Key-Log Economics*. Prepared for the Wilderness Society, August 2017.

Wuerthner, George. "Grazing Threatens Escalante River." *Wildlife News*, October 21, 2019. https://www.thewildlifenews.com/2019/10/21/grazing-threatens-escalante-river/.

Wyatt, Alexandra M. "Antiquities Act: Scope of Authority for Modification of National Monuments." Congressional Research Service, 2016.

GRAND STAIRCASE–ESCALANTE NATIONAL MONUMENT
https://www.blm.gov/programs/national-conservation-lands/utah/grand-staircase-escalante-national-monument

GRAND STAIRCASE–ESCALANTE PARTNERS
https://gsenm.org

GRAND CANYON TRUST
https://www.grandcanyontrust.org

RIO GRANDE DEL NORTE NATIONAL MONUMENT

PROCLAMATION

Obama, Barack. Proclamation 8946 of March 25, 2013. Establishment of the Río Grande del Norte National Monument. *Federal Register* 78 (March 28, 2013): 18783–87.

SOURCES

DeBuys, William. *Enchantment and Exploitation: The Life and Hard Times of a New Mexico Mountain Range.* Albuquerque: University of New Mexico Press, 2015.

Phillips, Fred M., G. Emlen Hall, and Mary E. Black. *Reining in the Rio Grande: People, Land, and Water.* Albuquerque: University of New Mexico Press, 2015.

Simmons, Marc. *New Mexico: An Interpretive History.* Albuquerque: University of New Mexico Press, 1988.

RIO GRANDE DEL NORTE NATIONAL MONUMENT
https://www.blm.gov/visit/rgdnnm

FRIENDS OF RIO GRANDE DEL NORTE, CONSERVATION LANDS FOUNDATION
https://conservationlands.org/friends/friends-of-rio-grande-del-norte

HANFORD REACH NATIONAL MONUMENT

PROCLAMATION

Clinton, Bill. Proclamation 7319 of June 9, 2000. Establishment of the Hanford Reach National Monument. *Federal Register* 65 (June 13, 2000): 37253–57.

SOURCES

"Backgrounder on Plutonium." U.S. Nuclear Regulatory Commission, March 2017. https://www.nrc.gov/reading-rm/doc-collections/fact-sheets/plutonium.html.

Blasdel, Alex. "'A Reckoning for Our Species': The Philosopher Prophet of the Anthropocene." *The Guardian*, June 15, 2017. https://www.theguardian.com/world/2017/jun/15/timothy-morton-anthropocene-philosopher.

Evans, James R., Marita P. Lih, Peter W. Dunwiddie, Florence E. Caplow, Richard Easterly, Peter J. Landholt, and Terry T. McIntosh. "Biodiversity Studies of the Hanford Site." The Nature Conservancy, 2003.

SELECTED RESOURCES

Findlay, John M., and Bruce W. Hevly. *Atomic Frontier Days: Hanford and the American West*. Seattle: University of Washington Press, 2011.

Gallucci, Maria. "A Glass Nightmare: Cleaning Up the Cold War's Nuclear Legacy at Hanford." *IEEE Spectrum*, April 28, 2020. https://spectrum.ieee.org/aerospace/military/a-glass-nightmare-cleaning-up-the-cold-wars-nuclear-legacy-at-hanford.

Hansman, Heather. "There's No Easy Fix for Our Nuclear Past." *High Country News*, December 10, 2018. https://www.hcn.org/issues/50.21/nuclear-energy-theres-no-easy-fix-for-our-nuclear-past.

Morton, Timothy. *Hyperobjects: Philosophy and Ecology after the End of the World*. Minneapolis: University of Minnesota Press, 2013.

HANFORD SITE
https://www.hanford.gov

HANFORD REACH NATIONAL MONUMENT
https://www.fws.gov/refuge/hanford_reach/

FRIENDS OF THE MID-COLUMBIA RIVER WILDLIFE REFUGES
http://friendsofmcrwr.org

MANHATTAN PROJECT NATIONAL HISTORIC PARK
https://www.nps.gov/mapr/index.htm

ORGAN MOUNTAINS–DESERT PEAKS NATIONAL MONUMENT

PROCLAMATIONS

Obama, Barack. Proclamation 9131 of May 21, 2014. Establishment of the Organ Mountains–Desert Peaks National Monument. *Federal Register* 79 (May 28, 2014): 30431–37.

Trump, Donald. Executive Order 13767 of January 25, 2017. Border Security and Immigration Enforcement Improvements. *Federal Register* 82 (January 30, 2017): 8793–97.

Biden, Joe. Proclamation 10142 of January 20, 2021. Termination of Emergency with Respect to the Southern Border of the United States and Redirection of Funds Diverted to Border Wall Construction. *Federal Register* 86 (January 27, 2021): 7225–27.

SOURCES

Chard, Chester S. "Pre-Columbian Trade between North and South America." *Kroeber Anthropological Society Papers* 1 (1950): 1–27.

DeBuys, William. *Enchantment and Exploitation: The Life and Hard Times of a New Mexico Mountain Range*. Albuquerque: University of New Mexico Press, 2015.

Edgington, Ryan H. *Range Wars: The Environmental Contest for White Sands Missile Range*. Lincoln: University of Nebraska Press, 2014.

"Donald Trump Announces a Presidential Bid." *Washington Post,* June 16, 2015. https://www.washingtonpost.com/news/post-politics/wp/2015/06/16/full-text-donald-trump-announces-a-presidential-bid/.

Garrett, Pat Floyd. *The Authentic Life of Billy the Kid*. Vol. 3. Santa Fe, N.Mex.: Sunstone Press, 1954.

Gladwell, Malcolm. "General Chapman's Last Stand." June 13, 2018. Season 3, episode 5 of *Revisionist History*, podcast. http://revisionisthistory.com/episodes/25-general-chapman%27s-last-stand.

"Historical Resources: Structures or Noteworthy Events That Occurred on the Landscape." Organ Mountains–Desert Peaks National Monument. Organmountains.org. https://www.organmountains.org/the-lands/historical-resources/.

Klar, Rebecca. "Interior Transfers Parts of Public Lands to Army for Border Wall Construction." *The Hill,* September 18, 2019. https://thehill.com/homenews/administration/462089-interior-transfers-parts-of-public-land-to-army-for-border-wall.

SELECTED RESOURCES

"The Lure of the Dripping Springs: Eugene Van Patten – Dr. Nathan Boyd." DesertUSA. https://www.desertusa.com/desert-new-mexico/ruins-dripping-springs.html.

Metz, Leon Claire. *Pat Garrett: The Story of a Western Lawman.* Norman: University of Oklahoma Press, 1983.

Simmons, Marc. *New Mexico: An Interpretive History.* Albuquerque: University of New Mexico Press, 1988.

Taylor, Mary Daniels. *A Place as Wild as the West Ever Was: Mesilla, New Mexico 1848–1872.* Las Cruces: New Mexico State University Museum, 2004.

Trevizo, Perla, and Jeremy Schwartz. "Records Show Trump's Border Wall Is Costing Taxpayers Billions More Than Initial Contracts." *Texas Tribune and ProPublica,* October 27, 2020. https://www.texastribune.org/2020/10/27/border-wall-texas-cost-rising-trump/.

Vasquez, Gabe. "The Border Wall: The Fight to Save our Culture, Wildlife, and Public Lands." January 30, 2018. Episode 1 of *The Nuestra Tierra Conservation Podcast.* https://www.nuestra-tierra.org/ntpodcast/2018/1/30/01-the-border-wall-the-fight-to-save-our-culture-wildlife-public-lands.

ORGAN MOUNTAINS–DESERT PEAKS NATIONAL MONUMENT
https://www.blm.gov/programs/national-conservation-lands/new-mexico/organ-mountains-desert-peaks-national-monument

FRIENDS OF ORGAN MOUNTAINS–DESERT PEAKS
https://organmountainsdesertpeaks.org

EL CAMINO REAL DE TIERRA ADENTRO NATIONAL HISTORIC TRAIL
https://www.nps.gov/elca/index.htm

BASIN AND RANGE NATIONAL MONUMENT

PROCLAMATION

Obama, Barack. Proclamation 9297 of July 10, 2015. Establishment of the Basin and Range National Monument. *Federal Register* 80 (July 15, 2015): 41967–74.

SOURCES

Carr Childers, Leisl. *The Size of the Risk: Histories of Multiple Use in the Great Basin.* Norman: University of Oklahoma Press, 2015.

D'Agata, John. *About a Mountain.* New York: W. W. Norton and Company, 2011.

Douglas, Sam Wainwright, dir. *Through the Repellent Fence: A Land Art Film.* 2017.

Edgington, Ryan H. *Range Wars: The Environmental Contest for White Sands Missile Range.* Lincoln: University of Nebraska Press, 2014.

Eilperin, Juliet. "With Obama's Help, Harry Reid Leaving an Indelible Mark in the Nevada Desert." *Washington Post,* July 7, 2015. https://www .washingtonpost.com/politics/with-obamas-help-harry-reid-leaving-an-indelible-mark-in-the-nevada-desert/2015/07/07/8131bd88-1e75-11e5-aeb9-a411a84c9d55_story.html.

Goodyear, Dana. "A Monument to Outlast Humanity." *The New Yorker,* August 22, 2016. https://www.newyorker.com/magazine/2016/08/29/ michael-heizers-city.

Macy, Joanna. "Guardians of the Future." Interview by Alan AtKisson. *Context Institute,* 1991. https://www.context.org/iclib/ic28/macy/.

Martineau, LaVan. *The Rocks Begin to Speak.* Las Vegas: KC Publications, 1973.

McPhee, John. *Basin and Range.* New York: Farrar, Straus and Giroux, 1981.

SELECTED RESOURCES

Nuclear Guardianship Library. "Resources for Developing the Political, Technical and Moral Understanding Required for the Responsible Care of Radioactive Materials for Many Generations." https://www.earthcitizens.net/nuclear-guardianship/.

Ryan, Cy. "Why New National Monument Could Derail Plans for Nuke Dump at Yucca." *Las Vegas Sun*, July 10, 2015. https://lasvegassun.com/news/2015/jul/10/nevada-official-says-new-national-monument-throws-/.

Sebeok, Thomas A. *Communication Measures to Bridge Ten Millennia*. Office of Nuclear Waste Isolation, Battelle Project Management Division, 1984.

"'There's No Understanding of My Work': Michael Heizer on His Monumental Art, in 1977." *ARTnews*, June 26, 2015. https://www.artnews.com/art-news/retrospective/theres-no-understanding-of-my-work-michael-heizer-on-his-monumental-art-in-1977-4398/.

Trauth, Kathleen Marie, Stephen C. Hora, and Robert V. Guzowski. *Expert Judgment on Markers to Deter Inadvertent Human Intrusion into the Waste Isolation Pilot Plant*. Sandia National Laboratories, 1993.

BASIN AND RANGE NATIONAL MONUMENT
https://www.blm.gov/programs/national-conservation-lands/nevada/basin-and-range-national-monument

FRIENDS OF BASIN AND RANGE
http://www.protectbasinandrange.org

GOLD BUTTE NATIONAL MONUMENT

PROCLAMATION

Obama, Barack. Proclamation 9559 of December 28, 2016. Establishment of the Gold Butte National Monument. *Federal Register* 82 (January 5, 2017): 1149–55.

SOURCES

Bernstein, Maxine. "Cliven Bundy's Public Lands Claim Is 'Simply Delusional,' Judge Rules." *The Oregonian*, April 9, 2019. https://www.oregonlive.com/crime/2019/04/cliven-bundys-claim-that-all-public-land-belongs-to-state-of-nevada-is-simply-delusional-judge-rules.html.

"Caldera National Monument Idaho Advocacy." Facebook. https://www.facebook.com/CalderaNationalMonument/.

Martineau, LaVan. *The Rocks Begin to Speak*. Las Vegas: KC Publications, 1973.

Nelson, Dustin. "Save Gold Butte." http://www.savegoldbutte.com.

Nuwuvi Working Group in collaboration with the U.S. Forest Service. "Nuwu Kanee, Nuwu Tooveenup (Our Home, Our Story): Nuwuvi (Southern Paiute) and the Spring Mountains." Text sent to author by Shanandoah Anderson.

Pendley, William Perry. "The Federal Government Should Follow the Constitution and Sell Its Western Lands." *National Review*, January 19, 2016. https://www.nationalreview.com/2016/01/federal-government-should-sell-western-land-follow-constitution/.

Ritter, Ken. "Bundy Insists U.S. Government Can't Own Land—No Matter Who's President." *Salt Lake Tribune*, January 9, 2018. https://www.sltrib.com/news/nation-world/2018/01/10/bundy-insists-us-government-cant-own-land-no-matter-whos-president/.

The Salt Song Trail. February 8, 2012, YouTube video, 20 minutes. https://www.youtube.com/watch?v=rg-bi83mMSI.

GOLD BUTTE NATIONAL MONUMENT
https://www.blm.gov/programs/national-conservation-lands/nevada/gold-butte

FRIENDS OF GOLD BUTTE
https://www.friendsofgoldbutte.org

SELECTED RESOURCES

FRIENDS OF NEVADA WILDERNESS
https://www.nevadawilderness.org/goldbutte

EPILOGUE

Biden, Joe. Executive Order 14008 of January 27, 2021. Tackling the Climate Crisis at Home and Abroad. *Federal Register* 86 (February 1, 2021): 7619–33.

Haaland, Debra. "Thirty by Thirty Resolution to Save Nature." January 8, 2020. https://haaland.house.gov/sites/haaland.house.gov/files/wysiwyg _uploaded/Resolution_30by30_02072020.pdf.

"Hearing to Consider the Nomination of the Honorable Debra Haaland to be the Secretary of the Interior." February 23, 2021, Senate Committee on Energy and Natural Resources. Archived webcast: https://www.energy .senate.gov/hearings/2021/2/hearing-to-consider-nomination-of-the-honorable-debra-haaland-to-be-the-secretary-of-the-interior.

Pennington, Emily. "Deb Haaland Says Public Lands Should Reflect America." *Outside Online,* April 28, 2021. https://www.outsideonline.com /2422775/deb-haaland-doi-public-lands

Index

Abbey, Joshua, 249
Acadia National Park, 35–36, 37, 40
access: conservation and, 57, 63;
   equitable, 32, 235–36, 283–84;
   to federal land, 261; to formerly
   public land, 31; to national
   monuments, 9, 13–15, 19, 40, 50,
   53–54, 63, 78, 136, 207, 235–36,
   267–68, 271–73; to national parks,
   37; to public land, 13, 35, 266, 271
Access Fund (nonprofit), 23
acequia parciantes, 184, 191
acequias, 176, 179
Acoma people, 152, 231, 281
Acoma Pueblo (Sky City), 231–32
Adena culture, 245
Alaska, xxi, 149–50, 158
Alto Diablo Peak, 108
Amador, Don, 53–54
American Forest Resource Council,
   73

American settlers, 177, 233, 244
America's National Monuments
   (Rothman), xiv–xv
Ancestral Pueblo ruins, 152–53
Andalex Resources Inc., 150
Anderson, Bob, 202
Anderson, Shanandoah, 259
Anderson Peak, 111
Antiquities Act: about, xiv–xv, xvi,
   xix–xxi; Biden and, 283; Bush
   and, 131, 133–34; Carter and, 149;
   Clinton and, 71, 149; flexibility of,
   52; intent of, xxv–xxvi; managing
   agencies and, xviii; nonuse of,
   123; Obama and, 11–12, 39–40,
   83; ocean environments and, 131,
   133–34; opposition to, xii, xv, 8, 9;
   reductions and expansions under,
   xxii–xxiii, 25; text of, 291–92;
   Trump and, 19–20, 151, 165
Apache Wars, 222

aquifers, 89
archaeological sites, xv, xix, 151–53, 248, 268, 292
archaeology, xiii–xiv
Athapaskan people, 69
Atomic Energy Commission, 201
ATV riding, 14, 23, 53, 62, 184, 269. *See also* off-road vehicles

B Reactor, 196, 202, 211
Babbitt, Bruce, 56, 202
Basin and Range (McPhee), 242
Basin and Range National Monument (Nevada), 239–255; *City* sculpture in, 239, 241, 244–46, 252; Indigenous people and, 254; landscape of, 241–42, 254–55; map of, 240; nuclear waste storage near, 246–52; Obama designates, 253; rock writing in, xxvii, 242–44, 247–50
Baxter, Percival, 37–38, 41
Baxter State Park (Maine), 31, 38
beagles, 201, 210
Bears Ears: A Native Perspective (publication), 6
Bears Ears Buttes, xii–xiii, 10, 19
Bears Ears Commission, 20, 25
Bears Ears Inter-Tribal Coalition, 6, 10, 11–12
Bears Ears National Monument (Utah), 3–26; author in, xi–xiii; Biden reinstates boundaries of, xxiv, 24–25; climbing at Indian Creek, 3, 5, 10, 20–21, 25–26; collaborative effort and, 52; effect of recreation on, 122; Ickes and,

8; Indigenous people and, 6–7, 9–14, 16–18, 52, 184; land use disputes in, 9–10, 12–15, 273; map of, 4; mining in, 166; Mormon settlers and, 7; Obama designates, xxii, 11–12; ranchers and, 21–22; Trump reduces, xxii, 12, 16, 18–20, 82–83, 166
Beatty (Nevada), 246
Beery, Wallace, xx
Beesley, Russell, 160, 164
Begay, Cassandra, 16–17
Begaye, Russell, 18
Beissinger, Steve, 114
Bell, James, 224–25
Belle Fourche River, xix
Benally, Rebecca, 14
Benally, Ryan, 14
Bennett, Bob, 9, 149
Bernhardt, David, 221, 262
Berryessa Peak, 47
Berryessa Snow Mountain National Monument (California), 45–64; birdwatching in, 54–56; BLM and, 56–57; Bob Schneider with Tuleyome and, 48–50, 52, 62; collaborations to create, 52–54; fires near, 45, 47–48, 58, 60–62, 279, 280; Indigenous people and, 61; management of, 58; map of, 46; wineries near, 50–52, 63
Biden, Joe, xxiii–xxiv, 24–25, 143, 166, 236, 282–83, 309
Big Chief mine, 92
Big Rock (in Rio Grande), 173, 175, 189–90
Big Spring Brook Hut, 30, 36

bighorn sheep, 87, 89, 111, 189, 232, 274
biking, mountain, 24, 40, 54, 234, 235
Billy the Kid (William Bonney), 222–25
Bingaman, Jeff, 178, 179
biodiversity: in Berryessa Snow Mountain, 54, 60; in Cascade-Siskiyou, 71–72, 77–78, 81, 85; in Mojave Desert, 114; monuments and, xix–xx, 283; in Papahānaumokuākea, 123, 126–27, 142
Bird Island (Nihoa), 123
bird-watching, 54–55, 195, 198
Bishop, Rob, 9, 11
black reef triggerfish (*humuhumu-nukunukuapuaʻa*), 138
bleaching, coral, 123–24, 137, 143
Blue Lake, 187–88
Blue Ridge, 58–59
Bluff (Utah), 15
Boasberg, James E., 134
bobcats, 33, 35
Bonney, William (Billy the Kid), 222–25
border wall, U.S.–Mexico, 203, 217, 221, 226, 232, 236–37, 282
Bossie, Andrew, 33
Bowen, Brian, 127, 128–29, 138–39
Bowlin Camp, 27, 29
Boyd, Nathan, 222
Brown, Matthew, 135, 136
Bryce Canyon National Park, 145
buckhorn cholla, 90, 96
Bullet Canyon (Utah), xi–xii, xiii, 13, 20

bunchgrass, 199–200
Bundy, Cliven, 257, 259, 260–61, 263, 269, 273, 276
Bundy family, 257, 260, 262
Bureau of Indian Affairs, 283
Bureau of Land Management (BLM): about, 283; Bears Ears, 12; Berryessa Snow Mountain, 57–58; Cascade-Siskiyou, 74–75, 82; designates wilderness areas, 7; Grand Staircase–Escalante, 56, 150, 158–59, 160, 166; Indian Creek, 5; monuments managed by, xvi, xvii, xviii; Pendley at, 262–63; public land administered by (or about), 261; Rio Grande del Norte, 178; Taos Pueblo tribe and, 186
Bureau of Reclamation, 60
burns, intentional, 61–62
Burt's Bees (company), 31
Bush, George H. W., xxi
Bush, George W., xx, xxiv, 131, 133, 134, 135–36, 304–5
butterflies, 75–76, 232

C Reactor, 209
Cache Creek, 50
Cache Creek Wilderness, 50
Cahuilla people, 102
Caldera National Monument, 266, 273
Caldera National Monument Idaho Advocacy group, 268–69
Caliente (Nevada), 252
California Bureau of Land Management, 56

California Coastal National Monument, 133
California lilacs, 63
Canyonlands National Park, 5, 8, 22
Carr Childers, Leisl, 242
Carson, Rachel, 115
Carter, Jimmy, xxi, xxiii, 149, 158, 301–2
Cascade Range, 71
Cascade-Siskiyou National Monument (Oregon and California), 69–85; biodiversity of, 71, 77–78, 81, 85; butterflies in, 75–76; Clinton designates, 69, 71; economic growth from, 79–80; impact of recreation on, 122; landscape of, 72–73, 75–76, 80–82; map of, 70; O&C land of, 73–74, 82–83; Obama expands, 69, 72, 73–74, 165; public view of, 84; Trump reviews, 69, 74, 82
Casey, Edward, 219
Castle Mountain Mine, 90–92, 94–95
Castle Mountains National Monument (California), 87–96; aquifer in, 89; bighorn sheep in, 89; gold mine in, 87, 89, 91–93, 95–96; Hart in, 93–94; map of, 88; Obama designates, 89, 90, 97
Catholicism, 230
cattle grazing, 14–15, 22–23, 157–59, 166, 168, 178, 242, 260, 263, 267–68, 270–71
Cayuse tribe, 207
Cedar Roughs Wilderness, 50
Cerro Viento (Windy Mountain), 183
Chaco Canyon, 188

Chacon, Raven, 245–46
Chan, Hing Ling, 139
Channel Islands National Monument, 133
chaparral ecosystems, 58, 60
Charlton Peak, 106, 108
cheatgrass, 199–200, 206
Chernobyl disaster, 250
Chihuahuan Desert, 232
Childers, Michael W., 163–64
chipmunks, 105–6
Chocolate Cliffs, 145
Church of Jesus Christ of Latter-day Saints, 7, 149
City (Heizer), 241, 244–45, 246, 250, 252, 253
Ciudad Juarez, 175
Clarke, Mark, 82
cliff dwellings, 6, 152–53
Cliff Palace (Mesa Verde), xiii
climate change, 60, 72, 100, 114–16, 130, 142–43, 251, 280, 282–84
climates, warming, 48, 61, 104, 110, 115
climbers/climbing, impact of, 11, 20, 22–24, 48–49, 116
Clinton, Bill: about monuments designated by, xx, xxiv; California Coastal National Monument, 133; Cascade-Siskiyou, 69, 71; Grand Staircase–Escalante, xxi–xxii, xxiii, 56, 149–151; Hanford Reach National Monument, 202; monuments proclaimed by, 302–4; Northwestern Hawaiian Islands Coral Reef Ecosystem Reserve, 123, 131
Coconut Island, 127

INDEX

Coleman, Arthur, 272, 276
Columbia River, 195, 196, 197, 201, 202, 205
Columbia River Gorge, 198
Comb Ridge, 18, 19
communication marker, 248–49, 251
Congress: establishes Canyonlands National Park, 8; establishes national monuments, xxi; establishes national parks, xvi, xviii; O&C Act, 73; Rattlesnake Mountain and, 207
conservation, xvii, xxi, xxiv, xxvi–xxvii, 39, 57, 62, 63, 78
conservation areas, 178–79
Conservation Lands Foundation, 225
conservation movement, American, 7–8
Constitution, U.S., 260
convict tangs, 138
Cook, Paul, 91
Coolidge, Calvin, xxiii, 297–98
coral reefs, 123, 142, 143
Coral Triangle, 126–27, 143
Cousteau, Jean-Michel, 131
coyotes, 198, 200, 201
creosote, 219, 230, 237, 259, 285
Cure Island (Kure Atoll), 123

Dance Hall Rock, 151
Deafy Glade trailhead, 45
Death Valley, xviii
deBuys, William, 191, 217
Department of Energy, 195, 196, 202
Department of Housing and Urban Development, 267

Department of Land and Natural Resources, State of Hawaii, 135
Department of Natural Resources, Taos Pueblo, 186
Department of the Interior, U.S., 73
Desert Peaks district, 226
Desert Space Foundation, 249, 250
Devils Postpile National Monument, xvi
Devils Tower National Monument, xv, xix
Diné (Navajo) people, 6, 9–10, 23–24, 152
Doña Ana Mountains, 227
Dorr, George, 35–36, 41
Double Negative (Heizer), 241, 244, 246, 250
Douglas, Fawn, 274, 275
Douglas fir (*Pseudotsuga*), 72–73, 74, 76
drilling, oil, xvii, xxvi, 7, 122, 166
Dripping Springs Resort, 221–23
drug trafficking, 217
Dutton, Clarence, 145, 160

eagles, 195, 198–99, 201, 213
economic factors: at Cascade-Siskiyou, 78–80; at Grand Staircase–Escalante, 64, 161; at Hanford Reach, 196, 211; in Hawaii, 125, 133–34, 139; at Katahdin Woods and Waters, 32, 39; in Utah, xxii, 8, 19
ecosystems: at Bears Ears, 5; at Berryessa Snow Mountain, 60; at Cascade-Siskiyou, 71, 78; at Castle Mountains, 89; conservation of, xxvi; at Gold Butte, 276;

at Grand Staircase–Escalante, 149; at Hanford Reach, 206; at Papahānaumokuākea Marine, 122, 128, 130

Edgington, Ryan, 247

effigy mounds, 250

egrets, snowy, 201

Eisenhower, Dwight, xxiii, 300

El Camino Real de Tierra Adentro, 225–26

El Capitan, xxv, 48–49

El Morro National Monument (New Mexico), xv, xix

El Paso (Texas), 230, 233

Eliot, Charles, 35

Eliot, Charles W., 35–36, 41

elk, 183, 208–9, 270

Enchantment and Exploitation (deBuys), 191

endangered species: in Berryessa Snow Mountain, 57; at Cascade-Siskiyou, 72; in Castle Mountains, 95; conservation of, xxvi; desert tortoise, 111; foothill yellow-legged frog, 49; at Organ Mountains–Desert Peaks, 232; at Papahānaumokuākea, 119, 121, 123, 129, 134; sage grouse, 163, 242

Endangered Species Act, 8

environmental cleanup, 209

environmental movement, 244, 263

Environmental Protection Agency, 7–8

environmentalists, xxvi, 9, 11, 79, 149, 157, 167, 184, 264, 269

Equinox Gold, 91, 95–96

erosion, xv, 21, 23, 237

Escalante Canyons Unit, 150. *See also* Grand Staircase–Escalante National Monument (Utah)

European settlers, 6, 206, 244, 263

Ewing, Josh, 15, 273

Exclusive Economic Zone (EEZ), 133, 134

expansions, monument: by Biden, xxiii–xxiv, 24–25, 143, 166; by Obama, 69, 72, 73–74, 76, 82–83, 134, 136, 139, 165

Falling Man Petroglyph Site, 268, 276

farmers, 24, 202, 206

Fat Man bomb, 196

Featherhat, Harlan, 165

Federal Lands Policy and Management Act (FLPMA), xxiii, 56, 273

fires: California, 45, 58, 60–61, 94, 279–280; Washington, 199–200, 203–4, 205–6

fish species, 123, 128, 130, 143. *See also specific types of fish*

fishing, 40, 139–140, 142, 143

Floyd, George, 281

flying squirrel, San Bernadino, 112–13

Fort Ancient culture, 245

four-wheelers. *See* ATV riding

Fremont County (Idaho), 267, 269

Fremont style rock writing, 244

French Frigate Shoals, 121, 127

Friends of Cedar Mesa, 15

Friends of Gold Butte, 274

Friends of Katahdin Woods and Waters, 33

Friends of Organ Mountains–Desert Peaks, 233

INDEX

frogs, yellow-legged, 49, 63
Fulks, Andrew, 50

Garcia, Ester, 177–80, 185, 191
Garden Valley, 239, 241, 252
Garrett, Pat, 224
Garrett, William, 272, 276
General Mining Law of 1872, 92
Geronimo, 219–20, 222
Gettysburg National Military Park, xxv
Gila Cliff Dwellings, xix
Glacial Lake Missoula, 198
Glacier Bay, xxiii
glaciers, 143, 198
Glass, Lamont, 207, 211
glass rods, 209–10
global warming, 115, 123–24, 137
gnatcatchers, black-tailed, 103, 104
Gold Butte National Monument (Nevada), 257–77; Bundy and, 257, 259–61; Indigenous people and, 259–60, 263–64, 274–77; landscape of, 261–62; map of, 258; monument opponents, 270–72; Obama designates, 259; Pendley and, 262–63
gold mining, 90–96, 272
Golden Gate National Recreation Area, xxv
Gomez, Sam, 180
González, José, 233
Graham, Charles Cary, xiii, xiv
granaries, 6, 153–54
Grand Canyon, xviii–xix, xxiii, 145, 149, 180
Grand Gulch (Utah), xiii

Grand Portage Band of Minnesota Chippewa, 18
Grand Portage National Monument, 17–18
Grand Staircase–Escalante National Monument (Utah), 145–68; ancient cultural areas of, 152–55; Biden reinstates boundaries of, xxiv; Clinton designates, xxi–xxiii, 149, 151; grazing in, 157–59; landscape of, 145, 147–48, 155, 157, 167–68; management of, 56, 159–62, 166–67, 271; map of, 146; mining and, 149–51, 158, 161, 162, 163, 164, 166–68; monument review of, 25, 163–64; ranchers in, 159; Trump reduces, xxii, 12, 18–19, 82–83, 150–51, 157, 165–66; visitors to, xv
Grand Teton National Forest, xx
Grand Teton National Park, xviii, xx
Gray Cliffs, 145, 154
grazing. See cattle grazing
Great American Outdoors Act, 283
Great Basin, 242
Great Basin Desert, 71, 247
Great Northern Paper Company, 38
Great Salt Lake, 244
Green Springs (Oregon), 83
greenhouse gas emissions, 142
green-tailed towhees, 107
Griffen Moon Timber Sale, 74
Grinnell, Joseph, 100–101, 103, 105–7, 110, 112, 114, 116
Grosvenor Arch, 151
groundwater, 111, 209
grouse, sage, 163, 204, 242
guano mining, 131

guzzlers, 111, 114

Haaland, Debra, 283–84
Haas, Dan, 193, 195–201, 202
Halstead, Robert, 252
Hamblin, Ron, 159
Hanauma Bay, 137–39
Hancock County Trustees of Public Reservations, 35
Hanford Reach National Monument (Washington), 193–213; Clinton designates, 202; eagles in, 198–99, 200, 201; fires in, 199–200, 203–6; Hanford Site, 195–97, 201–2, 207, 209–13; Indigenous people and, 207; map of, 194; native plant restoration in, 202–5; Rattlesnake Mountain, 207–8, 210–11
Hanford Site, 195–97, 201–2, 207, 209–13, 246–47, 251
Harding, Warren G., 297
Hargrove, Lori, 101, 103–6, 107, 110, 112–13
Hart (California), 93–94
Hart, Jim, 92, 93
Hart Peak, 91, 93, 95, 96
Hastey, Ed, 56
Hatch, Orrin, 149, 150
Hawai'i Institute of Marine Biology (HIMB), 127
Hawaiian Islands, 122, 128
Hawaiian Islands Bird Reservation, 123
Hawaiian Islands, Northwestern, 122–24, 129–31, 141–42
Hawaiian Islands Wildlife Refuge, 123

Headwaters Economics, 78
heap leaching, 94–95
Heinrich, Martin, 227, 234
heirs, land grant, 178, 184, 191
Heizer, Michael, 241, 244, 246, 252–53
Henry's Fork, 267, 270
Herbert, Gary, 12, 150
Herndon, Lucas, 233–34
herons, great blue, 186, 198, 201
hikers/hiking, impact of, xvii, 20, 62, 76–78, 80, 81, 103–4, 207–8, 210
Hitt, Bert and Clark, 92, 93
Hole in the Rock Road, 167
Holt, Nancy, 244
Hoover, Herbert, xviii, 298–99
Hopi people, 6, 10, 152
horseback riders, 62
Huchnom people, 61
hummingbirds, Anna's, 55–56
hunting, 14, 31–32, 38, 39, 40, 229
hyperobjects, 115, 210, 251

Ickes, Harold, 8
Idaho, 264–65
Iknayan, Kelly, 114
immigration enforcement, 232–33
Indian Creek, 3, 10, 14, 19–21, 227, 284
Indigenous people: Antiquities Act and, xxv–xxvi; assimilating, 274; Basin and Range and, 254; Bears Ears and, 6–7, 9–14, 16–18, 52, 184; Berryessa Snow Mountain and, 61; comanagement with federal government, 25; El Camino Real de Tierra Adentro, 226; Gold Butte and, 259–60,

263–64, 270–71, 274–77; Grand
Portage National Monument and,
17–18; Grand Staircase–Escalante
and, 165; Hanford Reach and,
196, 206; land seized from, 263–
64; meanings of land and time to,
254; New Mexicans, 233; Organ
Mountains–Desert Peaks and,
234–35; PLI and, 9, 11; Rattlesnake Mountain and, 207; sacred
areas of, 6–7, 14, 187, 196, 275–76;
slaughter and displacement of,
xiii, xxvii; in Utah, 6, 159; Zinke
and, 16, 18
Interim Safe Storage, 209
International Dark Sky Sanctuary, 33
invasive species, 114, 131, 157, 185,
199, 206
Island Park (Idaho), 264, 266–67,
269–70, 272–73
Island Park Preservation Coalition,
266–67

Jackson County (Oregon), 74, 78–79
Jackson Hole National Monument,
xx–xxi
Jake, Vivienne, 274–75, 276
Jepson Peak, 103, 104, 105
Jewell, Sally, 11, 63
John Muir Trail, 103
Johnson, Lyndon B., 301
Johnston Atoll, 127
Joshua Tree National Park, xviii, 89,
97
Joshua trees, 90, 96, 260
Juárez, Mexico, 233

Ka'ena Point, 126, 128–29, 141, 142

Kaibab Paiute people, 152, 274
Kaiona Beach, 121
Kaiparowits Formation, 148
Kaiparowits Plateau, 147, 150, 152,
158, 162, 164
Kamehameha, 135
Kanab (Utah), 160
Kane County (Utah), 164
Kaneohe Bay, 123, 127, 138
Katahdin Lake, 38
Katahdin Woods and Waters
National Monument (Maine),
27–43; author in, 27, 29–33, 36–
37; Baxter State Park near, 37–38;
Indigenous people and, 30; land
gifted to government for, xvii;
management plan for, 40; map
of, 28; night sky in, 33–34, 41–42,
285; Obama designates, 39–40,
52; Quimby and, 31–32, 284; St.
Clair and, 38–43, 277, 284
Kennedy, John F., 301
Key-Log Economics, 163
Kilbourne Hole, 217–19
kivas, 6
Klamath Mountains, 71
Klamath people, 69
Kosmoceratops, 147–48
Kure Atoll (Cure Island), 123, 127
Kwiria-Kaich, 102

la frontera, 217, 232
La Junta Point, 175, 176
Ladino, Jennifer K., xxv
Lafayette National Park (Maine), 36
Lake Berryessa, 49, 54, 58, 59, 60–61
Lake County stonecrop, 50
Lake Mead reservoir, 259

345

Lake Miwok people, 61
Lake Powell, 154
land: federal, 11–12, 56, 92, 150, 166, 260–64, 283; public, xiv, xvii–xviii, xxiii–xxiv, xxvi, 9, 150, 157–58, 181, 236, 262–64, 266, 271, 273, 275–76, 281, 284
land art, 244–45, 249–50
land donations, private, 35–38, 39
land grabs, xii, xvii, 38, 149
Land Grant Board, 178–79
Lanfair groundwater basin, 89
Las Cruces (New Mexico), 215, 217, 221, 226, 230
Las Vegas Band of Paiutes, 274
Las Vegas (Nevada), 247, 257, 261–62
Lassen Peak, 105
Latino Outdoors, 233
Lava Beds National Monument, 285
Laysan albatross (*moli*), 141
Laysan Island, 131, 141
Leavitt, Mike, 149
Lehi, Malcolm, 16
Leon, Richard, 83
light pollution, 33
Lili'uokalani, Queen, 135
Lincoln County War, 223
lions, mountain, 89, 232
Little Charlton Peak, 105, 106
Little Finland (Nevada), 261–62
logging, 7, 18, 31–32, 38, 72, 74, 78, 270
Lopez, Pablo, 234, 235
The Lorax (Seuss), 90
Lynham, John, 139–40

Macy, Joanna, 250–51, 254
Madison, James, 262

Malheur National Wildlife Refuge, 257, 260
mammoths, 234
management, land, 7–9, 163–64
management, national monument, xvi–xviii, xviii, 25, 40, 56, 58, 159–62, 166–67, 271–72
Manhattan Project, 195, 196, 217
Manhattan Project National Historical Park, 211
Manzanar National Historic Site, xxv
Mardon skippers (butterfly), 75–76, 78
Marianas Trench National Monument, 134
marine monuments, 133–34. *See also* Papahānaumokuākea Marine National Monument (Hawaii)
marine sanctuaries, 131
Mariposa County (California), 45, 47
Martineau, LaVan, 243, 247, 259, 274
Martinez, Cameron, 186–88, 254, 284
Martinez, Cristóbal, 245
Mason, Matt, 234
Massachusetts Lobsterman's Association v. Ross, 134
McNary National Wildlife Refuge, 193, 207, 211
McPhee, John, 242
meadowlarks, western, 205
Memorials Matter (Ladino), xxv
Meringolo, Denise D., xxv
Mesa Verde (Colorado), xiii, xiv, 188
Mexican-American War, 177
Mexico City, 226
Midway Island, 127, 131, 141

INDEX

mine reclamation, 95–96
mining: coal, xxii, 11, 20, 149–50,
    158, 162, 164, 166, 168; gold, 87,
    89, 90–96, 271, 272; guano, 131;
    prioritizing, 18; wilderness areas
    and, 7
Minnesota Chippewa Tribe, 18
missionaries, 102, 135, 176
Missoula floods, 198, 208
Moapa Valley (Nevada), 241
Mojave Desert, 89, 90, 93–94, 97,
    102, 111, 114, 247
Mojave National Preserve, 89
Mojave Trails National Monument,
    89, 97
Momyer Trail, 99, 101, 112, 116
monk seals (*ilio-holo-i-ka-uaua*),
    129–30
Montezuma Castle National
    Monument, xvi
Monticello (California), 60–61
Monticello (Utah), 14
monument reductions. *See* reduc-
    tions, national monument
monument reviews. *See* reviews,
    national monument
monuments, national, xv–xx, xxv,
    xxvii, 116, 281–83
Mormon Church, 11
Mormon settlers, 7, 159, 167, 168, 259
Morton, Timothy, 115, 210, 251
Mount Desert Island, 35
Mount Katahdin (Maine), 31, 37–38.
    See also Katahdin Woods and
    Waters National Monument
    (Maine)
Mount Olympus National Monu-
    ment, xxiii

Mount Saint Helens National
    Volcanic Monument, xxi
Mount Shasta, 81, 105
mountain biking, 24, 40, 54, 234, 235
mountain lions, 89, 232
Mt. Irish Archaeological District, 248
Muir, John, 264
Muir Woods, xix
mule deer, 201, 204–5
Murphy Timber Company, 74, 78, 82
Museum of Modern Art, 252
Museum of Vertebrate Zoology
    (MVZ), 100

N Reactor, 201
Napa County (California), 58
Napa Valley wineries, 51
National Conservation Lands, 56–57,
    158, 161
National Environmental Policy Act,
    263
national forests, xx, 187, 264, 280,
    285
national monument reductions. *See*
    reductions, national monument
national monument reviews. *See*
    reviews, national monument
National Oceanic and Atmospheric
    Administration (NOAA), xviii,
    135, 261
National Park Service (NPS), xvi–
    xviii, xxv, 18, 33, 56, 90–91, 158,
    211, 261, 269, 283–84
National Park Service Organic Act,
    273
national parks, xv–xvi
National September 11 Memorial,
    xxv

National Wild and Scenic Rivers
System, 176
Native Americans, xiii, 17, 165, 180,
184, 259, 270–71, 284. *See also*
Indigenous people
Native Hawaiians, 135–36
Natives Outdoors (nonprofit), 24
Natural Bridges National Monu-
ment, xix
nature, economic value of, 79–80
Navajo Code talkers, 284
Navajo Nation, 10, 17, 18, 24
Necefer, Len, 24
Nelson, Dustin, 270–71, 272–73
Nevada Museum of Art, 252
Nevada Test Site, 247
New Mexico. *See* Organ Mountains–
Desert Peaks National Monu-
ment (New Mexico)
New Mexico Outdoor Equity Fund,
236
New Mexico Wild (nonprofit), 181
NewCastle Gold, 91
Newspaper Rock, 19
Nez Perce tribe, 207
night sky, 33–34, 41–42
Nihoa (Bird Island), 121, 123
Nike missile site, 207
Nine Peak Challenge, 99, 104
NOAA Coral Reef Conservation
Program, 141
Nomlaki people, 61
Nordenskiöld, Gustaf, xiv
North Coast Wilderness Wild
Heritage bill, 50
Northeast Canyons and Seamounts
Marine National Monument,
134, 140, 143

Northwestern Hawaiian Islands,
122–24, 129–31, 141–42
Northwestern Hawaiian Islands
Coral Reef Ecosystem Reserve,
123, 131
nuclear bombs, 195, 211–12
Nuclear Guardianship Bill of Rights,
254, 284
Nuclear Guardianship movement,
250–51
nuclear reactors, 195–97, 201, 209,
211, 213
nuclear testing, 242
nuclear waste, 197, 206, 209–10,
246, 248–49, 251–53, 282
Nuestra Tierra Conservation
Project, 236
"Nuwu Kanee, Nuwu Tooveenup
(Our Home, Our Story)," 276–77
Nuwuvi (Southern Paiute) people, 6,
274, 276–77
Nuwuvi Working Group, 277

O&C Act, 73–74, 82–83
Oahu, 121–24, 142, 195
Obama, Barack: about monuments
designated by, xx, xxiv; Antiquities Act and, xxiii; designates
Basin and Range, 239, 252–53;
designates Bears Ears, xii, xxii,
11–12, 19; designates Berryessa
Snow Mountain, 54, 63; designates Castle Mountains, 89, 91,
97; designates Gold Butte, 259;
designates Katahdin Woods and
Waters, 39; designates Mojave
Trails, 89, 97; designates Rio
Grande del Norte, 178; designates

Sand to Snow, 89, 97; expands Cascade-Siskiyou, 69, 72, 73–74, 76, 82–83, 165; expands Papahānaumokuākea, 134, 136, 139, 165; presidential monument proclamations of, 305–8

observatories, research, 208, 212

oceans: importance to Native Hawaiians, 136; as national monuments, 142; ownership of, 131, 133

Office of Hawaiian Affairs, 135

Office of Mine Reclamation (State of California), 95

off-road vehicles, 14, 267–68, 270. *See also* ATV riding

Ohkay Owingeh (San Juan) Pueblo, 226

Old Grayback, 102

old-growth forests, 42

Olinger, Bob, 224–25

Olson, Steve, 47

Olympic Peninsula, 280

Oñate, Juan de, 230–32, 281

Operation Blockade, 232–33

Operation Hold the Line, 233

Oregon and California Railroad Company (O&C), 73–74, 82–83

Organ Mountains–Desert Peaks National Monument (New Mexico), 215–237; access to, 235–36; advocates for, 225–27, 234–35; Billy the Kid in, 223–25; Dripping Springs Resort in, 221–23; Geronimo legend at, 219–20; hunting in, 228–29; Indigenous people and, 234–35; Kilbourne Hole in, 217–19; map of, 216; Spanish colonists and Acoma Pueblo in,

230–32; Trump's border wall near, 215, 221, 232–33, 236–37

Oro Belle mine, 92

otters, river, 185, 189

Outdoor Retailer Show, 13

overfishing, 130, 142

overgrazing, 183, 230

owls, ferruginous pygmy, 232

Pacific Crest Trail (PCT), 69, 76–78, 81–82

Pacific Garbage Patch, 130, 137, 142

Pacific Ocean, 126–27

Pacific Remote Islands National Monument, 134

Pahranagat Valley, 249

Paiute (*Nuwu*) people, 259, 275

Papahānaumokuākea Marine National Monument (Hawaii), 119–44; Antiquities Act and, 131–34; Bush designates, 131; coral reefs at, 123–24; fishing industry and, 139–140; map of, 120; marine biodiversity at, 127–28; monk seals and, 129–130; Obama expands, 134, 136, 139, 165; preservation of Native Hawaiian culture at, 135–37; preservation of wildlife at, 122–23, 141, 142–44; sea turtles in, 119, 121; whales near, 124–26

paper mills/industry, 31–32, 42

Paria Townsite, 151

parrotfish (*uhu*), 138–39

Parry, Darren, 14

Patagonia (company), 13

Patwin people, 61

Pearl and Hermes Atoll, 131

Pearl Harbor, 195
Peña, Ángel, 225, 226–30, 233–34, 236, 276, 284
Peña, Gabriella, 226–29
Peña Nieto, Enrique, 215
Pendley, William Perry, 262–63
Penobscot (Penawapskewi) people, 30
Penobscot River, 30, 31
Perfect Kiva, 13
peridot, 218
permits: grazing, 184–85; for Papahānaumokuākea, 135, 136
Petrified Forest National Monument, xxiii
petroglyphs, xxvii, 6, 154–55, 228–29, 242–44, 247–50, 272–74, 276. *See also* rock writing
phytoplankton, 142
Picuris Pueblo, 184
Pilot Rock, 77, 80
Pink Cliffs, 145
pinyon, 178, 183
Piute Spring, 89
planting as restoration, 203–6
plate tectonics, 48, 63
plutonium, 195–97, 201–2, 206, 209–11, 246, 247
pollution, 33, 130, 137, 142, 195
Polynesians, 141, 143
Pomo people, 61
porcupines, 199, 201
Potrillo Mountains, 217, 227
Poverty Point National Monument, xxi
Pratt, Orson, 164
preservation, xvii–xviii, xxi, xxv–xxvii, 39, 57, 63, 71, 122, 143–44

presidential monument proclamations, xvi, 52, 293–309
pronghorns, Sonoran, 232
Protecting National Park Soundscapes (Reid and Olson), 47
protection of a landscape feature, xvi, xxiii, 63
Public Lands Initiative (PLI), 9–10, 11
Public Law 91-550, 188
Public Rangelands Improvement Act of 1978, 158
Pueblo (*Tiwa*) people, 176
Pueblo of Zuni, 10
Puebloans, 168

Questa (New Mexico), 177–78
Quimby, Roxanne, 31–32, 38–41, 42, 52, 284

radiation, 201
radioactive waste, 197, 206, 209–10, 246, 248–49, 251–53, 282
ranchers/ranching, 7, 9, 11, 18, 21–22, 158–59, 191, 200, 206
Range Wars (Edgington), 247
Rattlesnake Mountain, 210–11
Rattlesnake Mountain (*Laliik*), 197, 207–8
Rattlesnake Peak, 233
Rattlesnake Unit, 207
ravens, 111, 114
Reagan, Ronald, xxi
reciprocity ethic, 24
recreation: coexisting with preservation and conservation, xxiv, 24, 57, 78; negative effects of, 15, 22, 78, 122, 158–59, 168, 272–73;

INDEX

opening land to, 39, 242, 270; PLI and, 9; restricting, 31; scripted and unscripted, xvii

Recreation Committee (Monticello), 14

Red River, 175

Red Willow people, 187

Redd, Matt, 21–22

reductions, national monument: Antiquities Act and, xxii–xxiii, 25; at Bears Ears, xxii, 12, 18–20, 82–83, 166, 271; at Grand Staircase–Escalante, 12, 18–19, 82–83, 150–51, 157, 165–66

Reid, Harry, 239, 252

Repellent Fence (Twist, Chacon, Martinez), 245

resource extraction, 78

restoration plans, post-fire, 203–6

reviews, national monument: Bears Ears, xii–xiii, xxii, 18, 24–25; Cascade-Siskiyou, 69, 74, 82; Gold Butte, 260; Grand Staircase–Escalante, 25, 163–64; Katahdin Woods and Waters, 40–41; Organ Mountains–Desert Peaks, 217; Trump and, xxiv, 16

Rice, George, 14–15, 273

Rio Grande del Norte National Monument (New Mexico), 173–91; Cameron Martinez and, 186–89; colliding cultures in, 176–77, 190–91; Ester Garcia and, 178–80; Garrett VeneKlasen tour of, 181, 183–85, 186; map of, 174; Obama designates, 178; rafting in, 173, 175, 180, 185–86, 189–90; Rio Grande in, 175–76

Rio Grande Gorge, 175

Rio Grande Gorge Bridge, 181

Rio Grande (*Río Bravo*), 175, 185–86, 189–90, 215, 217, 221, 230, 284

Rio Pueblo, 189

robins, American, 108–10, 114

Robinson, Doug, 49

Robinson, Rebecca, 12

Robledo, Pedro, Jr., 231

Robledo, Pedro, Sr., 230–31

Robledo Mountains, 219, 220, 223, 227, 231

rock climbing. *See* climbers/climbing, impact of

rock writing, 247–48. *See also* petroglyphs

Rockefeller, John D., Jr., xx, 37, 41

The Rocks Begin to Speak (Martineau), 243

Rocky Mountains, 241

Rogue River tribes, 74

Roosevelt, Franklin D., xx, xxiii, 123, 133, 195, 299–300

Roosevelt, Theodore, xiv–xv, xix, xxiii, 123, 141, 293–95

Rose Atoll National Monument, 134

Rothman, Hal, xiv–xv, xvi, xx, 52

Rudabaugh, Dave, 223

sacred areas, 6–7, 14, 187, 196, 275–76

Saddle Mountain, 199–200

sage thrashers, 205

sagebrush, 204, 205–6, 239

Sagebrush Rebellion, 7–8

Salazar, Ken, 179, 180, 184–85

salmon, 195, 197

Salt Song Trail, 274

The Salt Song Trail (documentary), 274, 276

San Antonio del Rio Colorado Land Grant, 177

San Antonio Mountain, 104

San Bernadino East, 112

San Bernadino Mountains, 105, 108, 113

San Bernadino Peak, 113

San Diego Museum of Natural History, 101, 113

San Gabriel Mountains, 108

San Gorgonio Wilderness, 97, 100, 102–5, 108–9

San Jacinto Mountains, 101, 104–7, 110, 112–13

San Juan County (Utah), 3, 9–10, 11

San Juan Mountains, 175, 187

San Juan Pueblo, 226

San Juan Southern Paiute people, 152

Sand to Snow National Monument (California), 97–117; flying squirrel in, 112; map of, 98; Nine Peak Challenge in, 99–100, 103–4, 105, 106–7, 108, 110, 111, 113–14, 116–17; Obama designates, 89, 97; placement of, 97; ravens in, 111; robin in, 108–10; San Gorgonio in, 100, 102, 103; surveys and resurveys of, 100–101, 103–7, 110, 112–14

Sangre de Cristo Mountains, 177

Santa Rosa and San Jacinto Mountains National Monument, 97

Schneider, Bob, 48–50, 52–54, 58, 62, 63, 116

Schneider, Steve, 48–49

Scientific Forest Management Area, 38

Scorup, Al, 22

Seaborg, Glenn, 195

Sequoia and Kings Canyon National Parks, 105

Serpent Mound (Ohio), 245

serpentine soil, 49–50

settlers: American, 177, 233, 244; European, 6, 206, 244, 263; Mormon, 7, 159, 167, 168, 259; white, 184, 233, 271

Seuss, Dr. (Theodor Geisel), 90

Shaman Knob, 249

Shash Jáa Commission, 20

Shash Jáa Unit, 19–20

Shastan people, 69

Shavitz, Burt, 31

sheep, bighorn, 87, 189, 232, 274

Shields Peak, 110–11

Shivwits Band of Paiutes, 165

shrub-steppe habitats, 199, 202, 204, 212

The Sibley Guide, 107

Sierra de las Uvas, 226–27

Sierra de los Mansos, 235

Sierra Nevada, 71, 106, 241

Sieur de Monts National Monument (Maine), 36

Silent Spring (Carson), 115

Silva-Bañuelos, Jorge, 178

Siskiyou Mountains, 71

skiing, 29–32, 33, 35, 40–41

Sky City (Acoma Pueblo), 231–32

sky island species, 106, 110, 112, 113

slavery, xxvii, 282

Smithson, Robert, 244, 246

snorkeling at Hanauma Bay, 137–38

INDEX

Snow Mountain (California), 45, 47–48, 49, 58
Snow Mountain Wilderness, 48, 50
snowmobiling, 31–32, 39, 40
Solano County, 60
soldiers, American, 220
soldiers, Mexican, 220
Soledad Canyon, 237
songs, ownership of land recognized by, 259–60, 274–75
Sonoma County (California), 58
Sonoran Desert, 90, 97, 102, 232
Southern Paiute (*Nuwuvi*) people, 6, 274, 276–77
Spanish conquistadors, 233
Spanish Empire, 230
Spanish trade route, 226
sparrows: Brewer's, 205; lark, 205; Lincoln's, 110, 114; sage, 205; white-crowned, 104–5
species, invasive, 114, 131, 157, 185, 199, 206
Spiral Jetty (Smithson), 244
springs, natural, 81, 84, 89, 95, 111, 152, 157, 222
St. Clair, Lucas, 38–41, 42–43, 52, 277, 284
Standing Rock, 184
Steed, Brian, 166
storage facilities for nuclear waste, 246–50, 252–53, 282
Straight Cliffs, 167
Sun Tunnels (Holt), 244

Taft, William Howard, xxii–xxiii, 295
tailings, mine, 90–91, 94
Takelman people, 69

Taos Pueblo, 176, 180, 184, 186, 187, 188–89, 191, 254
tarantulas, 116–17
Thirty by Thirty Resolution to Save Nature, 283–84
Thompson, Mike, 50
Through the Repellent Fence (documentary), 245
timber companies, 38, 39, 79
timber harvests, 83
timber sales, 73–74
Tiwa language, 254, 284
Tohono O'odham people, 90
tortoises, desert, 111, 114
tourism: at Bears Ears, 14; at Cascade-Siskiyou, 71, 78–79; at Gold Butte, 270; at Grand Staircase–Escalante, 158; at Hanauma Bay, 137; at Hanford Reach, 210; at Island Park, 272, 273; at Katahdin Woods and Waters, 39; national parks and, xv–xvi; not allowed at Papahānaumokuākea, 122, 143
trapping, 38
Trask, Mililani, 136–37, 143
treaties, 7, 175–76, 190, 263–64
Treaty of Guadalupe Hidalgo, 177
Trek Mining, 91
Tri-Cities, 211
Trinity Site (New Mexico), 196, 210, 217
Truman, Harry S., 300
Trump, Donald: border wall and, 203, 215, 217, 221, 236; Caldera National Monument, 269; Castle Mountains and, 91; elected president, 11; modifies Northeast

Canyons and Seamounts, 140; nuclear waste repository and, 253; Organ Mountains–Desert Peaks National Monument, 215; reduces Bears Ears, xxii, 12, 18–20, 82–83, 166; reduces Grand Staircase–Escalante, xxii, 12, 18–19, 82–83, 150–51, 157, 165–66; reduces monuments, xxiii–xxiv, 131, 308; reviews monuments, xii, xxii, xxiv, 16, 24–25, 69, 74

Tudinu people, 96, 259

Tuleyome (nonprofit), 50, 52–54, 58

tuna fleets, 139–140

turtles, green sea (*honu*), 119, 121–22, 124, 143

Twist, Kade, 245

Uintah and Ouray Ute people, 6

Umatilla tribe, 207

UNESCO World Heritage Site, 136

Union of Concerned Scientists, 48

Unitt, Phil, 101, 103, 104, 105–6, 112–13

University of California, Berkeley, 100–101, 195

uranium, 197

U.S. Department of Energy, 246

U.S. Fish and Wildlife Service, xviii, 135, 193, 195, 202, 203, 261

U.S. Forest Service, xvi, xvii–xviii, 7, 12, 57–58, 113, 158, 178, 186, 261, 270

U.S.–Mexico border wall, 203, 217, 221, 226, 232, 236–37, 282

Utah Diné Bikéyah (UDB), 9–10, 12

Utah public land, 150

Ute Indian tribes, 10

Ute Mountain, 182

Ute Mountain Ute people, 6, 10, 16, 152

Ute people, 152

Valles Canyon, 226–29, 284

Valley of the Gods (Utah), 20

Van Patten, Eugene, 221–23

Vasquez, Gabe, 234–36

VeneKlasen, Garrett, 181, 183–85, 186, 191, 230

Vermilion Cliffs, 145, 154, 160

Viceroy Gold Corporation, 91

Vivian Creek trailhead, 101

Voices from Bears Ears (Robinson), 12

volcanic craters, 137, 217–19

Voyage to Kure (documentary), 131

Wabanaki nation, 30

Walla Walla tribe, 207

Wanapum tribe, 207

Wappo people, 61

water tables, 183

Watts, Ken, 266–67, 269–73

Wetherill, Richard, xiii–xiv

whales, 124–26

Wheeler Peak, 187

White Bluffs bladderpod, 197

White Bluffs (Washington), 196–97

White Cliffs, 145

White Mesa Ute people, 9

White Mountains, 105

White River, 242

White River Narrows, 243

White Sands Missile Range, 217, 225

White Sands National Monument, xviii

white settlers, 184, 233, 271

Whitfield, Sheri, 202–3
Wild and Scenic River designation, 50
Wilderness Act, 7
wilderness designations, 53, 57
*The Wilderness Society v. Donald
Trump*, 166
wildfires. *See* fires
wildlife studies, 100–101, 103, 105–6,
110, 112–14, 116
Wilson, Woodrow, xxiii, 36, 296
Windy Mountain (Cerro Viento), 183
wines, 50–51, 60, 63
Wintum people, 60–61
wolves, Mexican gray, 232
Women's Rights National Historical
Park, xxv
World War II, 8, 141, 195
World Wildlife Fund, 71
Wrangell–St. Elias, xxiii
wrens, 59

Wyoming, State of, xx

Yakama tribe, 207
Yellowstone National Park, xviii,
264, 269, 272
Yosemite National Park, 48–49
Young, Brigham, 164
Yucaipa, 99, 100
Yucca Mountain, 210, 246–49,
251–53
Yucca Mountain Nuclear Waste
Repository, 244, 247, 249, 251–53
Yuki people, 61

Zaldívar, Juan de, 231
Zebra Canyon, 156
Zinke, Ryan, 16, 18, 40–41, 82, 163,
166, 217, 221, 260
Zuni people, 6, 10, 152

Born in Ohio and a Midwesterner at heart, **MCKENZIE LONG** is a graphic designer and writer who lives in Mammoth Lakes, California. She is coauthor of two climbing guidebooks, a cross-country Mountain Bike National Champion, and a climber with multiple ascents of El Capitan in Yosemite. In 2019 she was named the Terry Tempest Williams Fellow for Land and Justice at Mesa Refuge.